Justice, Peace, and Human Rights

Justice, Peace, and Human Rights

American Catholic Social Ethics in a Pluralistic World

David Hollenbach

CROSSROAD · NEW YORK

1988

The Crossroad Publishing Company
370 Lexington Avenue, New York, N.Y. 10017

Printed in the United States of America

Library of Congress Cataloging-in-Publication Data

Hollenbach, David.
Justice, peace, and human rights.

Includes bibliographical references.
1. Social ethics. 2. Church and social problems—Catholic Church. 3. Catholic Church—Doctrines. 4. Pluralism (Social sciences)—United States. 5. Human rights. I. Title.
HM216.H54 1988 261.8'3 88-11854
ISBN 0-8245-0886-6 (pbk.)

To Rembert G. Weakland, O.S.B., and J. Bryan Hehir,
who have done so much to lead the church
in the ways of justice and peace

Contents

Preface

As the United States moves into the third century of its existence as a constitutional republic, two characteristics of the debate about the nation's future stand out as particularly significant for the Christian community. First, discussion of public affairs is increasingly driven to the level of basic ethical principle. This is evident whether the topic is the impact of technology and global interdependence on American jobs, the proper role of human rights considerations in U.S. relations with the Soviet Union and the developing nations, or the significance of nuclear weapons for the very meaning of war and peace. Questions of fundamental moral purpose and value occupy a central place in public discourse about economic, political, and military policy. Second, religion has reemerged as a significant force in the public arena both within the United States and internationally. The sociological thesis that the history of the modern world has been a one-way trip toward ever greater secularization appears increasingly dubious. The role being played by the Christian churches in American public life today is a vigorous and complex one. Both Christian participants as well as secular observers, however, often find themselves somewhat confused about how the churches ought to behave when they interact with American public life.

Within this context, the social role of the Roman Catholic church in the United States is a particularly important one. Catholicism is the bearer of a long tradition of ethical reflection rooted both in the gospel and in deep respect for human reason as a resource for moral analysis. The Catholic tradition's commitment to mediating the ethical meaning of the gospel to the larger culture through the use of human reason is especially relevant in a society that is as deeply pluralistic as the United States. At the same time, Catholic social ethics has been significantly more concerned since the Second Vatican Council with making its Christian theological foundations clear than it sometimes was in the past. This concern with the religious basis of the Catholic social ethic is a result of the broad renewal of church life and thought undertaken by the council. It has been further intensified by the perceived need to make the basic presuppositions of social ethics explicit if the church is to make its distinctive contribution to the life of our pluralistic society. In other words, growing appreciation of the realities of pluralism makes simultaneous reliance on the full resources of both faith and reason essential in Christian social ethics today.

This volume draws together a number of essays in which I have attempted to contribute to the development of Catholic social ethics in ways that respond both to the theological challenge raised by the council and to the cultural challenge posed by the pluralism of contemporary American moral experience and reflection. Part one discusses how the deepened recognition of the pluralistic context of social ethics has important consequences for the church's understanding of its mission in society and for the way Christians should understand the most basic norm of social morality, namely justice. Parts two, three, and four take up three more specific areas of social morality that have important public-policy implications—economic justice, human rights, and the question of the morality of warfare. These three sets of issues have been central in the public-policy initiatives undertaken by the Catholic church in the United States in recent years, particularly by its bishops. The second essay in part two and the first in part four were in fact originally written for conferences designed to assist the Catholic bishops of the United States in the projects of drafting their two recent pastoral letters on economic justice and nuclear strategy. Parts two, three, and four, therefore, are interpretations of the theological background of church activity in these areas. They also discuss some of the broader ethical and political implications of this activity. Finally, part five discusses why these social-ethical concerns must become more fully integrated into the daily pastoral life of the church. It analyzes the link between social ethics and three of the forms of ministry where the church acts most clearly as church: sacramental worship and liturgy, preaching and other forms of parish ministry, and religious education. This section is of particular relevance for the work of priests and ministers whose pastoral responsibilities are most important to the overall effectiveness of the church's ministry.

Though the focus of the book is on Catholic social ethics and social ministry, ecumenical concerns also play an important part in its arguments. Not all Christians, whether Roman Catholic, Protestant, or Orthodox, will agree with everything said here. But clarifying presuppositions is the first step in serious dialogue among the plural parts of the ecumenical community as well as in the civic sphere. It is my hope that there are more reasons for deepened ecumenical consensus than for lingering Christian division in the arguments of these essays.

The book as a whole is not a systematic and comprehensive treatment of Christian social ethics. Numerous theological questions and practical issues of great importance are dealt with only in passing if at all. For example, little is said about the overall content of the biblical teaching on the moral life of

Christians in society. Nor are practical questions such as environmental protection and the central issue of the social implications of the equality of women and men dealt with except tangentially. Also the reader will detect somewhat different perspectives on the same topic in several of the essays. This is a result of the fact that they were written over a number of years and revised only to eliminate unnecessary repetition. The original place of publication of each essay is indicated in the notes. It is an open question whether anyone today is capable of writing a systematic treatise on Christian social ethics that deals adequately with all the theological, philosophical, political, economic, military, and social questions this would involve. I, at least, am not ready to attempt to do so. The analysis and arguments in this book will, I hope, provide some illustration of the kind of work that still needs to be done if the Christian community is to address this larger set of questions more adequately.

Part One

The Challenge of Pluralism

Chapter 1

The Church's Social Mission in a Pluralistic Society

The involvement of the Roman Catholic church in social and political affairs has been undergoing a qualitative transformation since the close of the Second Vatican Council. The fact of such involvement is nothing new. For example, the special place granted the church in the Roman Empire by Constantine, the investiture controversy of the Middle Ages, and the history of the Papal States all show that the church has not been a stranger to the world of politics in the past. Similarly the church has long been deeply involved in responding to pressing social ills through direct Christian service. Hospitals, orphanages, schools, and efforts to aid the poor have historically been part of the church's understanding of its own mission. Since the council, however, the mode of the church's engagement in social and political life has entered a distinctive new phase whose contours are still in the process of taking shape.

The thesis of this essay is that the council launched this new phase through its recognition that the context for Christian social ministry is an inherently pluralistic world. The reality of religious, ideological, and cultural diversity was taken with great seriousness by the council, particularly in the two most important conciliar documents dealing with the social role of the church: *Gaudium et spes* (the Pastoral Constitution on the Church in the Modern World) and *Dignitatis humanae* (the Declaration on Religious Liberty).

The consequences of this new acknowledgment of pluralism have been multiple. First, it has pressed the church to a deeper reflection on how its social mission is rooted in the core of Christian faith and identity. Second, it has opened new questions about how to pursue this mission while also respecting the religious freedom of those who do not share the church's faith and tradition. These two issues will be the focus here. Other consequences of the new recognition of the pluralistic context for social mission are of equal importance. For example, this context calls for careful discernment of the relation between the Christian vision of society and contemporary political ideologies and careful reflection on how the universal mission of the church is to be embodied in the particular circumstances of the diverse nations and cultures of the globe. The questions of how the church's social mission is rooted in its religious identity and how this mission is compatible with respect for the religious freedom of others provide points of entry into the larger discussion of Catholic social ethics in a pluralistic world. Other dimensions of this larger discussion will be treated in subsequent chapters.

Social Mission and the Identity of the Church

J. Bryan Hehir, an astute interpreter and practitioner of the church's social ministry, has argued that "the decisive contribution of Vatican II was to provide a description of the church's role in the world which was properly theological and ecclesial in tone and substance."[1] Hehir's point is evident if one compares *Gaudium et spes* and subsequent postconciliar social teachings with the social encyclicals issued by the popes from Leo XIII to John XXIII. These earlier social teachings were almost exclusively framed in concepts and language of the natural-law ethic of scholastic philosophy. One searches in vain through the writings of the popes during the hundred years before the council for careful consideration of the biblical, Christological, eschatological, or ecclesiological basis of the church's social role.

There were several reasons for the preconciliar social encyclicals' almost exclusive reliance on philosophical rather than biblical and theological categories. This emphasis is in line with the Catholic tradition's high estimate of the power of human reason to discover the broad outlines of God's design for social life through reflection on human experience. This is the gist of the notion of natural law. At the same time the particular historical circumstances in which the church found itself following the French Revolution and the Enlightenment gave this appeal to reason and natural law a markedly defensive tone. The Enlightenment philosophers often appealed to the autonomy of human reason in a way that challenged the authority of the church and in some cases religion itself. In response Vatican I (1869–70) strongly affirmed the full compatibility of faith and reason. In his 1879 encyclical, urging renewal of the study of Thomas Aquinas, Leo XIII added that Christian faith does not detract from the dignity of human reason but rather "adds greatly to its nobility, keenness, and stability." Therefore those who follow St. Thomas in combining the guidance of faith with the use of reason "are philosophizing in the best possible way."[2]

This way of seeing the complementarity of faith and reason put the church in a position to declare that anyone who rejected the popes' conclusions about the proper ordering of society was not only unfaithful but also unreasonable. In addition, for this essentially apologetic strategy to be effective, it was necessary to avoid *direct* and *explicit* appeal to biblical and theological perspectives in proposing the Catholic vision of social life. In the words of Johann Baptist Metz, nineteenth- and early twentieth-century Catholic social teaching did not seek to *mediate* between faith and society but rather to *defend* Christian tradition against the corrosive currents of modernity. This defense "was carried on just in front of the fortress Church, on the territory of pure social ethics" (i.e., strictly natural-law ethics).[3] The Catholic insistence on the complementarity of faith and reason thus ironically came to be interpreted in a way that saw them moving on two parallel tracks only extrinsically related to each other. It became difficult to give properly *theological* reasons for the social teaching of the church or to give an account of how the deepest meaning of Christianity could speak directly to the problems of post-Enlightenment society.

During the decades immediately prior to the council, it became increasingly clear that this solution to the problem of the relation of the church and the modern world was both historically anachronistic and theologically unsatisfactory. On the historical level, the early social encyclicals had Western Europe implicitly in mind as the "world" to which the church's mission was to be directed. Further, they assumed that this world shared a unified intellectual heritage in which Christianity and culture had been harmoniously synthesized. Therefore new secular movements such as liberal democracy in the eighteenth century and socialisms of various stripes in the nineteenth century were regarded not only as betrayals of faith but as cultural heresies as well.

This reading of the historical context of the church's mission is no longer accurate in the twentieth century (if it ever was fully accurate). Differences of class, race, economic status, and political tradition have made the West a far from unified society with a harmoniously integrated culture. When one views the church's social mission in its full global scope this anachronism is even more evident. Cultural pluralism and social conflict are more adequate descriptions of the context of the church's social mission than the organic model of society assumed by neo-scholasticism. The council clearly recognized this:

> Although the world of today has a very vivid sense of its unity and how one person depends on another in needful solidarity, it is most grievously torn into opposing camps by conflicting forces. For political, social, economic, racial, and ideological disputes still continue bitterly, and with them the peril of a war which would reduce everything to ashes. True, there is a growing exchange of ideas, but the very words by which key concepts are expressed take on quite different meanings in diverse ideological systems.[4]

In addition the council was also cognizant of the methodological specialization of modern intellectual life and the fact that this has led to competing conceptions of the human person.

The realities of modern social conflict and scientific specialization have produced a kind of crisis of moral reason itself.[5] It has become increasingly difficult to sustain the natural-law tradition's robust confidence that intelligent exercise of reason by persons in different social locations, from diverse cultures, and with differing intellectual backgrounds will lead to identical conclusions about the way society should be organized. Therefore if the church is intent on making a contribution to debates about social, political, and economic life, it must state forthrightly and publicly its own most basic convictions about the nature and destiny of human beings. It must respond to the most basic questions about the meaning of human life in its social teaching as well as in doctrinal theology. The council highlighted a few of these questions:

> What is the human person? What is this sense of sorrow, of evil, of death, which continues to exist despite so much progress? What is the purpose of these victories, purchased at so high a cost? What can human beings offer to society? What can they expect from it? What follows this earthly life? . . . What recommendations seem needful for the upbuilding of contemporary society? What is the ultimate significance of human activity throughout the world?[6]

These are religious questions, demanding religious and theological answers.

During the decades preceding the council, Catholic theologians had been at work seeking to respond to these perennial questions in ways that spoke to the context of modern pluralism and skepticism. Far from abandoning the Catholic conviction about the complementarity of faith and reason, however, these theologians sought to appropriate the meaning of this complementarity more thoroughly. They sought to *mediate* the meaning of Christianity to a modern pluralistic and often conflictive society and to appropriate the positive values of this society into the life and thought of the church. For example, thinkers such as John Henry

Newman, Maurice Blondel, Pierre Teilhard de Chardin, and Karl Rahner (each in a different way) argued that God's grace is not *extrinsic* to human experience, understanding, society, or culture. Grace is immanent within history, beckoning it to transformation and redemption. It was but a short step from this retrieval of a more authentic understanding of the relation of nature and grace to the conclusion that the response of Christians to grace in faith should have a transformative and redemptive impact on history, society, and culture. In the years immediately preceding the council important theologians began publishing books with titles such as *The Theology of Earthly Realities* (Gustave Thils), *Catholicism: A Study of Dogma in Relation to the Corporate Destiny of Mankind* (Henri de Lubac), and *The Theology of Work* (Marie Dominique Chenu).[7] It had become clear, as Metz put it over a decade after the council, that the task of expounding the theology of the church's social mission "has to be carried on by using the very substance of the Christian faith."[8] The social mission is not a propaedeutic to or extension of the church's real purpose but is integral or essential to this purpose.[9]

The first result of the council's willingness to acknowledge the social and intellectual dividedness of the contemporary world, therefore, was to move the discussion of the church's social mission to the level of fundamental affirmations about Christian identity. The "social question" became a properly theological question. From one perspective this is a surprising result, for willingness to acknowledge the pluralism of contemporary society is often regarded as the first step toward religious indifferentism. But at the council the result was just the opposite. The church's social mission was more tightly linked to the Bible, to Christology, eschatology, ecclesiology, and other central doctrinal perspectives than at any time in recent centuries.

For example, *Gaudium et spes* stated that the religious mission and identity of the church "can serve to structure and consolidate the human community according to the divine law."[10] More specifically the council spelled out three dimensions of this social mission: the healing and elevation of the dignity of the human person, the building and consolidation of bonds of solidarity in society, and the endowment of daily human activity with a deeper meaning and worth.[11] The first three chapters of *Gaudium et spes* take up the themes of human dignity, human community, and the value of human activity in the world and develop them as the basis of the church's social mission. These three chapters all contain explicitly theological discussions of why the matter at stake is a religious and not purely secular concern.

Thus human dignity is rooted in the creation of human persons in the image of God. Though *Gaudium et spes* reaffirmed the natural-law argument that human dignity is evident, apart from faith, in the intelligence, freedom, and conscience possessed by all persons, it sought to make the direct links between these philosophical considerations and the biblical and theological notion of the *imago Dei.* Also, in a passage that has become central in the writings of John Paul II, the council went on to provide a Christological basis for the church's defense of this dignity. "Christ the Lord, Christ the final Adam, by the revelation of the mystery of the Father and His love, fully reveals human beings to themselves and makes their supreme calling clear."[12] In defending and promoting human dignity, therefore, the church is engaged in a properly religious task. Social mission is part of the religious mission of the church.

In the same way, while the council reaffirmed the traditional natural-law argument that human beings are social by nature, it went on to specifically theological arguments for the church's mission to build up the bonds of community and mutual interdependence among all people. This mission is founded on the command to love God and all one's neighbors. It reflects the Christian faith in God as a trinitarian unity of persons, which implies that personality is essentially relational. And social mission manifests the fact that God's saving grace draws persons into a communion of solidarity with one another, a communion that "must be constantly increased until that day on which it will be brought to perfection" in the kingdom of God.[13] The task of forging such bonds of reciprocal interdependence is not only intraecclesial but societal. The church, the council maintains, is a sacrament, a sign and instrument, of "intimate union with God, and of the unity of all humankind." Therefore participation in efforts to promote "an evolution toward unity, a process of wholesome socialization and of association in civic and economic realms . . . belong to the innermost nature of the Church."[14]

The council also affirmed the religious significance of all human endeavor, however secular it might conventionally be regarded. Even daily labor, when it is properly ordered, can be regarded "as unfolding the Creator's work" and as contributing "to the realization in history of the divine plan."[15] The fulfillment of this plan will only be accomplished by God's definitive act of establishing the kingdom and the creation of a new heaven and a new earth. This eschatological hope, however, does not decrease the importance of Christian engagement in the world. "The expectation of a new earth must not weaken but rather stimulate our concern for cultivating this one. For here grows the body of a new human family, a body which even now is able to give some kind of foreshadowing of the new age."[16] In fact all struggles to build a more just and humane social order are a participation in the paschal mystery of Christ's death and resurrection and in the activity of the Holy Spirit in our world.[17]

These are but a few of the explicitly theological perspectives that the council brought to bear in its reflections on the social mission of the church in the world. They show that this social mission is a religious one that flows from the heart of Christian faith. They have been developed and refined in the postconciliar teaching of the magisterium and in movements such as liberation and political theology. They represent the distinctive contributions that the church seeks to bring to the debates about social existence in a world increasingly conscious of itself as divided and pluralistic.

Social Mission and Religious Liberty

The movement of these religious and theological themes to the forefront of the church's understanding of its social mission has had a powerful effect on the level of social engagement by numerous Catholic groups. Since the council, the Catholic church has become an increasingly vigorous actor in the affairs of the polis. Base communities, men's and women's religious orders, lay persons and lay groups, bishops' conferences in various nations, and the pope in his world-wide travels have all intensified their engagement in the task of promoting justice and peace out of explicitly religious motivation. But it is not only the motivation of this activity that is Christian; the basic goals and objectives of social action are religiously based as well. The Christian vision of the kingdom of God is the overarching perspective shaping the church's public role in society on these various levels of activity. Here the reality of societal pluralism raises a second challenge that is forming the new mode of social mission since the council. Just as the acknowledgment of the irreducible pluralism of contemporary society has caused a reexamination of social mission in theological terms, this same pluralism raises the question of how to distinguish social mission from religious imperialism or theological triumphalism. The facts that the world is religiously diverse and that the Christian church is itself internally divided are obvious. How, then, is the Catholic community to seek to influence the public life of a local community, a nation, or the global economic and political order without imposing its theological vision through brute power? The tension between a theologically rooted social mission and the respect due to the religious freedom of one's fellow citizens has moved front and center since the council, sometimes in very concrete and painful conflicts.

There are two ways to avoid this tension, both of which would be unfaithful to the council itself. The first is to give in to the pressure to keep religion a private matter having little or nothing to do with the affairs of the commonwealth. Though one need not accept the thesis that modern history has been a one-way movement toward an increasingly secularized society, it is undeniable that modern social conditions tend to privatize religion.[18] The council called this tendency one of "the more serious errors of our age."[19] Belief that God is both Creator and Lord of all the universe is a direct challenge to such a domesticated or privatized definition of the church's task.

A second, opposite approach was also judged unacceptable by the council, namely that which seeks to secure a privileged position for the church in the public and political life of society. During the 1950s an intense debate took place among Catholic theologians about the church-state question. In the nineteenth and first half of the twentieth century the papal approach to the church-state issue was to advocate the establishment of Catholicism as the official religion of the realm wherever this was made practically possible through the presence of a Catholic majority. The council rejected this approach, bringing about a major development of doctrine within the Catholic tradition. The way this development was effected is of continuing relevance for the effort to understand the church's social mission. For though the church-state issue was resolved at the council in favor of religious liberty, the relation of the church to a religiously pluralistic society continues to need clarification.

The participants in the 1950s debate who continued to advocate a privileged political position for the church had a rationale for their position. They argued that since Roman Catholicism in fact possesses the true vision of the nature and destiny of humanity and the cosmos, this vision ought to form the basis for the whole of social and cultural existence. On the theological level this approach is known as "integralism." It stresses the *unity* of religion, daily life, politics, the sciences, the economy, and the whole gamut of human endeavor. It manifests the deep Catholic instinct to see all things human as potential mediators of the divine presence and grace. On this level its argument is similar to the postconciliar argument that the shaping of the social order in accord with the vision of the kingdom of God is "integral" to the preaching of the gospel.[20]

This is a theologically healthy instinct. It can, however, become perverse when interpreted to mean that all knowledge can be reduced to theology or that all social institutions ought to be extensions of the church. In the words of Karl Rahner, it can lead to a way of thinking that simply assumes that "human life can be unambiguously mapped out and manipulated in accord with certain universal principles proclaimed by the church and watched over by her in the manner in which they are developed and applied."[21] The temptation to this way of thinking has not disappeared since the council. It is as likely to be found among those on the political left as among those on the right. Indeed the fact that the church's social mission has become more immediately grounded in biblical and theological perspectives since the council may intensify the temptation to move in this direction. In order to avoid this danger it is important to note how the council sought to counter the privatization of Christian faith without falling into the ecclesiastical triumphalism of the integralist theology.

Dignitatis humanae unambiguously affirmed the right to religious freedom as a human and civil right. It defined the right this way: "This freedom means that all persons are to be immune from coercion on the part of individuals or of social groups and of any human power, in such wise that in matters religious no one is to be forced to act in a manner contrary to his own beliefs. Nor is anyone to be restrained from acting in accordance with his own beliefs, whether privately or publicly, whether alone or in association with others, within due limits."[22] The two aspects of the right (noncoercion of religious belief and nonrestraint of the exercise of belief) are analogous to the two religion clauses of the first amendment of the U.S. Constitution: nonestablishment and free exercise.

The relative weight of the two clauses of the first amendment has been and remains one of the most contentious points in U.S. jurisprudence. Broadly, the question is this: when does the free exercise of one person's religious freedom begin to restrict such freedom for others? A similar tension exists in the conciliar declaration. For along with its strong defense of immunity from coercion in religious matters, the council insisted that churches and other religious communities have a right to seek to influence public policy in ways that reflect their deepest convictions. In its words: "It comes within the meaning of religious freedom that religious bodies should not be prohibited from freely undertaking to show the special value of their doctrine in what concerns the organization of society and the inspiration of the whole of human activity."[23] In other words, the council includes the right of the church to engage in an active social mission and social ministry within its definition of religious freedom. This mission includes the effort to shape public policies, and these policies will necessarily affect the freedom and behavior of non-Catholics. Here the tension between social mission and religious freedom again comes into view.

If both privatism and integralism are to be avoided this tension must be understood at a deeper level than either of these unacceptable alternatives attained. John Courtney Murray's extensive writings on the subject, which prepared the way for the conciliar declaration, provide a route to such deeper understanding. Murray argued that affirmation of the right to religious liberty rests on a *complex* insight, an insight that has theological, political, moral, and juridical dimensions.[24]

Theologically, religious liberty is necessary to protect and secure the freedom of the church to pursue its mission. The response of human beings to God transcends the order of the political and cannot legitimately be brought under the control of the coercive powers of government. To do so would be to subordinate the church to the state. This theological principle correlates with the *political* principle of the essentially limited nature of governmental power. Government is not omnicompetent, and least of all is it competent in matters religious. The denial of such limits on governmental power is the seed from which all totalitarianisms spring. Governmental power is limited by its obligation to protect and support the transcendent dignity of the human person. One aspect of this dignity is freedom in matters religious. *Juridically and ethically,* religious freedom rests on the insight that law has a moral function but does not have the task of enforcing every humanly beneficial activity or of coercively forbidding every moral evil. Its role is the more limited but nonetheless crucial one of ensuring the basic conditions of social existence: public peace, justice, and those aspects of public morality on which social consensus exists. These are moral tasks, but they are not the whole of morality. The pursuit of the full moral good belongs to other communities within society such as families, voluntary associations, and churches. Their freedom to do so must be protected. The function of law, properly understood in its relation to morality, therefore, also supports the right to religious freedom.

In short, Murray argued that neither a purely theological, purely political, purely juridical, or purely ethical form of reasoning would yield an adequate understanding of religious freedom. The same can be said of an adequate understanding of the church's social mission.

Murray further maintained that the council's approach to religious freedom was a synthesis of the four levels of analysis made possible by the historical experience of the church in its engagement with the world. Synthesis by definition is not a deductive form of reasoning modeled after Euclidian geometry with its linear movement from axioms to theorems to corollaries, all summed up with a resounding *quod erat demonstrandum.* Synthetic reasoning proceeds by way of dialectic and analogy. It discovers correlations and similarities between different spheres of thinking and action. It depends on imagination, not simply the logic of ratiocination. It is therefore a persuasive rather than deductive enterprise, more like the rationality of classical rhetoric than logic or mathematics. And to be persuasive it must be rooted in experience, history, and culture. It is in fact a form of prudence or practical wisdom—a sense of the fitting.

This complex argument for the right to religious freedom can greatly illuminate the question of the way that the church should pursue its social mission in a pluralistic world. Just as the affirmation of religious freedom depended on establishing a *correlation* between theological, moral, political, and juridical concepts, the goals of social mission emerge from the discovery of such correlations between the vision of the kingdom of God and the shape of social-political existence. The movement from theology to social policy is one of reciprocal mediation of meaning between several different modes of understanding. Though the *ground* of the church's social mission is theological and moral, its actual practical objectives must also be shaped by social, political, economic, and legal analysis. If the distinctive contributions of these other modes of thought are not acknowledged, the relevance of the Christian vision to public life will remain obscure. At the same time, precisely because there are many different social and political analyses competing for adherents in a pluralistic society, fundamental theological perspectives must serve as criteria of discernment among them.

In other words, the virtues of prudence and Christian discernment are essential in the task of discovering the basic contours of the church's relation to the world. Murray maintained that the affirmation of the right to religious freedom was not a conclusion of theoretical reason and pure logic, but of practical wisdom schooled by historical experience. This practical-historical synthesis mediated secular wisdom to the church and theological insight to the spheres of politics and law. The church and the world both learned from each other.

The chief implication of this for the social mission of the church today is that the church's participation in public affairs must proceed according to a mode of dialogue and persuasion. Religious vision and theology have crucial roles to play in shaping a just and peaceful society. This role can be played, however, only to the extent that faith and theology are seen as participants in a drama that involves numerous other actors. The church is not the producer or director of this drama. God is—the God who created the worlds of politics, law, science, economics, and culture just as surely as God created the church and gave it a mission.

The new importance given to the theological basis of social ministry by the council means that theology has a new task—that of seeking a Christian interpretation of social reality and proposing concrete directions for Christian social action. In the council's view, such interpretation and action-proposals can be developed only through dialogue with the various interpretations and proposals present in a pluralistic society. The council was well aware of the interchanges between religion and secular modes of thought that had been beneficial to both in the past. The need for increased exchanges of this sort was judged even greater today.[25] The task here is neither defense of the church against the world nor conquest of the world by the church, but a mediation of understanding and criteria for action between them.

This task will be most fruitful when based on a relation of mutual respect and when it occurs in an atmosphere of freedom. Though there will surely be times when the church must take prophetic and uncompromising stands over against cultural tendencies or specific social policies, confrontation is not the ordinary relation between the church and the world as envisioned by the council. In fact one can extrapolate from the council's explicit words and suggest that even when the church takes vigorous positions on matters of public policy, it is likely to be most effective in securing social change when it presents cogent reasons for its position that are intelligible to those outside the Christian community. Speaking of the social ministry of bishops and pastors, the council recommended that "By unremitting study they should fit themselves to do their part in establishing dialogue with the world and with people of all shades of opinion."[26] The same words can be applied to the laity as well. Thus the new centrality of the Bible and theology in shaping the church's social mission should be accompanied by a strong spirit of respectful and rational debate. The complementarity of religious fidelity and public civility is the deeper meaning of the Catholic understanding of the relation of faith and reason that is particularly relevant in a pluralistic and conflicted world.

The two recent pastoral letters of the U.S. bishops exemplify both of the themes traced in this essay. Both the letter on the nuclear-weapons question and that on the U.S. economy insist that the church's involvement in these urgent social questions is not an unjustified meddling in politics. The bishops speak on these issues because it is part of their religious mission to do so. Also, the perspectives on peace and economic justice in the pastoral letters are firmly rooted in biblical sources and in the call of the kingdom of God. At the same time both letters seek to mediate these religious themes to a pluralistic society through reasoned reflection on fundamental moral norms.

The council's call for increased dialogue with the many competing social visions of a pluralist society has been particularly influential in shaping these documents. The process of drafting them involved broad consultation with numerous experts in theology, philosophy, and the social sciences, as well as with persons with rich practical experience in government, business, labor, and the military. The issuing of successive drafts with the invitation to all interested parties to submit responses represents a new style of social teaching that places maximum emphasis on dialogue and debate.

Finally, both documents not only propose general moral principles that should shape military and economic activity but also advance a number of more specific recommendations about public policy, such as the call for a policy of "no first use" of nuclear weapons by the United States and the adoption of economic policies that seek full employment. These policy recommendations cannot be deduced from theology or fundamental moral principles. They involve prudential judgments among the competing strategic and economic concepts that form the framework of the contemporary policy debates. The bishops do not propose these recommendations as the only possible moral positions on these issues. They do not, in other words, attempt to close off debate on these policies either within the church or in society at large. Rather they make these recommendations precisely in order to bring the Christian moral perspective into active engagement with this debate.

Karl Rahner has observed that if the teaching office of the church restricts itself to the enunciation of general moral and religious principles for social existence, these teachings "become remarkably abstract and thus singularly ineffective. They are very often recognized as wholly right and yet seem so inept that we are left helpless when faced with a concrete choice."[27] Therefore Rahner urged that the church must have the courage to move to a more concrete level in addressing the pressing social issues of the day. Such a step does involve certain risks, such as identifying the official church too closely with contingent policy options. However, it also has considerable advantages. It exemplifies how Christians should translate their fundamental convictions into concrete decisions. It provides a key means for engaging the church in the debates about national priorities, debates that are crucial for the cause of justice and peace. On balance the U.S. bishops have concluded that the advantages outweigh the risks. This judgment is itself rooted in pastoral prudence and discernment. It acknowledges the legitimacy of pluralism on the level of policy but it seeks to engage this pluralism in serious moral argument. It is a prime example of the conciliar commitment to dialogue as the means for mediating the Christian vision to a pluralistic world. Much work remains to be done to give greater depth and breadth to the new form of social mission that has been developing since the council. The essays that follow in this book are efforts to carry this work a step farther.

Chapter 2

Modern Catholic Teachings Concerning Justice

The 1971 Synod of Bishops of the Roman Catholic church introduced its reflections on the meaning of justice in world society with a statement that has become the platform and legitimation for a whole series of new initiatives in sociopolitical life by Roman Catholics. The bishops stated:

> Action on behalf of justice and participation in the transformation of the world fully appear to us as a constitutive dimension of the preaching of the Gospel, or, in other words, of the Church's mission for the redemption of the human race and its liberation from every oppressive situation.[1]

Since this statement was made almost two decades ago, it has been quoted repeatedly in the discussions about the role of Christians in the social and political spheres. These discussions have frequently been heated, and sometimes rather confused. Several crucial issues are at stake in the continuing debate.

First, how is the justice which is "constitutive" of the mission of the church to be understood? Political philosophers from Plato to John Rawls have proposed a wide array of definitions of justice.[2] Many of these rather technical theories of justice are implicitly present in the contemporary debates over the proper role of the church in the formation of public policy. Justice can be described most generally in the ancient phrase *suum cuique*—to each what is due. This principle, however, can be specified and concretized in quite different ways, leading to quite different notions of justice. The principle can be interpreted as a call for respect toward a structured system of *roles, offices,* and *powers* in society, usually unequal ones. (Plato: "You remember how when we first began to establish our commonwealth, and several times since, we have laid down, as a universal principle, that everyone ought to perform the one function in the community for which his nature best suited him. Well, I believe that principle, or some form of it, is justice."[3]) The same general norm can imply obligation to respect some form of *excellence*, *achievement*, or *merit*. (Aristotle: "Everyone agrees that in distributions the just share must be given on the basis of what one deserves, though not everyone would name the same criterion of deserving: democrats say it is free birth, oligarchs say it is wealth or noble birth, and aristocrats say that it is excellence *[aretē]*."[4]) *Suum cuique* can be interpreted as a principle of respect for what belongs to each person, namely for *property*. (John Locke: "The great and chief end, therefore, of men's uniting into commonwealths, and putting themselves under government, is the preservation of their property."[5]) The principle can lead to a call for affirmative action by individuals and society aimed at meeting the basic *needs* of all. (Marx: "From each according to his ability, to each according to his needs."[6]) Finally, it can be interpreted, as it perhaps most commonly is by contemporary North Americans, as demanding equal *liberty* and *opportunity* for all. (John Rawls: "First, each person is to have an equal right to the most extensive basic liberty compatible with a similar liberty for others. Second, social and economic inequalities are to be arranged so that they are both (a) reasonably expected to be to everyone's advantage, and (b) attached to positions and offices open to all."[7])

The pluralism of interpretations of justice, moreover, is not simply a diversity of theoretical accounts produced by philosophers. It is a problem that arises within Christian moral theology and Christian life. Men and women within the contemporary church who consider themselves agents of justice both act and understand their action in quite diverse ways. The experience, motives, and goals of a Christian American lawyer or politician, a curial monsignor promoting Vatican *Ostpolitik*, a North American feminist theologian, and a member of a Brazilian base community all lead to conceptions of the promotion of justice that are at least functionally different if not substantively so. This pluralism of definitions of justice is not resolved in any simple way by stating that the promotion of justice is an integral part of the Christian faith. If the synod's statement is to be saved from falling into the limbo reserved for slogans and platitudes, there is an urgent need to clarify the meaning of justice that it presupposes.

Second, recent debates among theologians, bishops, and activists of various ideological hues have also revolved around the fear that this statement may lead some to identify action for justice with the preaching of the gospel and the mission of the church in an illegitimately reductive manner. The fear is voiced in a number of ways: concern that some are confusing the development of a more just society with the radical newness of the kingdom of God that comes only from grace and the redemptive action of God; dismay that too close an identification of the virtues of justice and faith will lead to an attempt to reestablish a clericalist control of society in an updated version of medieval Christendom; distress over an alleged confusion of the "values of the gospel" with the orientations of a social-political ideology. These fears are met with counterclaims that any attempt to drive a wedge between commitment to the alleviation of injustice and the life of Christian belief destroys the integrity of Christian life, saps the prophetic power that Christians are called by God to evince, and denies the inseparability of the two great commandments of love of God and love of neighbor.[8] If further light is to be brought to these contemporary debates among Christians, a clarification of the relation between belief in the gospel and the meaning of justice is sorely needed.

This essay will attempt to clarify both the meaning of justice and its relation to Christian belief by placing the synod's document in the context of discussions of social justice in the Catholic tradition during the one hundred years that preceded it. The bishops' statement represents only one notable development in a long tradition of Catholic reflection and teaching on social and political questions. The modern phase of the Catholic social-ethical tradition, from Leo XIII to the present, is especially rich in refined and critical thought on the nature of justice and its relation to Christian belief. This tradition's understanding of these questions has grown, developed, and changed in significant ways during the past hundred years. A study of these developments may be of considerable help in clarifying both the meaning of the synod's statement and the basic social and political obligations of Christians.

Relational Justice and Christian Love

In 1891 Leo XIII issued his encyclical *Rerum novarum* and initiated a new phase in social and political self-understanding of the Roman Catholic church. The years immediately preceding the publication of this document were in many ways like our own time. They were years in which the church was gradually coming to an awareness that major social change was under way—the transformation of traditional patterns of social life by the process of industrialization. Leo XIII's stated goal was to specify the "principles which truth and justice dictate" for dealing with the "misery and wretchedness" caused by these changes. This goal was to be pursued by an effort "to define the relative rights and mutual duties of the rich and the poor, of capital and labor."[9]

The discussion of justice in terms of relative rights and mutual duties is characteristic of the entire modern Catholic tradition. It is based on the conviction that one cannot specify the meaning of *suum cuique* without examining the social relationships, patterns of mutuality, and structures of interdependence that bind human beings together in communities. The normative notion of justice adopted by the modern tradition, which has its historical origins in biblical, Augustinian, and Thomistic thought, is an essentially social concept—it is relational and mutual. Though justice demands respect for human rights as the imperious claims of individual dignity and worth, these rights are always "relative." More precisely, they can be neither specified nor understood apart from the web of social interdependence that entails mutual obligation and duty. This apparently innocuous affirmation is in fact highly significant. For example, Leo XIII's approach immediately distinguishes modern Catholic social thought from the liberal natural-rights tradition of the eighteenth century which so much influenced the drafters of the United States Constitution. The mutual interdependence of persons on each other in family life, in work, and in political life is viewed as the foundation and matrix for the realization of human freedom and dignity. Respect for freedom and dignity, therefore, involves more than not interfering with the activity of persons. Obligations of justice include positive duties to aid persons in need, to participate in the maintaining of the public good, and to share in efforts to create the kinds of institutions that promote genuine mutuality and reciprocal respect.

This more positive approach to the meaning of justice is rooted in the tradition's acceptance of the Aristotelian and Thomistic view of the essentially social nature of persons. The major encyclicals from Leo XIII to the present make frequent appeals to both philosophical and empirical arguments to establish such a social definition of human nature. The documents, however, also make frequent appeals to a bond of love that lies at the root of the obligations of justice. The stress on mutuality as intrinsic to the meaning of justice is a clear evidence of the influence of a Christian morality of love in what often appear to be thoroughly philosophical discussions of justice. The effect of this presence of the norm of love in the papal writings has been twofold.

First, it has led to continuing stress on concern and respect for individual human persons in their uniqueness and their concrete needs. The fundamental norm of the tradition, as John XXIII put it, is that "individual persons are necessarily the foundation, cause, and the end of all social institutions."[10] Within the Catholic tradition respect for human dignity, human rights, and human need cannot be adequately understood without reference to the Christian moral norm of agape (love) and its concern for concrete persons, especially those in need. The demands of justice are thus not primarily the conclusions drawn from a general philosophical principle expressed in propositional form. They arise from the claim or call that the dignity of persons makes on the freedom of others. Justice is rooted in the fact that the very existence of a human person confronts others with a certain "ought" that demands respect and support. "An age-old tradition calls the execution of this 'ought' 'love' and it understands this love as the acceptance, the willing, supporting, and fostering of the other's subjectivity, selfhood and freedom."[11] This is not to identify justice with love. It seems clear from a number of recent discussions that the principle of justice has a different role to play in moral argument than does the principle of love.[12] This theory of justice, however, seeks always to remain attentive to the particularity of persons because of the presence of this agapeistic grounding. The statement of Augustine that "justice is love serving only the loved object, and therefore ruling rightly"[13] is paralleled closely by Pius XI's claim:

> According to the Apostle, then, all the commandments, including those which are of strict justice, as those which forbid us to kill or to steal, may be reduced to the single precept of true charity. . . . Both justice and charity often dictate obligations touching on the same subject matter but under different aspects.[14]

Thus both philosophical arguments about the social nature of the person and religious appeals to the Christian norm of love of neighbor together rule out all individualistic standards of justice and all those which do not take into account the special claims of persons in need.

Second, the influence of the norm of agape has caused the tradition to place special emphasis on interpersonal and social mutuality in its discussions of justice. Justice calls for social relationships and a kind of social organization that open the way to the fulfillment of the person which can only occur in unity and solidarity with others. Mutual interdependence is not merely a physical, psychological, or economic fact. It is a moral obligation. This interdependence can be realized only in that form of solidarity and mutuality that Pius XI called "social love."[15] Again, though love is not a substitute for justice, without it justice becomes a lifeless theory and can neither be adequately conceptualized nor effectively realized in action. As *Quadragesimo anno* put it, echoing Thomas Aquinas:

> Justice alone can, if faithfully observed, remove the causes of social conflict but can never bring about union of minds and hearts. Indeed all the institutions for the establishment of peace and the promotion of mutual

> help among persons, however perfect these may seem, have the principal foundation of their stability in the mutual bond of minds and hearts whereby the members are united with one another. . . . And so, only then will true cooperation be possible for a single common good when the constituent parts of society deeply feel themselves members of one great family and children of the same heavenly Father; nay, that they are one body in Christ, but severally members one of another.[16]

This emphasis on the social role of love has exerted an important influence in the tradition's discussions of the concrete claims of justice.

In all the documents of the tradition, then, the theory of justice is rooted in a philosophical view of the nature of the person as essentially social and simultaneously in an explicitly Christian notion of love as mutuality and as response to persons in the concrete, especially those in need. These theological and philosophical foundations thus point toward the definition of justice in terms of mutually and reciprocally binding obligations. What is *due* to a person or a group is to be determined by the kinds of relationships that shape and influence the life and action of that person or group. Human dignity—the fact that human beings are not things or mere means—always exists *within* these various concrete relationships. The justice or injustice of these relationships is to be judged in terms of the way they promote human dignity by enhancing mutuality and genuine participation in community or, put negatively, by the way they abuse human dignity by reifying persons and excluding or marginalizing them from the relationships without which humanity withers. This vision of mutuality and participation was at the basis of Leo XIII's moral protest against an industrial economy in which "a small number of very rich men have been able to lay upon the teeming masses of the poor *[infinitae proletariorum multitudini]* a yoke little better than slavery itself."[17] It is also the foundation of the 1971 synod's perception of the present international socioeconomic situation:

> Serious injustices . . . are building around the world of human beings a network of domination, oppression and abuses which stifle freedom and which keep the greater part of humanity from sharing in the building up and enjoyment of a more just and more fraternal world. . . . These stifling oppressions constantly give rise to great numbers of "marginal" persons, ill-fed, inhumanly housed, illiterate and deprived of political power as well as of the suitable means of acquiring responsibility and moral dignity.[18]

The notion of justice present in the tradition appeals to the mutuality characteristic of agape in its negative judgments on these patterns of proletarianization and marginalization.

The foundation of the concept of justice in mutuality and love is extraordinarily attractive, especially to contemporary Christians predisposed to be highly critical of the present social configuration of power and wealth. It is a vision capable of inspiring participation in efforts to bring about change. It is also, however, a very general and abstract norm, so general as to provide little more than an attitudinal orientation toward the complexities of social, economic, and political activity. Important as this attitudinal orientation undoubtedly is, the *vision of the foundation of justice* in interdependent responsibility and mutual love needs to be differentiated into a *theory of justice* that determines the relative rights and mutual duties of persons with some degree of specificity. In the words of Paul Ramsey, this vision needs to be "in-principled."[19]

The Importance of Societal Models

The willingness to specify such differentiated and relatively concrete norms of justice is one of the characteristics that has distinguished Roman Catholic social thought from the social ethics of much of twentieth-century Protestantism. The popes and their theological advisors achieved this specificity by an appeal to natural law, that is, by a claim to be able to determine the essential dimensions of the human person and of life in society. By an appeal to rational reflection, the tradition has proposed certain specific human rights, such as the rights to life, food, housing, assembly, etc., as concrete demands of justice and as equally binding on all persons regardless of their religious convictions.[20]

The writings of the popes from Pius IX to Pius XI, however, have also proposed a number of relatively specific moral norms of natural law that are much less attractive to most contemporary Christians. For example, Leo XIII and Pius XI made a very strong defense of social inequality as a characteristic of the natural structure through which human mutuality and interdependence should be realized. In their view some form of social, political, and economic inequality was a necessary element in any order of human relationships that would protect human dignity through stable patterns of mutual dependence.

The appeal to mutuality and response to concrete persons becomes operative as an ethical standard for social life only when it is, so to speak, filtered through a model of society that is used to interpret the causes and effects of possible forms of social and political action. The difference in the model of society employed in different phases of the tradition has led to radically different conclusions about the concrete actions demanded by justice. In trying to determine the meaning of that justice which is a proper expression of Christian faith and love, it is thus necessary *both* to keep in full view the social anthropology and norm of love that has been a constant throughout the tradition *and* to rethink the way this basic norm is to be made concrete through an interpretation of the structures of social interaction. To see the difference in the kinds of conclusions regarding equality to which the tradition has come during the past hundred years, one need only contrast the statement of Vatican II that "with respect to the fundamental rights of the person, every type of discrimination, whether social or cultural, whether based on sex, race, color, social condition or religion, is to be overcome as contrary to God's intent" with Leo XIII's belief that "inequality of rights and of power proceeds from the very author of nature 'from whom all paternity in heaven and on earth is named.' "[21]

The disrepute into which "natural-law" arguments have fallen in recent years among a fair number of Roman Catholic ethicists and theologians is in part traceable to a rejection of some of the conclusions that have been drawn by the tradition on the basis of its interpretation of human nature through appeals to right reason. Such recent Catholic criticism of natural-law thinking frequently echoes one of Reinhold Niebuhr's strongest objections to the traditional Catholic approach to social ethics:

> It rests upon an untenable faith in the purity of reason and it is merely another of the many efforts which men make to find a vantage point of the unconditioned in history. The effect of this pretended finality of "natural law" is obvious. It raises "ideology" to a higher degree of pretension, and is another of the many illustrations in history of the force of sin in the claim of sinlessness.[22]

The lessons that contemporary representatives of this tradition have learned from some of the exaggerated claims made in the past have led to a new caution in claims concerning the possibility of identifying the concrete demands of justice with precision. A kind of epistemological humility has been characteristic of more recent church statements. For example, Paul VI observed:

> [Christian social ethics] no doubt will see its field restricted when it comes to suggesting certain models of society, while its function of making critical judgment and taking an overall view will be strengthened by its showing the relative character of the behavior and values presented by such and such a society as definitive and inherent in the very nature of human beings.[23]

This is a rather remarkable statement coming from the chief spokesman for the tradition that more than any other has claimed to base its moral teaching on the ability to identify at least some of the moral norms which are "definitive and inherent in the very nature of human beings."

The new cautiousness and humility in the attempt to specify what is just and what is unjust has come about for several reasons, all of them evident in Vatican Council II's *Gaudium et spes.* Chief among these was the council's recognition that persons "can come to authentic humanity only through culture, that is, through the cultivation of natural goods and values. Wherever human life is involved, therefore, nature and culture are intimately connected."[24] "Nature" understood as a pregiven structure of human existence and social life does not, therefore, provide a norm of authentic humanity. It must be "cultivated," developed, and enriched through the exercise of human freedom.

The stress on the development of moral norms through cultural activity raises a second major question in the most recent Catholic statements on the meaning of justice. At the council the Catholic tradition came to a new recognition that the openness of human freedom implies a plurality of possible concrete norms of behavior. Moral norms, including the norms of justice, cannot be determined apart from careful scrutiny of the cultural milieu in which they are affirmed to be normative. No cultural or societal arrangement can contain or exhaustively realize the drive toward transcendence which is the fundamental characteristic of the human person.[25] On this basis the council acknowledged that the cultural and social realization of human transcendence and dignity "necessarily has a historical and social aspect" and that "in this sense we speak of a plurality of cultures."[26]

This recognition of pluralism as an expression of the transcendence of the human spirit is the basis of a redefined understanding of the role of reason in the most recent Roman Catholic social statements. These statements acknowledge that scientific thinking, including that of the human sciences, is governed by plural methodologies, and that various insights that can be gained from the use of social analysis, political theory, and social philosophy are necessary but not sufficient components in the enterprise of determining the meaning of justice. No single method for analyzing the problems of social interaction can produce a concretely normative set of conclusions about the demands of justice. Sociological and political analysis, contrary to the implicit assumptions of Leo XIII and Pius XI, cannot provide a model of society that will in some way fully embody the norm of justice in a definitive way.[27] This rules out, at least in principle, claims such as those made by earlier popes that a social system based on private property or on a hierarchical distribution of authority and power is the only rational arrangement and therefore the only just arrangement. The same holds true for similar claims made for any concrete socialist system.[28]

This conclusion is reinforced by the acknowledgment that class, status, race, and social role have important influences on what one admits to be a conclusion of reason. In public argument about social, economic, and political questions, "the very words by which key concepts are expressed take on quite different meanings in diverse ideological systems."[29] In short, the pluralization of reason and the constant danger of ideological and self-protective definitions of justice are recognized. This new caution represents an advance beyond the tradition's past proclivities to identify the patterns of historically conditioned social arrangements with unconditional obligations of justice.

This development presents major problems, however, for it threatens to paralyze action by placing all decisions about social policy under the shadow of relativism. An opposite but correlative danger is that the frustrations induced by the difficulty of discerning concrete norms of justice will lead to uncritical and ultimately counterproductive responses to urgent problems. The task that this places before the church, and especially before moral theologians, has been well stated by James Gustafson:

> The task of theological and ethical work becomes that of finding a justification both for religious belief and for moral decisions which do not deny the relativities of history, but which provide an objectivity short of absolute claims. In ethics the task is to find some degree of order, continuity, and structure within historical change.[30]

The attempt to discover such order, continuity, and structure indicates a way of reading the modern Catholic social tradition that may be of help in the present difficult situation. It has been suggested that the tradition's conclusions concerning the concrete demands of justice have drawn from the social-relational concept of human existence, interpreted in particular ways because of the presence of a historically conditioned social model. Christian faith has no stake in defending a specific social model, be it feudal, capitalist, socialist, or liberal democratic, unless this model either especially promotes or especially threatens the basic Christian ethical conviction concerning the normative character of social interdependence and reciprocal love. The remainder of this essay, then, is an attempt to distill ethical norms from the tradition's fundamental ethical stance that are as specific as possible but not totally historically relative owing to the undue influence of conditioned social theories and models.

Three Kinds of Justice

The centrality of the tradition's concern for the mutual claims of concrete persons is evident in its distinction of three modes or types of justice: commutative justice, distributive justice, and social justice.[31] These three modes of justice are distinguished by the different types of human relationship and interdependence to which they refer. Commutative justice concerns the claims that exist in relations between individual and individual or between groups that are essentially private and nonpolitical, such as voluntary associations. Commutative justice is the form of justice that demands fidelity to agreements, contracts, or promises made between persons or groups outside the political or public process. The obligation of commutative justice is one of fidelity to freely formed mutual bonds and of fairness in exchange. It is rooted in the fundamental equality of persons, an equality that implies that no one may ever presume an arbitrary sovereignty over another by setting aside contracts or promises which have bound two free beings into a relation of mutual interdependence. It implies further that if contracts or agreements are to be just, they must be genuinely free. This latter condition of commutative justice is used extensively throughout the tradition to argue that wage agreements cannot be in accord with commutative justice when a worker is compelled to accept an insufficient wage simply because the only alternative is no wage at all.[32] Commutative justice, then, is an expression in the sphere of private interaction of both the genuine dignity of all persons and the need for a mutuality based on equality in their relationships and agreements.

The other two types of justice—distributive justice and social justice—concern the relative rights and mutual duties that obtain between persons in public society, especially the state and civil society as a whole. Distributive justice specifies the claim which all persons have to some share in those goods that are essentially public or social. Such goods as the fertility of the earth, the productivity of an industrialized economy, and the security provided by advanced systems of health care and social insurance are seen by the documents of the tradition as the products of the social system as a whole. They are not the property of any individual or class in an exclusive sense, for all members of society are at least indirectly involved in their production through membership in public society. Even though participation in the creation of these public goods may be minimal or, in the case of children, infirm or aged persons, presently nonexistent, the tradition claims that membership in the human community creates a bond between persons sufficient to ground a right for all to share in the public good to the minimum degree compatible with human dignity.

Distributive justice is the norm that states the obligation of society and the state to guarantee this participation by all in the common good.[33] The norm of distributive justice, then, specifies the demands of mutuality and interdependence in those relations that determine the opportunity of every person to share or participate in essentially public goods. It establishes the equal right of all to share in all those goods and opportunities that are necessary for genuine participation in the human community. It establishes a strict duty of society as a whole to guarantee these rights.

Social justice concerns institutionalized patterns of mutual action and interdependence that are necessary to bring about the realization of distributive justice. Within the Roman Catholic ethical tradition, social justice has a meaning somewhat more technical than that in contemporary common usage. It refers to the obligations of all citizens to aid in the creation of patterns of societal organization and activity that are essential both for the protection of minimal human rights and for the creation of mutuality and participation by all in social life. In other words, social justice is a political virtue. It is distinguished from the other forms of justice because it is based on that form of human interdependence which occurs through the state. Citizens have a personal obligation, mediated through political obligation, to help create a society in which the concerns of agape can be made effective, namely concerns for concrete needs of all persons and for the creation of reciprocal interdependence. Social justice also states the obligation of the state both to promote distributive justice and to make those legal claims on all citizens that are entailed by this task.

These three forms of justice are evidently interrelated and mutually limiting. All three express the demands of agape. All three contain an egalitarian core: equal claims to mutual freedom and fidelity to contracts in the case of commutative justice, equal rights to mutual participation in the public good in the case of distributive justice, and equal obligation to aid in the creation of social and political structures for participation and mutuality in the case of social justice. These common elements are the foundation of the way the tradition establishes preference rules by which the conflicts between the prima facie claims of the three types of justice can be reconciled. Precisely because commutative justice cannot be realized in situations of drastic economic or social inequality between the partners to a contract or agreement, distributive justice is invoked to set limits to the kind of agreements that can be justly made regarding wages, for example, or to the legitimate accumulation of title to property. When economic or social power is distributed in a grossly unequal way, commutative justice in the economic sphere becomes a factual impossibility. Thus property rights and the operation of a free labor market are morally limited by the interrelated demands of commutative and distributive justice. In addition, the creation of the conditions necessary for both commutative and distributive justice depends on concerted action by society as a whole through its public institutions, especially government. These institutional and political dimensions of the obligations involved are expressed as the claims of social justice.

This distinction between types of justice together with the common root of all three types in agape and mutuality has provided the tradition with a relatively refined language and conceptual framework for the discussion of complex social problems. It is a framework which is at once rooted in the distinctively Christian moral norm of agape and refined through critical reflection on the diverse dimensions of human interaction. It is an approach that provides a degree of "objectivity short of absolute claims" within the relativities of history that Gustafson sees as one of the goals of Christian ethical reflection.

The employment of these three interrelated concepts of justice during the last hundred years of the tradition has been influenced by the tradition's understanding of the power of human reason to identify those social and political structures through which mutual interdependence is most adequately realized. As noted above both Leo XIII and Pius XI were convinced that an unequal distribution of power, authority, status, and wealth was essential to the preservation of a just social order. Because of his identification of the anticlerical and terroristic tactics of Bakuninist anarchism in Italy with the growing egalitarian spirit of his time, Leo XIII frequently adopted arguments based on a hierarchical, semifeudal social model in spelling out the concrete meaning of justice.[34] The hierarchical model of society thus serves as a kind of mold into which the insights of the tradition concerning mutuality and participation are poured. The potential that the norms of justice and love have as sources of major social reform or even revolution were thus severely curtailed in Leo XIII's writings. For example, in *Rerum novarum,* Leo XIII stated that neither distributive justice nor social justice could demand that persons sacrifice possessions appropriate to their proper place within the stratified social hierarchy. In his words:

> No one is commanded to distribute to others that which is required for his own needs and those of his household, nor even to give away what is reasonably required to keep becomingly his condition in life, "for no one ought to live other than becomingly." But when what necessity demands has been supplied and one's standing fairly been taken thought for, it becomes a duty to give to the indigent what remains over.[35]

Thus Leo XIII does not interpret the demands of distributive justice in a way which leads to basic changes in the distribution of status and role that are seen as necessary to the protection of social harmony.

In the more recent phases of the tradition, from Pius XII to the present, this commitment to a basically paternalistic framework for the realization of justice has been gradually abandoned. Especially since John XXIII, official Roman Catholic social teaching has been willing to challenge the adequacy of *any* social model or social structure which denies to persons that minimum level of well-being or degree of participation in the social good which is necessary for the realization of *reciprocal* interdependence and *mutual* human dignity.[36] For example, John XXIII abandoned Leo XIII's reference to what is "becoming" or suitable to one's social status in determining what wealth is superfluous and thus subject to the legitimate claims of the poor. "The obligation of every person, the urgent obligation of the Christian, is to reckon what is superfluous by the measure of the needs of others."[37] Human need takes priority over claims which derive from a stratified system of role-distribution in society.

The same willingness to judge social models and systems by the standards of mutual human dignity was evident in the 1971 synod's affirmation that social and political participation for all is a genuine demand of justice. Justice cannot be realized in a society in which some citizens are prevented from sharing in the decisions that shape the basic structures which determine their fate. "Participation constitutes a right which is to be applied both in the economic and in the social and political field."[38] The realization of participation will take different forms in different social political situations. In this context it is clear, however, that any appeal to the exigencies of a particular social arrangement as grounds for excluding some persons or classes from the process of social decision-making is ruled out by distributive and social justice.

In summary, then, the tradition has made a major shift over the last hundred years in the normative status that it grants to particular social models. In Leo XIII the hierarchical model of society served as a framework for the interpretation of the demands of mutuality and reciprocity. This framework entered into the definition of the meaning of justice and the specification of relative rights and mutual duties. Since John XXIII—especially in *Octogesima adveniens* and *Justitia in mundo*—the situation has been reversed. The norms of agape—mutuality and concern for persons in their particularity and uniqueness—are used to evaluate critically both social models and social systems.

In the newer framework, commutative, distributive, and social justice remain indispensable for the specification of the claims of love. Justice demands equality and fairness in all private transactions, wages, and property ownership. It demands equal opportunity for all to participate in the public goods generated by society as a whole, such as social security, health care, and education. It demands that all persons share in material well-being at least to a level that meets all basic human needs, such as those for food, clothing, shelter, association, etc. And finally it demands that all persons are under an obligation to share in the creation of those public institutions which are necessary for the realization of these other claims of justice.

Justice and Christian Faith

Viewed in the framework of this analysis it becomes clear that the theory of justice presented in the tradition is a *Christian* theory of justice. Though Catholicism makes no claim to have insight into the nature of justice which is inaccessible to non-Christians, the theory it advocates comes out of the fundamental norm of Christian love. Commitment to the hierarchical model of social order as a demand of reason surely prevented the standard of agape from having its full impact in earlier years. The unwillingness of the recent statements to adopt *any* social model as in itself normative has brought the norm of agape into the forefront of the discussions of justice. By retaining many of the insights of Leo XIII and Pius XI concerning the relationships between commutative, distributive, and social justice, however, the tradition has been able to avoid falling into the kind of appeal to love that shapes attitudes but has little to say about the complexities of social policy and economic life.

The tripartite notion of commutative-distributive-social justice, understood in this way, does not provide immediate answers to the complex problems of social existence, but it does provide principles of discernment and quite specific guides for judgment. Justice explicates the response that love calls for in the differentiated but related relationships of social and interpersonal interdependence. Discernment and judgment concerning the concrete actions called for in particular situations depend, therefore, on the mutuality and concern for individual persons which is love and on the analysis of interaction of different types of human relationships expressed in the tripartite principle of justice.

The position adopted at the 1971 synod pushes the argument for an explicitly Christian notion of justice to an even deeper level. The affirmation that the doing of justice is constitutive of Christian faith is rooted in the way the bishops developed the relationship that exists between faith and love. The God in whom Christians believe is a God of love. Out of love God established his covenant with humanity and promised to be forever "the liberator of the oppressed and the defender of the poor."

Thus the call to respond to this God of the covenant is a permanent call "to turn away from self-sufficiency to confidence in God and from concern for self to a sincere love of neighbor." Because God has identified with all persons through the covenant, especially with the "least brethren,"[39] and because every person is a true image of God, response to God in faith and response to the neighbor in love and solidarity are inseparable. Therefore, "the Christian finds in every person God's own self and God's absolute demand for justice and love."[40]

This theological and religious framework is at the very root of the Christian vocation to justice and the meaning of justice elaborated in the most recent phase of the modern Catholic tradition. The tradition has recognized the problematic and pluralistic definition of justice present in contemporary social and political philosophy. It also recognizes the profound problem of apathy that afflicts contemporary society. Its answer to both the definitional and the motivational problems is an appeal to Christian faith—to the biblical story of Jesus and its continuation in the redemptive presence of grace in time:

> The uncertainty of history and the painful convergences in the ascending path of the human community direct us to sacred history; there God has revealed himself to us, and made known to us, as it is brought progressively to realization, his plan of liberation and salvation which is once and for all fulfilled in the paschal mystery of Christ.[41]

The paschal mystery of Christ is the very core of Christian faith—belief in the redemptive and exemplary significance of Christ's death and resurrection. The synod's statement that action for justice is constitutive of the preaching of the gospel can thus be inverted without doing violence to its substance: faith in the paschal mystery of Christ is a constitutive dimension of both Christian action on behalf of justice and of the effort to formulate a Christian definition of justice.

This Christian pursuit of justice will be action rooted in solidarity with all persons, especially the poor. It will be action conformed to the demands of mutuality and reciprocal interdependence expressed in the norms of commutative, distributive, and social justice. It will be action that acknowledges the claim of every unique individual to those material and social goods necessary for the satisfaction of basic human needs: food, clothing, housing, health care, social security, decent working conditions, etc.

These claims of justice are not known only by Christians. But Christian faith, as interpreted by the developing Roman Catholic tradition, implies that these obligations of justice are religious obligations for all who profess this faith.[42] The norms of justice we have been discussing are not derived simply from a natural philosophical ethic, nor are they of peripheral concern to the Christian community as an organized institution. There is, in short, a Christian theory of justice and an explicitly Christian obligation to seek this justice, both of which are rooted in the covenant love of God for all persons and in the fulfillment of this love in the death and resurrection of Christ.

The roots of this approach to justice in the paschal mystery suggest one final reflection on the developing Catholic social tradition. This view of the possibility of achieving mutuality and reciprocal interdependence in society clearly calls for significant changes in both individual behavior and institutional arrangements. Solidarity and concern for concrete persons implies a kind of self-surrender and self-sacrifice that is contradictory to the self-interest which is the linchpin of so much modern political theory. This norm of justice may appear to be utopian, idealistic, and even naive. It need not be interpreted this way, however.

First, this theory of justice affirms the equal claims of all persons to those goods and the kind of participation in society which are essential to their dignity as persons. The call to self-sacrifice touches only privilege and superfluity, not essentials and basic human needs. The call to self-surrender is not a call to self-immolation but rather a call to a form of solidarity and reciprocity in which the true fulfillment of self is to be found. Those who disagree that fulfillment is to be found in this way are unjustified in calling this theory naive or utopian. They may call it wrong or untrue if they wish. Such an objection, however, is an objection based on an ultimate interpretation of the meaning of human fulfillment, not a judgment of whether such a community of mutuality is possible or not.

Second, Christian faith affirms that the full achievement of this mutuality and reciprocity is an eschatological hope, to be realized only in the kingdom of God. Human sinfulness and the finiteness of persons make the historical realization of justice always imperfect and partial. Thus this theory of Christian justice can concede that it is in a certain sense utopian.[43] Christian faith is eschatological faith and the Christian pursuit of justice involves an eschatological hope. The movement from the imperfect justice of the present to the perfect justice of the kingdom is thus a movement sustained and guided by faith. This faith, however, is not simply a formless trust. It has a content and shape: that of the paschal mystery of Jesus Christ. The movement of history toward its culmination in the kingdom of God is a movement that follows the pattern of death and resurrection.[44] The pursuit of justice is itself part of this movement.

Eschatological hope, therefore, does not weaken the obligations of justice. Precisely the opposite is the case. Christian faith in the ultimate coming of God's kingdom is a call to share in the death and resurrection of Christ. Christian justice is a specification of how this sharing is to be made present in the relations between persons in history. This implies that the struggle for justice—for a justice both defined and motivated by Christian faith in the paschal mystery—is an expression of the presence of grace and eschatological hope. By the very nature of their faith Christians are called to be continually attentive to the emergence of new possibilities for reciprocal mutuality. They are called to continue this struggle in the face of setbacks, discouragement, and even defeat. These are the consequences of the definitional and motivational links that relate faith and justice to each other internally. Efforts toward the fulfillment of minimum human needs and the realization of structures of genuine mutuality are consequences of faith in Jesus Christ. They are religious obligations of all Christians and of the church as an organized actor in society.

Part Two

Economic Justice and the World of Work

Chapter 3

Human Work and the Story of Creation

This essay will address the encyclical letter *Laborem exercens* from the viewpoint of theological ethics. There is a certain irony in the assumption that a theologian might have anything useful to say about the significance of work. Can one think of a reality that is more of "this world" than human labor and toil? If one supposes that religious belief and the worship of God are preeminently activities of the Sabbath—the day of rest—then work would seem to be quite beyond the pale of the theologian's concern. The same irony is present in the idea that a religious leader like Pope John Paul II might be able to add anything useful to an appreciation and understanding of work. Indeed, in Hannah Arendt's interpretation of the Western history of ideas about work and politics, the Christian religion has contributed to a significant devaluation of these two chief poles of public life. According to Arendt, the Christian ethic, "while it is incapable of founding a public realm of its own, is quite adequate to the main Christian principle of worldlessness and is admirably fit to carry a group of essentially worldless people through the world."[1]

Laborem exercens forcefully challenges the presupposition that Christian faith is concerned with the Sabbath to the exclusion of interest in the everyday or interested in the *vita contemplativa* to the detriment of the *vita activa*. The pope's claim to be able to make some contribution to our understanding of the meaning and value of work is based on two complementary aspects of the Christian doctrine of creation: God is the active creator and sustainer of all that is, and human beings are created and sustained by God in their very being and their every action. In view of the encyclical, the divine action of creation and the created human activity of work are not related to each other as Sabbath to weekday or as sacred to profane. There is a dynamic interrelation between God's action as creator and the human activity of work. As the encyclical puts it, "The word of God's revelation is profoundly marked by the fundamental truth that the human person, created in the image of God, shares by his work in the activity of the Creator and that, within the limits of his own capabilities, the human person in a sense continues to develop that activity, and perfect it as he advances further and further in the discovery of the resources and values in the whole of creation."[2] In other words, human work "is a participation in God's activity."[3]

This claim is a bold one, both from the point of view of Christian theology and from the perspective of our ordinary experience of what work is really like. Theologically it runs the risk of arrogantly inflating the significance of what we humans can do and who we humans really are. Karl Barth, the great theologian of the "otherness" of God, has warned us against the pretense that can be operative in such claims about human work. Though Barth would agree that a human being can in some sense participate in the activity of God, he insists that "this does not mean that he becomes a co-creator, co-saviour or co-regent in God's activity. It does not mean that he becomes a kind of co-God."[4] In addition to this possible arrogance, such claims for the significance of human work risk trivializing our understanding of the creative action of God. In cultures where work is alienated or increasingly meaningless for large numbers of people, the close linking of human work with the activity of God is no compliment to God. Further, such linkage could bestow a false aura of religious legitimacy to social patterns that should be challenged or simply overthrown by those who not only believe that God is creator but also that God is good.

Laborem exercens is not unaware of these dangers. For example, it calls for a perspective on human work that shows "the maturity called for by the tensions of mind and heart"[5] which permeate work life in the present day. It asserts that its interpretation of the value of labor "will require a reordering and adjustment of the structures of the modern economy and of the distribution of work."[6] It challenges all patterns of work that alienate the worker from work when it affirms that "in the first place work is 'for persons' and not persons 'for work.'"[7] It also argues that capital or the means of production are *instruments* for the enhancement of human creativity and human fulfillment. They must never be allowed to become the determining forces in the economic process.[8] It directs these criticisms at both "rigid capitalism" and at the state capitalism of bureaucratic collectivism.[9] The encyclical challenges the present international distribution of labor as a threat to human dignity and says that "both within the individual political communities and in their relationships on the continental and world levels there is something wrong with the organization of work and employment, precisely at the most critical and socially most important points."[10]

These criticisms of present structures of work are advanced in the name of an understanding of the relation between God as creator and the human person as creature. The present essay will focus on a limited part of this argument: the theological interpretation of the interconnection between human work and the creative and preserving action of God. It will be argued that the encyclical's approach to this theological question is useful but incomplete, and that this incompleteness leads to an oversimplification of the issues that arise in a Christian ethical approach to the problems of the domain of work.

The argument will have three phases. First, the encyclical's use of the book of Genesis will be considered, for the theology of *Laborem exercens* rests squarely on this biblical source. Second, some suggestions will be made about how a more complex understanding of the tensions and conflicts of the world of work is called for in a theology based on a more nuanced reading of the first book of the Bible. Finally a few suggestions will be advanced about the ethical implications of these first two considerations. Thus this essay will not deal with many of the valuable points raised in the encyclical. It has the modest purpose of exploring the theology of *Laborem exercens* and a few of the ethical consequences of this theology.

The Implications of Genesis 1–11 for a Theology of Work

Laborem exercens bases its analysis of the significance and proper ordering of human labor on a number of intellectual sources. It relies on the past social teachings of the church on related socioeconomic questions and claims fundamental continuity with this tradition.[11] True to the Roman Catholic natural-law tradition with its emphasis on the significance of human experience and reason as sources for theology and ethics, *Laborem exercens* affirms that philosophical and sociol-scientific analyses play a legitimate and important role in shaping its conclusions. John Paul II, however, asserts that the church's contribution to the discussion of work is formed "not only in the light of historical experience, not only with the aid of the many methods of scientific knowledge, but in the first place in the light of the revealed word of the living God."[12] As René Coste has noted, the pope's aim is the presentation of a "truly theological anthropology of work."[13]

The keystone of the encyclical's theological discussion is its interpretation of the first chapters of the book of Genesis. An indication of the importance of the Genesis accounts in the pope's reflection is the fact that twenty-one of the document's ninety-one footnotes contain references to the first book of the Bible. Indeed the encyclical is quite explicit about the relevance of Genesis to its understanding of work: "The church finds in the very first pages of the book of Genesis the source of her conviction that work is a fundamental dimension of human existence on earth. An analysis of these texts makes us aware that they express—sometimes in an archaic way of manifesting thought—the fundamental truths about the human person in the context of the mystery of creation itself."[14] Thus, without excluding what can be learned about the structure and dynamics of work from all the human sciences, John Paul II relies on biblical sources to support his assertion that what the encyclical presents as "a conviction of the intellect is also a conviction of faith."[15] In other words, it is the pope's appeal to the biblical sources and their interpretation in living Christian tradition that warrants his claim to a distinctive though not exclusive competence to speak on the meaning and values of human work.

There are several verses from Genesis to which the pope repeatedly refers in developing the theme of human work as a participation in the creative activity of God. Most prominent among these are three verses in the so-called Priestly account of creation found in Genesis 1, i.e., verses 26–28.

> 26Then God said, "Let us make *adam* in our image, after our likeness; and let them have dominion over the fish of the sea, and over the birds of the air, and over the cattle, and over all the earth, and over every creeping thing that creeps upon the earth." 27So God created *adam* in his own image, in the image of God he created him; male and female he created them. 28And God blessed them, and God said to them, "Be fruitful and multiply, and fill the earth and subdue it; and have dominion over the fish of the sea and over the birds of the air and over every living thing that moves upon the earth."

These verses provide a central part of the foundation of the encyclical's theology of work. John Paul II employs them to support the link he sees between human work and the creative activity of God.

In the Image of God

First, human beings in some way reflect and embody the nature of God. This is the meaning of the affirmation that human beings are created "in the image of God." Throughout the history of Christian thought the creation of humankind as *imago Dei* has been interpreted in a variety of ways. It has been taken to mean that, like God, human beings are persons rather than animals or things. That is to say, humans are capable of self-conscious awareness.[16] In a closely related interpretation, humans are seen as images of God through their possession of both reason and freedom, faculties which give them the capacity for both self-determination and moral responsibility.[17] Others have interpreted the divine image as the human capacity for interpersonal relationship, for friendship, for community life in society, and for love.[18] None of these readings of the meaning of the image of God in human persons is excluded by *Laborem exercens*. Rather, John Paul II has focused on an interpretation that is more explicitly suggested by the biblical text itself. Human persons are like God through their commission to subdue the earth and have dominion over the rest of creation.

The significance of work is directly linked to the creation of humankind in the image of God through this interpretation of the *imago Dei*. In the words of the encyclical, "The human person is the image of God partly through the mandate received from the creator to subdue, to dominate, the earth. In carrying out this mandate, humankind, every human being, reflects the very action of the creator of the universe."[19] The encyclical thus understands all the creativity of civilization and the economy as an expression of the image of the Creator in the human creature. Whether work be agricultural or industrial, physical, or intellectual, more traditional in form or in the technologically advanced spheres of electronics and scientific research, the encyclical affirms that all forms of creative activity by which nature is brought to the service of human ends are an expression of the image and likeness of the Creator in the human creature.

The biblical language that speaks of human "dominance" over nature and of the commission to "subdue the earth" has been criticized as a prime source of ecological irresponsibility in Western society and culture.[20] Recent biblical studies have shown, however, that the attitude toward nature expressed in Genesis 1:26–28 is one of stewardship rather than exploitation.[21] John Paul II has elsewhere expressed his sensitivity to the responsibility humans have for the preservation of the natural and biological worlds. In his first encyclical letter, *Redemptor hominis*, he affirmed that this same biblical passage commissions the human race to be "master" and "guardian" rather than "exploiter" and "destroyer" of nature.[22]

It is unfortunate that this emphasis has not been reiterated in *Laborem exercens*. This omission has occurred, it seems, because the encyclical's primary purpose is to emphasize what it calls the "subjective dimension" of work. The *imago Dei* motif is brought forward to emphasize that in work human beings must remain true agents and that both the means of production and the fruit of labor are at the service of those who work. A person's activities in work "must serve to realize his humanity, to fulfill the calling to be a person that is his by reason of his very humanity."[23] Thus the theological interpretation of human "dominance" over nature supports the encyclical's fundamental principle that work is not simply "merchandise" to be bought and sold. Rather, the account of creation set forth in Genesis 1 stands as a critique of any economic system in which persons are "treated on the same level as the whole complex of the material means of production."[24] The great strength of the encyclical lies in its willingness to direct this critique against both national economic systems and against transnational and international economic arrangements that violate this principle.

The major theological contribution of the encyclical, therefore, lies in the grounding it provides for a very positive evaluation of human work through the interpretation of the *imago Dei* as expressed in the subjectivity of workers. This is undoubtedly a most important theme in the Genesis narratives. Indeed there are additional episodes in these narratives that can further reinforce the positive evaluation of work and the critical principle of the subjectivity and dignity of workers which the pope wants to emphasize. For example, Genesis 2:15 describes God placing the first human being in the Garden of Eden with the charge to "till and keep it." Thus work is part of human life in its created, paradisiacal state. It is created by God as "very good." It is not merely the result of human sin. The geneology contained in Genesis 4:17–22 portrays the origins of civilization, with the emergence of urban culture, animal husbandry, the arts, and technology. These developments are regarded as signs of God's continuing blessing on the creativity of humankind. In Genesis 8:22 God promises to Noah that this blessing shall continue "as long as the earth remains," and Genesis 9 extends the promise of God's preservation and blessing in an "everlasting covenant" with "all flesh that is upon the earth."

The Reality of Sin

Despite the legitimacy and value of the encyclical's powerful biblical argument for the dignity of both work and worker, the picture that it offers us seems to me to be an incomplete one. The absence of the qualifications on the meaning of human "dominance" over nature that are called for by a critical exegesis of the whole creation narrative raises a question about the overall use of Genesis in *Laborem exercens.* The narratives of Genesis 1–11 are a rich and complex whole. They present a description of human existence and the human predicament by recounting a set of highly compressed narratives about cosmic and human origins. The full biblical theology of the relation between Creator and human creature must take the whole of the Genesis creation story into consideration and also situate it in the context of the rest of the Old and New Testament.

The exposition of such a fully developed biblical theology of creation and work is beyond the scope of this essay. In responding to *Laborem exercens* from the perspective of theological ethics a more limited point can be made. Elaboration of the theology of the participation of human work in the creative activity of God calls for greater attention to the aspects of the Genesis narrative that focus on the problematic and even sinful dimensions of human agency and human action. The Genesis account of human origins, taken as a whole, is less sanguine about the ease with which human civilization and human productivity can be brought into harmony with the creative and preservative blessing of God than *Laborem exercens* appears to be.

The Genesis narratives are myths and certainly not to be confused with scientific or historical documents. The value and religious significance of these myths derive from their ability to form and express an appreciation of the ultimate shape of human existence as a whole. As Paul Ricoeur has put it, "the 'Adamic' myth is the anthropological myth *par excellence*."[25] The accounts of the origins of cosmos and humanity found in Genesis are narratives that recount events from primal time in order to describe the *present* condition of human existence. These mythic narratives are attentive not only to the potentialities inherent in a world that has been created as radically good. They also evoke the limits of human capacities and the hardships to which human beings are subject. They describe the origins not only of human creativity but also of human "deviation" or "going astray."[26] Moreover, as the biblical scholar Claus Westermann has shown, the context for the initial elaboration of the Genesis narratives was that of danger, the struggle for survival, and the experience of the self as threatened.[27] The subsequent recounting of the creation myths "had the function of preserving the world and of giving security to life"[28] by situating danger, threat, and sin in the larger context of a good God and a good creation. A fully adequate interpretation of the depiction of human agency and human work as they are portrayed in Genesis must take this into account.

Laborem exercens takes note of the fact that the Genesis accounts include evocations of the limits, burdens, and threats to human creativity. The encyclical points out that, because of the disobedience of Adam and Eve to the command of God, human work is often full of toil: "In the sweat of your face you shall eat your bread" (Gen 3:19). Work is sometimes sterile and unproductive: "Thorns and thistles it shall bring forth to you" (Gen 3:18).[29] These references to the ambiguities of the situation of human agency and labor, however, are considerably less developed in the encyclical than they are in the creation account in the first eleven chapters of Genesis.

There are five major events in the total narrative of origins that mythically portray the emergence of sin and the destructive capacity of human agency: the disobedience of Adam and Eve and their consequent expulsion from the Garden of Eden (Gen 3), Cain's murder of his brother Abel (Gen 4:2–16), the marriage of the "sons of God" with the "daughters of men" and the limitation on the span of human life because of this infraction (Gen 6:1–4), God's destruction of the earth by flood as a result of pervasive wickedness in human hearts (Gen 6:5–7:24), and scattering of the peoples of the earth and the confusion of their languages as a result of the people's attempt to build a city "and a tower with its top in the heavens" (Gen 11:1–9).

It is not the purpose here to present a detailed interpretation of these passages. Two brief observations will serve to show their importance for an understanding of the relation between human work and the creative activity of God. First, an underlying motif in the narratives is the distortion of the capacities of human freedom and agency that follows from a failure to recognize the limited nature of these capacities. This is most evident in the serpent's temptation of Adam and Eve by holding out the possibility that they might become "like God" (Gen 3:5). It is present in the overstepping of the boundary between the divine and the human expressed in the myth of the marriage of the "sons of God" with the "daughters of men." It reappears in the story of the Tower of Babel, where the desire of the people to "make a name" for themselves (Gen 11:4) leads them to try to climb the heavens through the tools of their own technology.[30] The motif of the creation of human persons "in the image of God" is thus held in tension with the powerful warning that human superiority over nature is the occasion of a perpetual temptation to try to become "like God" through knowledge, sexuality, technology, or other human capacities. Though created in God's image, human beings are creatures, not God or even demigods. If they deny their creatureliness they obscure the *imago Dei* as well.

Second, the Genesis myths concerning the origin of sin directly link the distortion of the relation of creature to God with the distortion of the relations within the human community as well. Among the consequences of the effort of the first couple to become "like God" is a distortion of the relation of mutuality and equality that characterizes their existence as created by God into a relation of domination and subordination (Gen 3:16).[31] The story of Cain and Abel should be understood as a further elaboration of this distortion of human relationships which follows upon the failure of humans to accept their creatureliness. The words that God addresses to Adam after he has eaten the forbidden fruit, "Adam, where are you?" are directly paralleled by the words God addresses to Cain after the murder of Abel, "Where is Abel, your brother?" The alienation from God that follows upon the effort to transcend the status of creature is paralleled by the alienation from fellow-humans that follows on the effort to escape the responsibility of being our "brother's keeper." And finally, the Tower of Babel story not only portrays an act of rebellion against humanity's earthbound nature but also gives an account of how human history has become a battleground of conflict and misunderstanding because of this rebellion.

On the basis of his exegesis of all these passages from Genesis, Westermann has concluded that the breakdown in the participation of human activity in the creative action of God and the breakdown in the life of human society are inseparable from each other.

> In the biblical account of the origins sin is not the narrow, individualistic notion that it has become in church tradition. It is viewed in a broader perspective. It is seen as that other limit, that inadequacy or overstepping of limits which determines the whole of human existence. Sin shows itself in many forms in all areas of human life and not merely in a personal confrontation of man and God. It is to be reckoned with in all aspects of the human community, where man is at work as well as in the world of politics.[32]

The first eleven chapters of the book of Genesis thus evidently contain an interpretation of human capacity and agency that is in marked tension with the theology that sees human work and dominance over nature as manifestations of the image of God in human beings. The theology underlying *Laborem exercens*' valuation of work is indeed warranted by the Genesis narrative of origins. *Laborem exercens,* however, does not present us with the *whole* of the biblical perspective on the potentialities and limits of human creativity in work. The problem of presenting a complete and unified interpretation of the biblical perspective on *any* question of fundamental human importance is notoriously difficult. The biblical sources are internally pluralistic and cannot be simply harmonized into a tightly integrated theological framework.[33] The fact that there is a certain selectivity in the way *Laborem exercens* reads the book of Genesis, therefore, should not be surprising. Nevertheless, a balanced theology of work calls for greater attention to the aspects of the biblical story that are deemphasized in the encyclical. In what follows a few suggestions will be made about how such balance might be sought.

The Theology of Work on a More Complete Biblical Basis

Historical-critical analysis of the narratives of origins has concluded that there are two main sources upon which the redactor of Genesis has relied in constructing the text as we have it in the canonical Bible. The theology of *Laborem exercens* relies heavily, one might say almost exclusively, on passages that can be traced to the so-called Priestly redactor or P source of the sixth–fifth century B.C. By contrast, the narratives of Adam and Eve's disobedience, of Cain and Abel, of the marriage of the "sons of God" and the "daughters of men," and of the Tower of Babel can all be traced back to the older tenth–ninth century B.C. author known as the "Yahwist."

This earlier Yahwistic theology is considerably more attuned to the ambiguities of human creativity and work than are the emphases added by the Priestly author. Gerhard von Rad has called the Yahwist "the great psychologist" among the biblical writers. Like his Christian successors Augustine, Pascal, and Reinhold Niebuhr, the Yahwist's theology includes deep reflection on the "riddles and conflicts" of human behavior and the "mistakes and muddles" present in the human heart.[34] The Priestly author, on the other hand, is more the architect than the psychologist. He is concerned with establishing a well-integrated social system with temple cult, theocratic governance, and religious law as the soul of this system. In the words of Bernhard Anderson, "the Priestly writer does not portray sympathetically the human side of the historical drama: the people's conflicts, frustrations, anxieties, doubts. He lacks the 'human interest' that we find in the Yahwist's story of Paradise Lost or in the narrative of Abraham's supreme test of faith; for his concern is with the laws and institutions that were given to the people in the climactic period of Sinai."[35]

Westermann, among others, has pointed out that the Priestly tradition originated in the context of that phase of Jewish religion which had as its primary focus the rebuilding of the temple in Jerusalem and the reestablishment of Jewish society after the Babylonian exile.[36] The positive valuation of human creativity in the Priestly source is directly linked with the religious developments taking place in response to the author's social-historical context. The Priestly tradition elaborates a theology of human creativity that is considerably more expansive than one which would affirm that the building of temples is the prime focus of human work. Nevertheless the connection between an almost entirely positive valuation of the fruits of human culture and the religious aims of the priestly author is not accidental. The priestly theology is a theology for a religiously centered and organically integrated society.

One should not be surprised to discover a similar conjunction of religious and sociocultural interests in a contemporary document like *Laborem exercens.* Pope John Paul's preference for the Priestly strand in the book of Genesis can be explained at least in part by the analogies that exist between the social-historical context of the Priestly author and the context that has shaped the pope's thought. Both have experienced severe restriction on the religious and national aspirations of their people—the Priestly author through exile in Babylon and the pope through the restrictions imposed on the Polish people by a succession of foreign powers. Both are convinced that the preservation of nationhood and the preservation of religious identity are closely interconnected. Thus both defend a close connection between cultural creativity, historical tradition, and religious fidelity. The highly positive estimation of the value of human creativity as an expression of the image of God in human existence serves to link religion and culture closely together in both the Priestly theology and the theology of *Laborem exercens.* Their theologies of work are developed as components of this understanding of the organic link between religion and culture.

John Paul II has made this larger cultural concern most evident in an address at the headquarters of UNESCO. In this address he stated that the justification for his presence in a forum such as UNESCO was "*the organic and constitutive link* which exists between *religion* in general and Christianity in particular, on the one hand, and *culture* on the other hand. This relationship extends to the multiple realities which must be defined as concrete expressions of culture in the different periods of history and all over the world."[37] The social paradigm for the pope's reflections is that of a society in which Christianity and social, economic, and cultural life are closely interwoven. This model of social-religious-cultural integration governs the pope's analysis of work. It also serves as the basis of *Laborem exercens'* repeated appeals for solidarity among workers and for collaboration and cooperation among all components of the economy. John Paul's theology, in other words, gives primacy to organic unity and integration among the diverse elements of social, economic, and religious life. An organically unified social life is seen as an expression of both the fullness of what it means to be human and the depths of what it means to be Christian. It is in this sense that one can say that the theology of *Laborem exercens* is a Priestly theology.

The Yahwistic account of human and cosmic origins is much less optimistic about the ability of the human race to achieve this kind of harmonious integration than is either the Priestly author or *Laborem exercens.* The story of the Tower of Babel, which von Rad has called "the keystone to the Yahwistic primeval history" presents us with a picture of the very antithesis of human community bound together by bonds of solidarity and cultural integration.[38] The potential of work, technology, culture, and even religion to become sources of conflict and destruction is a leitmotif of the Yahwist narratives. Because all these achievements of human creativity can and in fact sometimes do lead to rebellion against God and murder of fellow-humans, the Yahwist continually reminds humankind of its limits: "You are dust, and to dust you shall return" (Gen 3:19). A balanced theology of work must take this perspective into account.

Where, then, does this leave us in the effort to understand the participation of human work and creativity in the creative action of God? One possibility would be to say that we are left free by the biblical sources to choose between the Priestly or Yahwist emphases according to the needs of our own cultural or economic situation. Such an approach is to some extent inevitable, for a complete unification of these diverse emphases in a single theology is not finally possible. If the biblical witness, however, is to serve as a challenge to the cultural milieu and not simply as a legitimation of it then this kind of selectivity cannot be a fully adequate response to the pluralism of biblical theologies. An alternative approach would be to try to find some sort of compromise between the alternatives contained in the two biblical sources examined here. This could take the form of a search for a least common denominator or for a theological midpoint between them. The danger of this solution is the elimination of theological tension that it entails. The biblical view of the relation between human and divine creativity is not some neutral perspective halfway between Priestly optimism and Yahwist pessimism. It includes both of these emphases.

The Tension between Goodness and Perversity

The beginnings of a solution to this problem can be uncovered if we consider the fact that the two traditions we have been discussing have in fact been woven together by the editors who produced the book of Genesis in the final form that it takes in the Bible. It is this document, in the context of the whole Bible, that is normative for a Christian theology of work and human creativity. The Genesis account as a whole presents us with the biblical picture of the origins and potential of human work. Thus it is possible to read Genesis as an account of two *aspects* of human creativity rather than as a simple juxtaposition of two different accounts of human creativity.

The most probing recent discussion of the relationship between the two aspects of the mythic narrative is that of Paul Ricoeur. Ricoeur has shown that the Yahwist myth of the "Fall" and expulsion from the Garden, together with its consequences of murder and cultural conflicts, is a narrative way of evoking an experience of a fundamental "rift" in human existence. This "rift" is the deep tension between the ontological goodness of the God-created human being and the actual perversity that is written on the pages of human history. It is the experience expressed in the classic words of Rousseau: "Man is born free, and everywhere he is in chains."[39] In the Yahwist strand of the Genesis narrative the goodness of created humanity is evoked by the portrayal of a state *before* the advent of murder and historical conflict. Evil is not a necessary consequence of created human nature but rather the result of the free human attempt to transcend the limits of creaturely goodness. Evil and sin are real and powerful realities, but they are the contingent results of human freedom rather than the necessary outcome of human nature. Thus the Yahwist's account of the conflicts that emerge in the free exercise of human creativity is set against the background of the affirmation that "sin is not our original reality, does not constitute our first ontological status; sin does not define what it is to be" a human being.[40] The Yahwist account, in other words, makes its assertions about the capacities of human creativity in the negative mode: the human quest for knowledge leads to loss of innocence—but it need not be so; the productivity of technology leads to strife and cultural conflict—but it need not be so; the religious quest to be like God and to ascend the heavens leads to rivalry and murder—but it need not be so. These same assertions about the goodness of human capacity and creativity are made by the Priestly tradition in directly affirmative and positive terms. The Priestly author focuses in the first place on the ontological status of human capacities—they are very good—rather than on their actual exercise in history and in civilization. The Priestly tradition has taken the Yahwist's affirmation of the contingency of sin and evil and transformed it into a positive theological assertion of the ontological goodness of human capacities and human nature. As Ricoeur has put it, the Yahwist's "it need not be so" is "the radical intuition which the future editor of the second creation-story (Gen 1) will sanction by the word of the Lord God: 'Let us make man in our image, after our likeness.' "[41]

These two traditions, therefore, are reflecting on human existence and human capacities for creativity from two different points of view. The Priestly tradition is principally concerned with the created being or essence of humanity. To apply a category drawn from another time, the Priestly theology is rooted in an ontological and metaphysical interest. The Yahwist, on the other hand, is preoccupied by the historical and social expressions of these capacities in all their ambiguity. His theology is rooted in the categories of historical, social, cultural, and religious critique. An adequate theology of work cannot disregard either of these perspectives. Pure ontological reflection on the created goodness of the human person risks irrelevance to actual historical conflict and oppression if it ignores the Yahwist's sensitivity to such historical realities. On the other hand, purely historical reflection on the outcomes of the exercise of human creativity in society risks leading one to the conclusion of Qoheleth: "Vanity of vanities! All is vanity. What does a man gain by all the toil at which he toils under the sun?" (Eccles 1:2–3). An adequate theology of work and human creativity needs *both* a deep sensitivity to the capacity of human beings to be cocreators with God *and* a ruthlessly realistic assessment of the conflicts and oppressions that human freedom can and does create. Without the first the theology has no basis for hope and thus cannot be Christian. Without the second the theology will not be capable of generating an ethic that is usable in human history—the time between Paradise and the coming of the kingdom of God.

Conclusion: An Ethical Implication

The implications of this analysis for ethical reflection on human work are multiple. By way of conclusion a single brief comment on the ethical approach of *Laborem exercens* will be offered here. It is developed more fully in the following two chapters. The encyclical presents a strong case for an ethic that seeks to promote cooperation, collaboration, solidarity, and harmony among all persons involved in the work process.[42] The same concerns are evident in the pope's discussion of international and transnational economic processes.[43] These ethical emphases are rooted in the encyclical's theology of both the genuine creativity of human work and its emphasis on the capacities of human beings for genuinely communal cooperation. The creation of human beings in the image of God is the ultimate foundation for such an ethical standpoint. This ethic is also capable of providing real support for some important new developments presently underway in national and international economic discussions. This aspect of the encyclical deserves support and gratitude.

It can be asked, however, if *Laborem exercens'* ethic is adequate for use in situations where collaboration, solidarity, and cooperation are unlikely or impossible. From the foregoing analysis it is evident that John Paul II has deemphasized the conflictual elements of the Genesis account of human existence and human work. In another series of reflections on the book of Genesis he has made clear his conviction that the Priestly tradition represents a theological advance over the Yahwist. In the pope's words the Priestly source "is much more mature both as regards the image of God, and as regards the formulation of the essential truths about man. . . . Man is defined there, first of all, in dimensions of being and existence *('Esse')*. He is defined in a way that is more metaphysical than physical."[44] John Paul II, in other words, gives primacy to a style of theology that is more metaphysical and ontological over theological approaches that are more historical.[45] This approach is quite capable of denouncing all situations that do not conform to the structure of human personhood as this structure is discerned through ontological analysis. Its danger, however, is that it will lack the categories that are necessary to guide action in nonideal circumstances.

To paraphrase Ricoeur, the gap that exists between the ideal possibilities of created human nature and the realities of history is paralleled by a gap between a description of personhood set forward in ontological terms and an ethic that can guide action in the midst of conflict.[46] *Laborem exercens*' contribution lies in its description of and theological support for the possibilities of human creativity. It is less developed in its approach to the practical and political questions that arise in the actual struggle to realize these possibilities. This limitation is rooted in the document's theology.

Both the traditional ideologies of liberal capitalism and Marxist socialism, each in different ways, are more attentive to the realities of conflict and struggle in the world of work than is *Laborem exercens*. The encyclical is certainly aware of the need for worker struggle, and it reaffirms such techniques of struggle as labor unions, the strike, and the right to a just wage. What remains unclear is how these legitimate rights are to be exercised in practice according to the encyclical's ethic of collaboration and solidarity. More detailed analysis of the practical possibilities and actual impediments to such collaboration is needed if the gap between ontology and ethics is to be bridged. A theology that is based on a more complete reading of Genesis than that found in *Laborem exercens* would help make it clear that such detailed analysis is essential in a religious vision of work as cocreation.

Chapter 4

Unemployment and Jobs: A Social, Theological, and Ethical Analysis

The need for Christian social ethics to attend to the conflicts and tensions inherent in socioeconomic life can be illustrated by examining a question of considerable importance in the United States today—that of unemployment and job-generation. From Leo XIII to John Paul II, papal social teaching has addressed no set of concrete issues more consistently and systematically than those of just wages, adequate working conditions, and other topics connected with the domain of human labor. These issues have also occupied a major place in the past teachings of the U.S. Catholic bishops and the writings of Catholic scholars in the field of ethics. In addition, the problem of unemployment is a central one in the public discussion of economic justice in the United States today. So it is certainly fitting that the 1986 pastoral letter of the U.S. bishops, *Economic Justice for All,* gave considerable emphasis to the questions of unemployment and jobs in developing a framework for understanding the ethical aspects of economic activity in the United States today.[1]

This essay will provide somc analytic background that supports the normative stance of *Economic Justice for All* toward the problems of unemployment and job-generation. The essay's argument has three phases. First, the multiple dimensions of the problem of unemployment in present-day American society will be sketched and the challenges this problem poses for citizens and policymakers will be outlined. Second, the theological significance of work discussed in the previous chapter will be further developed to suggest why the issue of unemployment is such an important one for Christian social ethics. Third, the implications of the ethical norms of justice and human rights for the employment question will be developed. This final section will also make several proposals concerning both personal responsibilities of Christians and ethically appropriate public policies for dealing with the question of unemployment and jobs. The theoretical roots of these ethical norms will also be explored in greater depth in succeeding chapters.

Dimensions of the Problem

One can distinguish at least four different kinds of unemployment on the basis of their causes. The first is the "frictional unemployment" which is the consequence of the fact that in an economy like ours, where people change jobs periodically, some of them will be out of work at any given moment. There are, of course, serious disputes about how much of this frictional unemployment is a necessity in our economy.

The second is the cyclical unemployment that increases as the economy contracts and decreases as the economy expands through the business cycle. Here again there are disputes about how to respond to this kind of unemployment. New Deal style approaches call for a variety of job-creating initiatives such as government expenditures to stimulate the demand for work and direct public-works projects. Supply-side policies seek to generate jobs by encouraging private investment through reduced taxes. The experience of recent years suggests that neither of these theories provides an all-purpose cure for cyclical unemployment.

A third sort of unemployment has been called chronic or structural unemployment. In Paul Samuelson's textbook definition, it is that form of unemployment "which cannot be cured by expansion of over-all monetary demand, but which is attributable to lack of proper skills, location and attitudes among youth, the aged, the illiterate, minorities, the residents of depressed areas, and the technologically displaced."[2] This is the unemployment of people whose chances of finding a job are slim or nonexistent in any phase of the business cycle because they lack the skills or other prerequisites for finding work in our kind of economy. Various responses to chronic unemployment have been attempted since the 1960s, most notably those created by the passage of the Comprehensive Employment and Training Act (CETA). These programs have generated considerable controversy. Despite notable weaknesses, however, there is evidence that they did accomplish at least part of their purpose.[3]

All three of these forms of unemployment have been the subject of considerable reflection and analysis for many years. We have built up a body of theories—both economic and moral—on how to deal with them. Pluralism reigns, but at least people have some sense of what the issues are, and the church has some experience in reflecting upon them from an ethical point of view. In recent years, however, a fourth type of unemployment has become a central topic of discussion in the United States. There is a growing body of opinion that the United States stands at a moment of basic transition in the way its economy works. Those with less optimistic dispositions or a greater sense of the dramatic are inclined to see it as a moment of crisis. Whether transition or crisis, something seems to be happening to the United States job market as a result of very complex interactions between the processes of technological change and the shifting patterns of the international division of labor.

It seems certain that the recent high rates of unemployment in the United States have in part been caused by these technological and international shifts. Each of the economic recoveries of recent years has left the United States with a higher unemployment rate than the recovery that preceded it. This suggests that we are faced with a new and more threatening form of structural unemployment, caused by a combination of the effects of the exporting of jobs to countries with lower wages, the transfer of sophisticated and efficient technology to these countries, and the displacement of industrial jobs by a smaller number of jobs in the high-tech and service sectors within the United States itself.

Conclusions on how to deal with unemployment in the United States are therefore dependent on an understanding of these new technological and international dynamics. And here there is even less agreement than on the remedies prescribed by theories developed in response to the three other more traditional types of unemployment. This has put the church in a difficult position as it attempts to offer moral guidance and contribute to the formation of public opinion.

A few examples will illustrate the problem. In their study of plant closings and the unemployment that necessarily accompanies them, Barry Bluestone and Bennett Harrison call for greater governmental limits on the mobility and export of capital in the interest of protecting American jobs.[4] This view is opposed by Lester Thurow, who argues that locking up capital and workers in low-productivity industries insures economic decline and ultimately greater job loss.[5] Therefore Thurow argues in favor of shutting down low-productivity "sunset" plants more rapidly and relocating workers in growing "sunrise" industries as the best way to protect jobs—exactly the opposite conclusion from that reached by Bluestone and Harrison. This debate also has international dimensions. Insuring jobs in America's aging smokestack industries against competition from products produced abroad in more modern plants with cheaper labor will require protectionist legislation. Bluestone calls for a limited amount of such protectionism. Thurow sees this as a formula for saving

American jobs only in the short run, and at the cost of keeping "the rest of the world poor."[6]

There are further issues in the discussion of the present economic transition that also complicate the ethical task. Groups as diverse as a team of editors from *Business Week,* in their study on *The Reindustrialization of America,*[7] and the United Auto Workers, in their "Blueprint for a Working America,"[8] have called for a new form of public planning in the economy in the interest of improving productivity and saving jobs. Both groups call for a partnership of labor, management, and government in planning how to target credit for investment that will enhance productivity and preserve jobs. The *Business Week* team notes that such cooperation depends on whether or not the three groups "can break out of their ideological shells to adopt a program that appears to rub, at certain seams, against the idea of a free market."[9] The UAW plan resembles the *Business Week* proposal in urging the institution of a limited amount of collaborative planning to guide investment into job-producing sectors. However, in a characteristic difference of vocabulary, the UAW plan speaks of getting labor, management, and government together "to bargain" on the direction this targeted investment should take, while *Business Week* speaks of "cooperation" between the three groups. The *Business Week* group is concerned over labor's adversarial relationship to management. The UAW, on the other hand, fears that since the funds for investment must come from somewhere they are quite likely to come from the salaries of the working class. Thus the UAW blueprint insists that "not only is top-down planning by a private or public elite undemocratic, but it won't work well. We need democratic decision making."[10] The *Business Week* team acknowledges that the burdens of reinvestment costs must be distributed fairly and that the success of any planning effort will depend on the degree to which it reaches out to include chronically unemployed minorities and avoids exacting sacrifice from those least able to bear it, that is, from the poor.[11] Though the concern for fairness is evident in both these proposals, they reveal a conflict among the interests of the industrial working class, of the poor and minorities, of management, and of local communities that are significantly dependent on an aging heavy-industry base.

In addition, most of these proposals have included calls for programs to retrain significant numbers of workers for new jobs. The reason such retraining is needed is that many of the new jobs to replace those lost in basic industry and manufacturing will be in high-technology areas such as microelectronics, robotics, and other fields dependent on a highly skilled work force. Robert Reich has argued forcefully that production which depends on the assembly line and relatively unskilled labor "can be accomplished more cheaply in developing nations."[12] The problem with these proposals for retraining industrial workers for high-tech jobs is that such high-tech training programs are the ones that the chronically unemployed are least prepared to enter, because of the low level of basic verbal and quantitative skills among this group. Retraining for high-tech jobs, if pursued alone, threatens to increase class differences within the United States. It could lead us to a divided society where one class operates computers and manufacturers silicon chips and the other works in low-skill, low-wage service jobs. The *Business Week* team rightly concluded that "the country's economic health is increasingly determined by 'invisible' investment in human capital," i.e., in the education of a skilled work force.[13] But the skills needed are not only in the high-tech areas, but also on more basic levels. Bluestone and Harrison have argued that there are significant needs for new investment and output in the United States in the areas of housing, energy, mass transit, freight-rail transit, and health. Investment in these areas could fill social needs and generate a significant number of jobs with diverse skill requirements.[14] Training on a diversity of skill levels thus seems called for if the unemployment problem is to be dealt with adequately.

Finally, all of these proposals for new investment, collaborative planning by management, labor, and government, and programed retraining are criticized as unworkable by a number of commentators. Neoconservative authors such as George Gilder oppose such steps as excessive politicization of the market. Gilder believes that the solution lies in reliance on the entrepreneurship of innovative small companies and a tax structure that will make them viable. Amitai Etzioni argues further that planned reindustrialization is impossible because we have no way of knowing what sectors of the economy are "sunrise" sectors until they have already risen, and because the Japanese model of guided change is incompatible with American culture.[15]

In short, the current reality of unemployment has multiple causes diagnosed in a variety of ways. The efforts to generate new jobs must be on a variety of levels and no single initiative will serve as a panacea. Indeed, there are serious conflicts between steps that would relieve the problem of unemployment in one segment of society and those that would relieve it in another. For example, high-tech investment may generate jobs for the more highly skilled but eliminate jobs for the less skilled. Policies to protect American jobs will threaten jobs in other countries, including the poor countries of the Third World. Proposed solutions to the unemployment problem in the United States will also have a significant impact on the employment picture in other industrialized nations and on the possibilities for economic diversification and development in less-developed countries. It is within this complex context that the bishops have sought to develop their pastoral letter providing theological and ethical guidance for policy.

The Theological Significance of Work

Before turning to the task of examining how Christian moral principles can be of help in reaching decisions about priorities in the face of these tensions and tradeoffs, it will be useful to address the question of why unemployment is a matter of such concern in the first place. In the light of the economic considerations just sketched and the mounting evidence that there is a long-term trend toward increasing unemployment in industrialized societies, Gregory Baum has raised this fundamental question:

> Should the Church in the face of a society with chronic unemployment demand full employment and continue to promote a piety that leads to dedication and diligence, or should the Church recognize that there is no return to full employment and hence produce a spiritual outlook that enables people to remain humanly and psychically well even if they do not work? Has the time come when the Church must transcend the work ethic?[16]

Baum's question suggests that we might be faced with the need to develop a whole new approach to unemployment by moving toward a spiritual and cultural stance that gives increasing significance to leisure and decreasing significance to work. He implies that we might address the problem by focusing on the virtues of leisure rather than the vices of unemployment.

This same question has been raised in a radical way and answered positively by some social philosophers who synthesize Marxist and Freudian perspectives on labor. Herbert Marcuse, for example, quoting C. B. Chisholm, maintains that

> the true spirit of psychoanalytic theory lives in the uncompromising efforts to reveal the anti-humanistic forces behind the philosophy of productiveness: "Of all things, hard work has become a virtue instead of the curse it was always advertised to be by our remote ancestors. . . . Our children should be prepared to bring their children up so they won't have to work as a neurotic necessity. The necessity to work is a neurotic symptom. It is a crutch. It is an attempt to make oneself feel valuable even though there is no particular need for one's working."[17]

In dealing with this issue let me indicate at the outset that I believe that Baum's question should be answered with a strong negative and that Marcuse's conclusions are quite thoroughly wrong. Their challenges to the work ethic, however, have the value of pressing the issue at hand to the foundations of our understanding of the meaning and value of work in human life. In dealing with the issue of unemployment and jobs, Christian ethics must give careful attention to such questions of fundamental meaning and value. It will do so by beginning with the understanding of the significance of work contained in the Bible and Christian tradition, and by showing the relationship between these Christian theological warrants and contemporary social experience.

As the previous chapter noted, the Bible contains two quite different valuations of work, one of which views work as a very positive expression of human creativity and the other which sees it as a burdensome toil and punishment for sin. Both of these themes are present through the history of Christian theological reflection on the meaning and value of work. Francis Schüssler Fiorenza has summarized this history succinctly and has shown that it has clear parallels in contemporary social experience.

> In the religious tradition, work has both a positive and a negative evaluation. It is seen as creative, as a service to community, and as a divine vocation. Yet it is also negatively evaluated as a punishment for sin. In contemporary society, a similar ambivalence exists. On the one hand, work is seen as important for the individual's self-concept, sense of fulfillment, and integration into society. On the other hand, there is an increasingly instrumentalistic attitude toward work: persons work not so much for the sake of the work itself, but for the rewards of work.[18]

These two different views of work, however, are not simply juxtaposed as contradictory elements within the Christian tradition. Both in the Bible and in subsequent theological tradition, the positive, creative potential of human work is regarded as more fundamental in the sense that it is the intention of the Creator that human labor itself be a creative expression of human dignity. Like human beings, work and economic activity were created "good . . . very good." The conflict and alienation that distort the world of work are seen as the consequences of human sin and therefore as counter to the structures of human existence as created by God. This sinfulness, moreover, is not simply the result of individual choice. It has become embedded in the economic and social institutions of human communities. As Fiorenza points out, both Christian tradition and contemporary human experience reveal that the value of work is ambiguous and unstable precisely because it is deeply shot through with the tension between God's creative purposes for humanity and humanity's sinful distortion of these purposes. Nevertheless, work is also a sphere of human existence that is open to the healing, redeeming, and emancipating action of the redemption offered by Christ. The negative evaluation of work, therefore, is not to be accepted as a coequal with the positive interpretation of its meaning in Christian theology. These negative dimensions of the world of work are realities to be resisted and overcome, even though Christians believe that this final overcoming of conflict and alienation will occur fully only in the kingdom of God.[19]

From these theological considerations it should be clear what the response of Christian theology to Baum's question ought to be. The Marxist-Freudian perspective of a Marcuse echoes a *part* of the Christian tradition's valuation of work, but only a part of it. Alienated labor, drudgery, and servile toil are not discoveries of the disciples of Marx and Freud. They were well known to Moses and to the prophets and sages of Hebrew tradition. These biblical authors, however, did not propose a "rationality of gratification," a "libidinous morality," or an ethic of leisure and play as the alternative to the alienation and frustration of the work world.[20] Rather, they saw *work in its created wholeness and healed redemption as an energetic contribution to the common life of society, an active form of human participation in human community.* From a biblical and Christian theological point of view the overcoming of sin is not simply the result of the derepression of human instinct but rather the creation of authentic channels by which persons can contribute their energies to the creation and maintenance of the human community itself. Through such contributions individual persons in turn are enabled to discover the meaning and value of their own lives as images of God the creator. While avoiding any overly romantic view of the creative capacities of most human beings, a Christian theology of work should insist that work's prime meaning is the bonding to community which it can foster. *This* kind of work ethic is close to the heart of Christian faith.

Biblical and theological perspectives such as these have strong echoes in the conclusions reached by social psychologists and anthropologists who have studied patterns of employment and unemployment in contemporary industrial societies. It is clear that forms of work can change significantly from one historical period to another. Nevertheless, there can be no human civilization apart from the continual creation and maintenance of that civilization by human agents. Though human work may become more "knowledge-intensive" and less "muscle-intensive" in postindustrial societies, to deprive people of work is to thwart their exercise of creativity and to exclude them from active participation in the communal human project of civilization. Work in our society is partly an instrumental means to the income necessary to meet one's basic human needs and to broaden one's leisure-time possibilities. Were this instrumental function of work its prime meaning, then our goal would be clear: a sort of generalized welfare-leisure system for all. Not only is such a proposal an affront to the actual experience of most of the unemployed in the United States and the world today, but it also flies in the face of the conclusions of recent systematic analyses of this experience. It is clear from sociopsychological research that the human suffering of unemployment arises as much from the isolation and loss of a sense of social participation that it produces as from the loss of income it brings.[21] This research confirms the biblical picture that portrays work as having the dual purpose of fulfilling physical human needs and creating community, civilization, and culture.[22] On these theological and sociopsychological grounds, therefore, the bishops rest their case that persons are harmed and society is distorted by unemployment. These perspectives imply that even though unemployment insurance and transfer payments in the form of welfare are clearly demanded to meet the basic needs of the unemployed, the more basic issue is that of overcoming unemployment.

In their pastoral letter, the American bishops have appealed *both* to these theological perspectives *and* to the sociopsychological research that shows the congruence between theology and contemporary reality. Without the appeal to the Bible and theology the bishops would have failed to show why they, as *bishops*, are concerned with these questions in the first place. Without the evidence from present experience and its systematic interpretation in the social sciences they would be subject to the charge that their theological message is irrelevant to the contemporary situation. Though the bishops clearly need not fear that many will challenge the assertion that unemployment is a serious social problem, they do need to be concerned that the assessment of why it is a problem becomes properly framed. For the way that the question is asked will have much to do with the way it is answered.

Ethical Principles: Justice and the Right to Employment

Recent church teachings on the ethical principles that should shape both the Christian and secular response to issues of social policy have increasingly been set down in the language of human rights. This use of "rights language" has been just as characteristic of discussions of unemployment and jobs as it has of other moral issues that arise in the trajectory of human life from womb to tomb. Indeed papal, conciliar, and episcopal teachings on which the 1986 pastoral letter draws have repeatedly affirmed that human persons have a right to employment that makes an urgent and imperative demand on society in all its parts. For example, *Pacem in terris* stated, "When we turn to the economic sphere, it is clear that human beings have the natural right to free initiative in the economic field and the right to work."[23] *Gaudium et spes* affirmed "every person's duty to labor faithfully and also his right to work."[24] Both of these statements were referred to by the U.S. Catholic bishops in their 1975 statement, "The Economy: Human Dimensions." The bishops stated, "Opportunities to work must be provided for those who are able and willing to work. Every person has the right to useful employment, to just wages and to adequate assistance in the case of real need."[25] This statement was repeated a number of times by individual bishops testifying before congressional committees on behalf of the USCC in favor of the Humphrey-Hawkins Full-Employment Bill.[26] This indicates a firm commitment in Catholic social teaching to a policy that would guarantee a job for everyone able to work. This commitment is a practical implication of the theological and sociopsychological perspectives outlined above.

However, the matter is not quite this simple. Immediately following the sentence in which *Gaudium et spes* sets forth the duty and right of every person to work, the council qualified its meaning somewhat: "It is the duty of society, moreover, *according to the circumstances prevailing in it, and in keeping with its proper role*, to help its citizens find opportunities for adequate employment."[27] The qualifying phrases in this sentence suggest that there may be different ways of implementing the right to employment in different social circumstances. But the council did not elaborate on what these might be. In *Laborem exercens* there is a similar ambiguity. Though Pope John Paul II does not refer explicitly to a right to employment in this letter, he does state forcefully that unemployment "in all cases is an evil" and "the opposite of a just and right situation." He also states that "the question of finding work or . . . suitable employment for all who are capable of it" is a fundamental issue. John Paul II introduces the notion of the "indirect employer" into Catholic social teaching in discussing the employment question, a notion that includes "all the agents at the national and international level that are responsible for the whole orientation of labor policy." This is a very broad concept. It is made somewhat more precise by the pope's statement that "in the final analysis this overall concern weighs on the shoulders of the state," provided this is not interpreted as a call for "one-sided centralization by the public authorities." Finally he specifies what the content of this responsibility is: "to act against unemployment."[28]

Recent church teachings, then, clearly argue for the presence of an obligation that society make efforts to provide employment for all. At the same time, the means for fulfilling this obligation are left unspecified. Similarly unspecified are the agents responsible, though governments have a special role provided they avoid statist approaches. Because of this hesitancy in offering detailed plans for implementing the right to employment, recent church teachings might be open to the charge of timidity or inconsistency. Before one concludes that the authors of previous church documents are guilty of this charge, it would be well to remember these words of Dietrich Bonhoeffer:

> What then . . . is an "ethic" which by definition makes a theme of the ethical? And what is an ethicist? We can begin more easily by saying what, in any case, an ethic and an ethicist cannot be. An ethic cannot be a book in which there is set out how everything in the world actually ought to be but unfortunately is not, and an ethicist cannot be a man who always knows better than others what is to be done and how it is to be done.[29]

Bonhoeffer's words put us on guard against an approach which would suggest that an adequate ethical perspective on employment will be one which simply *declares* that there should be work for all. This is inadequate, because neither Christian ethicists nor bishops nor the church as a whole are in a position to create employment by fiat. And neither is anybody else. A Christian ethical approach to the right to employment must be concerned with providing guidance on the priorities we should adopt as we confront the hard choices and tradeoffs that are necessarily present in the formation of social policy. A Christian ethical approach to employment and job generation must recognize that we are dealing with a multiplicity of values in dynamic relation and tension with one another. It will then go on to try to discern which balance between these values seems most in harmony with human dignity and a Christian vision of the fullness of human community.

The task, then, is to move beyond moral proclamation to careful analysis of modes of implementing the right to employment. Concern with implementation is itself a genuinely moral concern, not simply a technical or political one. It is therefore both a proper and necessary part of ethical argument. The moral content of the concern for implementation becomes evident if we examine the right to employment more carefully from the viewpoint of moral philosophy and political theory.

The right to work belongs to that class of rights known in normative political theory as socioeconomic rights. Socioeconomic rights, which also include the right to food, to adequate housing, to health care, and to social security, are contrasted with civil-political rights such as freedom of religion, expression, assembly, and due process of law. One of the keys to the distinction between the two sets of rights is the difference in what must be done to implement them. The right to religious freedom is implemented by a combination of constitutional law and judicial action that restrains the state or other persons from interfering with religious belief and expression. It is a negative right, an immunity from coercion, guaranteed juridically. Implementation of a social right such as the right to work is a considerably more complex task in our society. An interlocking series of positive steps by the society as a whole must be taken if this right is to be secured in practice. It is a positive right, an entitlement or empowerment that demands action rather than restraint on the part of both society and the state.[30]

It should be noted, however, that the difference between the two types of rights is partly a matter of the kinds of institutions that *already* exist within a society. The creation of institutions for the protection of civil-political rights in the West, such as constitutional government, involved a whole series of vigorous positive steps, from the time of the Magna Carta down to the present, including revolution and the development of an immensely complex judicial system. The institutional machinery for the protection of civil-political rights is in place in the West and therefore their implementation today is a relatively easy task compared to the implementation of socioeconomic rights. Securing the right to work is more difficult because the implementing institutions are not so fully developed and because we do not have clear and convincing ideas on how to bring them into existence in fully functional form. In a highly interdependent world economy the implementation of the right to employment involves not only economic and political issues of great complexity within the United States, but similar issues of even greater complexity on a world scale. So, when past church documents stop short of specifying detailed methods for the implementation of the right to work, this is in large part because we are much less clear about the institutions needed than we are for the implementation of civil and political rights.

From a theological point of view, a second aspect of the problem of implementing the right to employment comes into view. As noted above, the Christian tradition contains a twofold understanding of work. Work is understood primarily as a positively valued sphere for the expression of human participation in community. But the world of work is also a sphere in which human sinfulness in the form of arrogance, greed, or sloth can lead to alienation, oppression, and domination. The consequences of this sinfulness are present not only in the toilsome burden of some forms of industrial labor. They are also powerfully present in the exclusion from community and denial of creativity that is an important dimension of the reality of unemployment.

Unemployment, therefore, is not *simply* a result of our limited understanding of the appropriate institutional means for overcoming it. It is also the consequence of human perversity both on the level of the economic choices made by individuals and of the economic patterns that institutionalize the dominance of some groups over others. From a theological point of view, unemployment must in part be regarded as the result of a denial of human interdependence by society and by the powerful groups within it. And Christians who are true to the belief that sin will be fully eliminated from the human heart only in the final coming of the kingdom of God must be prepared to face the reality of the brokenness of human community in the economic sphere. We will not eliminate unemployment by the declaration of the existence of the right to a job, but by participation in the sustained struggle to overcome the distortions of human community and work introduced by human duplicity and selfishness.

Does this mean, then, that we should abandon any effort to present ethical guidance on the problem of overcoming unemployment and generating jobs in the American economy? Do the limits of our understanding of the institutions that are needed to implement the right to work and the regretful acknowledgment of the presence of sin in our economic activity mean that we should be resigned to the continuing reality of high unemployment rates? I think the answer to this question is a resounding *no*. It is precisely the acknowledgment of these limits that will enable Christian ethics to make an important contribution to this debate by focusing its reflection on the real problem in all of its apparent intractability. The powerful biblical and theological vision of the positive function of work in the lives of all human beings must remain a central focus of a Christian economic ethic. Also the healing of human brokenness that will be fulfilled in the kingdom proclaimed by Jesus has already begun among us, and we must look for signs of its presence in the evolving economic order. Finally, we must formulate clear moral guidelines that will direct social life in the direction of this healing and that will rule out those policies and patterns of economic activity which we can see as clear impediments to employment for all.

The fundamental framework used by the bishops to move from the affirmation of the human importance of work and the conviction that unemployment is an evil to moral-action guides for dealing with this evil is the theory of justice that has been elaborated within the Catholic social tradition. Reinhold Niebuhr has described justice as the moral norm governing "the claims and counterclaims of historical existence."[31] In the discussion of the problem of unemployment, we are faced with more than a few claims and counterclaims, such as unemployment vs. inflation, jobs in the United States vs. jobs abroad, the role of the market vs. the role of the government, the distribution of jobs and income vs. the enhancement of productivity through capital investment. A satisfactory approach to these conflicts will not result from simply choosing sides in each of the debates. Nor will it come by saying all the claims are important and should be granted equal moral status. What is needed is a way of determining the proper ordering of these claims and the priorities that should exist among them as we seek to structure the economic system in a way that respects human dignity, resists human sinfulness, and responds to the call to the kingdom of God. In *Rerum novarum* Leo XIII described justice as the principle that helps define "the relative rights and mutual duties of the rich and the poor, of capital and labor."[32] This is what is needed in the discussion of unemployment: a description of relative rights and mutual duties that can help us discern which elements of the many proposals for dealing with the present transition in the American economy are more satisfactory from a Christian ethical point of view.

The chief elements of the Catholic tradition on the meaning of justice were discussed in an earlier chapter. Here it will be enough to take note of some of the key aspects of this understanding of justice that are relevant to the most pressing issues in the current debate as it touches the employment question.

First, the most fundamental thing to be said about justice in Roman Catholic thought is that it is concerned to establish the conditions that are necessary to enable all persons to participate in the economic activity of society. This is another way of saying that justice demands respect for the dignity of all persons. But it highlights the fact that human dignity is not a quality that persons simply possess provided nobody else takes it away from them. The realization of human dignity requires that one participate in social life. The dignity of the person is the dignity of a social being. Therefore both the possibility and the actuality of social participation are crucial to human dignity. Thus, in recent Catholic teaching, the overcoming of injustice is closely identified with the enhancement of social patterns of active participation in the political, economic, and cultural life of society and the overcoming of all forms of discriminatory exclusion on the basis of race, sex, national origin, or other arbitrary standard. Though it is clear that some persons will be more active participants than others in each of these spheres, there is a minimum level of access that must be made possible for all: "Participation constitutes a right which is to be applied in the economic and in the social and political field."[33] In discussing the implementation of the right to employment Christian ethics both can and should insist that the creation of institutions for the enhancement of economic participation is of the highest priority and that racial or sexual discrimination in employment can never be justified.

In relating the notion of justice-as-participation to the jobs question, several more specific points are important. First, justice in the employment sphere means that persons should have the opportunity to contribute to society through economic activity in concert with others. Justice is not just a matter of seeing to it that people's private needs are fulfilled. Work—especially work in an industrial or postindustrial society—is for the community as well as for oneself. The charge has been heard frequently of late that Catholic social thought has stressed the distribution of wealth and ignored the production of wealth. While there is a measure of truth in this charge, it is not the whole story. The notion of "social justice," which has a technical meaning in Catholic moral theology, refers to the obligation of all persons to contribute to the production and protection of the common good of society. In the words of Pius XI, "It is of the very essence of social justice to demand from each individual all that is necessary for the common good."[34] This statement assumes that the common or public good needs to be created and protected. In all but hunter-gatherer societies this is clearly true in the economic sphere. It is especially evident in an advanced industrial economy. Social justice, as understood by Pius XI, would, in my opinion, be better designated "contributive justice"—that form of moral obligation which calls on persons to contribute to the generation of the public good by aggregating their activity, to the extent they are able, with that of others in a productive way. This is the active meaning of justice-as-participation. It helps us see that justice in employment is as much a matter of creating the public good of a society as it is a matter of distributing it.

It should also be noted that the public good that contributive justice calls on us to create in the economic sphere must be measured by indices more complex than that of the gross national product. The GNP measures one element of the public economic good. But there are other highly important public goods or evils that result from the way the productive side of the economy is organized, including full employment, equal opportunity, environmental quality, or the lack of all these goods. The conditions of contributive or productive justice are not limited to the generation of the GNP, but involve these other important public concerns as well. In measuring whether the economy is productive, these other values must be taken into account.

The norm of justice, therefore, implies that the public good to which all are obliged to contribute is a social as well as a narrowly defined economic one. The justice of the productive side of the economy cannot be measured solely by its output in goods and services, important as these surely are. The organization of production also has very important effects on employment levels, patterns of discrimination, and environmental quality. Economists are fond of calling these effects "externalities." But if we are honest in evaluating what the economy is "producing" these effects must be regarded as internal to economic activity and subject to scrutiny in the light of the overarching norm of justice. Just as enterprises that damage environmental quality or whose products are potentially threatening to human health are legitimately subject to governmental regulation, so is the structure of the productive side of the economy a legitimate governmental concern from the standpoint of its impact on employment levels.

Recent debates have made it clear that there are significant disagreements about when governmental regulation in the interest of environmental quality begins to become counterproductive for the overall well-being of the community. Such disputes are inevitable in the domain of job creation as well. But Christian ethics can make a forceful point here without stifling debate and smothering pluralism: it is the responsibility of our society—jointly through management, labor, government, and community groups—to evaluate and in some measure regulate their economic behavior in light of its impact on employment. To fail to do so would be to say that some people simply don't count as members of the human community, namely those who are unemployed. Such a failure would also be a way of saying that the actual productive capacity of unemployed skilled workers or the potential capacity of those with lower skills are of little or no value as we seek to negotiate the present economic transition. This would deny the reality of human interdependence in community that is at the very foundation of social morality.

The norms of justice also have important implications for our understanding of the distributive side of the economy. An image commonly used in discussions of distributive justice is that of slicing up a pie and handing out the pieces. While this may be an adequate image for discussing the distribution of incomes, it gives a false picture of the distribution side as a whole. A job, for example, is not like a piece of pie that someone gives me, or like a paycheck that I take home with me. A job is not a consumer good. It is something I go to, something I engage in with many others in highly complex, structured activity that is linked with a vast interlocking system. From this point of view it is really more accurate to speak of participating in the work of society than of having a job. The distribution of jobs, therefore, concerns the way that participation in the economic process is structured—how it provides access to work for all or just for some, whom it excludes and whom it includes. Though it is clear that the kind of participation open to different persons can and should be different, the notion of justice on the distributive side demands that the same kind of structural concerns with patterns of active participation in the economic life of society be brought to bear here as were discussed above in considering the productive side. This parallel is no accident, for it is an illusion to think that the process of production and the process of distribution operate independently of each other. In fact they are closely interconnected and mutually reinforcing.[35]

This means that the demands of distributive justice will not be met simply by proposing some form of income policy such as a negative income tax, guaranteed annual income, or other welfare reform proposals, essential as these surely are. Distributive justice will not be realized simply by a more compassionate policy on transfer payments. Such transfers are called for in justice in the cases of those with special needs such as the ill, the aged, and the handicapped. These economic disadvantages are in some sense beyond the control of the persons affected, and society at large has a duty to help ameliorate their effects. However, in the case of persons who through no fault of their own have been placed in a seriously disadvantaged position by socially correctable maldistribution of opportunity and power, transfers are at best a palliative for injustice. They do not represent distributive justice in any full sense. Therefore any debate about income policy in our society should be placed in the context of this larger question of employment. The argument will not be likely to please either labor or management. It may displease labor, for it suggests that the preservation of existing industrial jobs at high hourly wage rates is not the be-all and end-all of distributive justice. At the same time it is likely to disgruntle management for it implies that the bottom line on the quarterly report is hardly an adequate index of their performance.

These considerations provide a few indications of what it means to recognize that the right to employment is a social right whose implementation depends on a moral analysis of the responsibilities of diverse actors in a complex social system. By situating this right in the context of the structures of participation on both the productive and distributive sides of the economy, we are in a position to acquire some insight on how to move from declaring the existence of this right toward implementing it. Such implementation will depend on how the patterns of capital investment both produce and distribute jobs. The issues of what kind of capital investment is taking place, what levels of employment and unemployment are present in the United States, and how employment and unemployment are distributed among different demographic groups are inseparable from one another. When the jobs question is looked at from an ethical point of view, these issues must be looked at in their interconnectedness rather than separately.

A political consideration will bring this argument to a tentative conclusion. There is a strong tendency for the individual parts of this interconnected whole to become identified with the political agendas of particular groups in society. The business and financial communities place strong emphasis on capital investment in the interests of increased productivity leading to profit maximization. Organized labor frequently has the protection of existing jobs, wages, and benefits as its prime focus. Minority groups and advocates of the poor press for new job creation, including public job programs and training programs. As both the UAW and *Business Week* studies mentioned above have noted, a continued fragmentation of these groups along ideological lines carries us away from rather than toward a solution to major problems besetting the economy today. While it would be naive to think that these groups either can or should adopt a common perspective, it is certain that all of these groups must contribute to finding a just solution to the problem of unemployment.

Government also has an important role to play in balancing the competing claims of these diverse groups. It has long been a tenet of Catholic social thinking that the government has as one of its prime tasks the coordination of the activities of diverse groups in society in a way that is productive of the common good. As Paul VI put it, "As a social being the human person builds up his destiny within a series of groupings that demand, as their completion and as the necessary condition for their development, a vaster society, one of a universal character, the political society."[36] At the same time, however, it is clear that "statist" solutions are excluded by the principle of subsidiarity which insists that the government "furnish help *(subsidium)* to the members of the body social, and never destroy and absorb them."[37] This principle defends institutional pluralism while also granting a limited role to the government in the economic sphere. It implies that job generation is a task for all the relevant institutionalized groups of American economic life: labor, management, and government working together.

The recent appeals for more collaborative relations between labor and management are in line with the main thrust of Catholic social ethics[38] and with the interpretation of justice advanced here. There will, without doubt, be conflict among the interests of these groups. Therefore the cooperation envisioned must be based on a distribution of real power that enables these groups to make their legitimate perspectives part of the formula on which compromise is reached. A number of the recent critics of the adversarial relationship between labor and management seem to expect labor to do all the cooperating in the form of reduced demands. Though "give-backs" may be needed in some cases, and plant closings may be the only solution in others, such decisions should not rest solely in the hands of management. The interests of the workers involved, the long-term health of the firm or industry as represented by management, the effects on local communities, and the common good of the society as a whole that is the concern of government should all have an influence on decisions that affect the generation and distribution of jobs. Though the adversarial relationship must be reduced, a condition for *just* cooperative relations is a *genuine* influence for the cooperating partners. Paternalism, whether by the government or by management, must be avoided. Concretely this implies, for example, the need for advance notice when plants are to be closed and for adequate plans for retraining and relocating workers when such closings are necessary. All the partners in the collaborative relationship have responsibilities to help provide for this retraining and relocation when it is necessary. It is not the responsibility of management, labor, local or national government alone, but neither are any of these groups free to wash their hands of this problem, which is likely to become more prevalent in the years ahead.

This generalized call for a new collaborative and participatory approach to our economic problems should not be confused with socialism or state capitalism. It is rather a "mixed" economy model, which seeks to institutionalize the representation of the diverse interests of a pluralist society in the investment and job-generation process. The key to this kind of development of a *new form* of mixed economy lies in giving each of the sectors of labor, management, and the several levels of government some say in the structure of the production and distribution of jobs. It will embody a new form of justice-as-participation, a form that is called for by the transition which our economy is undergoing.

Chapter 5

Justice as Participation: Public Moral Discourse and the U.S. Economy

When the church ventures to preach or teach about the relevance of the gospel to the public life of a pluralistic society, it can expect to become involved in a certain measure of controversy. This controversy is likely to be particularly lively when the preaching or teaching touches people's pocketbooks. And the potential for quite nasty disputes is perhaps greatest when the discussion moves beyond questions of how people should voluntarily use their money, talent, and other economic resources to questions of public policy. For these policies affect people's freedom, inevitably broadening freedom of choice for some and limiting it for others.

In November of 1986 the U.S. Roman Catholic bishops issued their pastoral letter entitled *Economic Justice for All: Catholic Social Teaching and the U.S. Economy.* The drafting process involved broad consultation and wide public debate. It is hoped that dialogue will continue in both the church and the larger society. All this has reinforced my conviction that the church has the capacity to be what James Gustafson has called "a community of moral discourse" as well as the ability to stimulate such discourse in the broader society.[1] Serious and sustained discussion of the moral dimensions of American economic life can be very productive.

A Culture Confused about Justice

At the same time, the bishops' project has revealed deep fissures in the moral content of American culture. These fissures are also evident in the research summarized and interpreted in the recent study of contemporary

American social values by Robert Bellah and his coauthors, *Habits of the Heart*.[2] The fault lines that lie just beneath the surface of our national life are the result of competing convictions about the meaning of the central moral and political norms of social life. Should these fault lines give way, the social earthquake could be great indeed.

In particular the debate has vividly revealed the conflicting notions of justice held by Americans. The purpose of this essay is to analyze what the bishops' letter says about the meaning of justice and to relate the moral argument of the letter to several other contemporary interpretations of the meaning of justice. This essay will argue that a renewal of the biblical and civic republican strands of American culture would contribute greatly to achieving a more just society. The biblical and republican traditions converge in understanding justice as a form of active participation in social life, while injustice is at root a kind of exclusion from human community. The notion of justice as participation will be proposed as the possible basis for a new cultural consensus that can help the nation address the urgent problems that face it.

Disagreements about moral and religious questions will, by definition, be present in every pluralistic society. When the disagreements concern the most fundamental norms of social and political life, however, the situation begins to look ominous. Almost thirty years ago John Courtney Murray observed that discourse on public affairs must inevitably move from debate on specific decisions or policies upward "into realms of some theoretical generality—into metaphysics, ethics, theology." Unfortunately, he added, "this movement does not carry us into disagreement; for disagreement is not an easy thing to reach. Rather, we move into confusion," a situation in which "soliloquy succeeds to argument" and prejudice and suspicion replace civil discourse and reasoned debate.[3]

The fury with which some critics publicly denounced the successive drafts of the bishops' letter as Marxist in fact and totalitarian in implication is evidence, I think, of the confusion present in the debate. For example, one of the more vociferous of these critics suggested that the letter "is secretly smuggling an egalitarian, socialist concept into Catholic thought" and has adopted "an un-American concept of justice."[4] This kind of language is a symptom of a very real disease in our society. Murray named this disease "barbarism," a state where argument about justice in public affairs either "dies from disinterest, or subsides into the angry mutterings of polemic, or rises to the shrillness of hysteria." When such things happen, Murray said, "you may be sure that the barbarian is at the gates of the city."[5]

More recently, Alasdair MacIntyre has offered a somewhat similar diagnosis of the state of our public moral discourse. In MacIntyre's view, post-Enlightenment ideas and social institutions have destroyed the possibility of giving any universally plausible and rational account of the foundation of morality. He describes our situation as one in which moral language is frequently used, but this usage is most often to express disagreement. There seems to be "no rational way of securing moral agreement in our culture."[6] As a result of the culturally fragmenting effects of modern individualism, we have lost a coherent moral vision as well as the kind of coherent institutions of communal life needed to sustain such a vision. "Modern moral utterance and practice can only be understood as a series of fragmented survivals from an older past and . . . the insoluble problems . . . generated for modern moral theorists [will] remain insoluble until this is well understood."[7]

For MacIntyre, this moral breakdown is both most evident and most dangerous in our inability to achieve agreement about the meaning of justice—the central virtue of political life. We lack the fundamental prerequisite for being a political community at all, and raw Nietzschean power threatens to replace reason and justice as the guiding force in social life. In short, our situation is that of a new "Dark Ages." MacIntyre's diagnosis is considerably more pessimistic than Murray's, for he concludes "the barbarians are not waiting beyond the frontiers; they have already been governing us for quite some time."[8]

The Recovery of Virtue

The prescription MacIntyre offers for this disease is the cultivation of the virtues of social life in small, local communities, a kind of modern equivalent of the monasticism of Saint Benedict. Only in more intimate communities of this sort can we hope to recoup the intellectual and moral resources needed for genuinely civil existence. Before attempting to discern the meaning of justice "writ-large," i.e., justice in the life of society as a whole, the meaning and reality of justice "writ-small" must be cultivated, i.e., justice as a virtue of persons and small groups.

This appeal for the retrieval of the primacy of virtue and character strikes a sympathetic chord in the Christian understanding of the moral life. Indeed, the bishops' pastoral letter stresses the importance of personal virtue in any just society. Thomas Aquinas's Christian appropriation of the Aristotelian discussion of the virtues shows that this is a typically Roman Catholic emphasis. In addition, the letter borrows from the Lutheran and Calvinist understandings of personal vocation to ground the economic responsibilities of all members of the Christian community—workers, homemakers, managers, financiers, and government officials. The church itself, moreover, must be a community that nurtures and sustains both the virtues of each of its members and their vocations to be disciples of Christ in the midst of daily life.

Nevertheless, renewal of the sense of vocation and of personal virtue is not the whole of what the bishops have set out to do. Their purpose is not only to encourage the personal moral and religious development of Christians but also to address the larger economic institutions and policies of the nation.[9] In order to do this successfully in a pluralistic society they need a moral language that is intelligible and plausible to those who do not share their tradition. If one accepts MacIntyre's analysis of contemporary Western culture, no such language exists, and the bishops' second goal is unrealizable.

Stanley Hauerwas, a theologian strongly influenced by MacIntyre, has argued that the effort by Christians to shape public policy within the presuppositions of a liberal, pluralist society is not only futile but theologically illegitimate. In Hauerwas's theology, the church's social task is to bear faithful witness to the story of Jesus, not to cast about trying to find moral arguments that will be persuasive to non-Christians. Hauerwas fears that if the church seeks too much influence in shaping the policies of a pluralist society, its commitment to Jesus Christ will inevitably be contaminated and coopted by the falsehood and violence that are evident in "the world." In his words,

> Once "justice" is made a criterion of Christian social strategy, it can too easily take on a meaning and life of its own that is not informed by the Christian's fundamental convictions. It can, for example, be used to justify the Christian's resort to violence to secure a more "relative justice." But then we must ask if this is in fact the justice we are to seek as Christians.[10]

Hauerwas concludes that the church should cease and desist from the attempt to articulate universal moral norms persuasive to all members of a pluralistic society. It should return to its proper task of building up the Christian community of faith, love, and peace. The church does not "have" a social ethic to guide the life of society as a whole. It should "be" a social ethic; its own life of faithfulness should bear witness to what the world should be but unfortunately is not.[11]

Hauerwas's positive affirmations about the importance of faithfulness to the story of Jesus, costly discipleship, and strong bonds of mutual service within the Christian community are fully affirmed in the bishops' letter. The letter makes a major effort to ground its discussion of economic ethics in the scriptures, in the liturgical life of the community of faith, and in the call to conversion and discipleship. It also goes quite far in confessing the sinfulness of the institutional church's own internal economic life in areas such as fair wages, responsible stewardship of resources, and the like. Its disagreement with Hauerwas is with his *exclusive* concern with the quality of the witness of the Christian community's own life. In the traditional categories of Ernst Troeltsch, the bishops refuse to take the "sectarian" option of exclusive reliance on the witness of the Christian community that Hauerwas recommends. They continue to rely on a "church-type" ecclesiology. They believe that the church has a responsibility to help shape the life of society as a whole. And the fulfillment of this responsibility calls for dialogue and argument about the norms of justice that should govern the life of our pluralistic society.

The theological argument between sect-type and church-type versions of the relation between the Christian community and the larger society is an ancient one. I will not attempt to deal with it here. One brief statement will have to suffice. The bishops succinctly sum up the reasons for their conviction that a fruitful relationship can exist between the Christian community and our pluralist culture:

> Biblical and theological themes shape the overall Christian perspective on economic ethics. This perspective is also subscribed to by those who do not share Christian religious convictions. *Human understanding and religious belief are complementary, not contradictory.* For human beings are created in God's image, and their dignity is manifest in the ability to reason and understand, in their freedom to shape their own lives and the life of their communities, and in the capacity for love and friendship.[12]

Note well: they do not say that human understanding and religious belief are *identical,* but rather that they are not in opposition to each other. Furthermore, a relationship of complementarity means that human wisdom and Christian belief must be mutually enriching and mutually corrective of each other. The church can and should learn from the world; the world can and should learn from the gospel and the whole Christian tradition.

This methodological presupposition, however, does not solve the substantive question, raised by Murray and MacIntyre, concerning the fundamental norm for public life and public policy. If our pluralistic society is fundamentally "confused" about the meaning of justice, and if it has lost the ability to reach agreement on such meaning, then one wonders what it means to say that the human understanding of justice and the Christian vision are complementary. If the meaning of justice has been fractured into incompatible fragments, each being advocated by a particular ideological camp, then the nice synthesis of faith and culture suggested in church-type ecclesiologies is an illusion. We would be forced back to the sectarian option of a community of faithful witness, not because of Hauerwas's theological objections, but because our society lacks a shared culture to which faith can relate. We would face what George Lindbeck, with a good Lutheran sense of irony, has called the "sectarian future of the church."[13]

From Cultural Confusion to Public Argument

Is this the case? My answer depends on a distinction—a distinction between a judgment about the quality of the present popular debate on the meaning of justice in our society, and a conclusion about the future possibilities for this debate that are being opened up by several moral and political philosophers.

First, the current popular debate. If one looks at popular opinion about the meaning of economic justice in our society, it is evident that there is no consensus. There are deep disputes about the merits of the free market, about the desirability or effectiveness of programs designed to aid the poor and the unemployed, about the level of inequality that is tolerable or desirable, about the legitimacy of affirmative-action programs, about the relation between equality of opportunity and equality of outcomes, and about the relation between our responsibilities to vulnerable U.S. workers and to those who work in industries abroad that compete for the jobs of U.S. workers. The economic debates in the Congress are so often stymied because they are riddled with conflicting claims. There is no agreement about which of these claims takes priority.

A certain amount of this is, of course, an inevitable part of the democratic political process. It would be dangerous to think that a single set of moral insights could be invoked to settle all these disputes. The wish for a fully rational political process can easily become a wish for a single intelligence to direct it. That way lies tyranny.

Tyranny, however, is not the only way to avoid paralysis and the breakdown of debate into pure interest-group, single-issue politics. The alternative is the development of a fundamental consensus about the *premises* of public debates, shared convictions that enable us to replace confusion and prejudice with real arguments. In Murray's words:

> The whole premise of the public argument, if it is to be civilized and civilizing, is that the consensus is real, that among the people everything is not in doubt, but that there is a core of agreement, accord, concurrence, acquiescence. We *hold* certain truths; therefore we can *argue* about them. It

> seems to have been one of the corruptions of intelligence . . . to assume that argument ends when agreement is reached. In a basic sense the reverse is true. There can be no argument except on the premise, and within the context of agreement.[14]

Murray called this consensus the "public philosophy," a phrase borrowed from his contemporary, Walter Lippmann.[15] The authors of *Habits of the Heart* see their work as a venture in public philosophy, which William Sullivan has described as "a tradition of interpreting and delineating the common understandings of what the political association is about and what it aims to achieve."[16] Murray argued that the core of the public philosophy is a passionate conviction, rooted in clear understanding, about what is "due to the equal citizen from the City and to the City from the citizenry according to their mode of equality." In other words, the central conviction in the consensus that should shape public argument is an understanding of and devotion to justice, the "ground of civic amity . . . the ground of that unity which is called peace. This unity, qualified by amity, is the highest good of the civil multitude and the perfection of its civility."[17]

In 1960 Murray acknowledged somewhat ruefully that such a public philosophy was at least precarious and quite probably nonexistent in the America of his day. Nevertheless he refused to give up so easily, for no constitutional commonwealth can succeed in the absence of this kind of consensus. If we lack the public philosophy we need, we must recreate and regain one:

> The further conclusion will be that there is today a need for a new moral act of purpose and a new act of intellectual affirmation, comparable to those which launched the American constitutional commonwealth, that will newly put us in possession of the public philosophy, the consensus we need.[18]

We need, in the words of the bishops that echo Murray, a "new American experiment," a new way of thinking about justice and new institutions to secure it for all. The bishops state that by drawing on the resources of the Catholic Christian tradition they hope to make a contribution to this new consensus about the meaning of justice and a new experiment in achieving it. They are seeking to retrieve the central values of biblical faith and civic virtue to contribute new moral purpose to American economic and cultural life.

The bishops are not alone in sensing the need for a renewal of public philosophy at this critical juncture in the history of the United States.

Since the publication of John Rawls's *Theory of Justice* in 1971, there has been a veritable explosion of serious analyses of the meaning of justice by moral and political philosophers in this country. The theoretical approaches of these thinkers cover a wide spectrum, perhaps as wide as the diversity to be found in debates on the level of public opinion. For example, the libertarianism of Robert Nozick stresses the primacy of the right of private property and freedom of exchange in the marketplace. Rawls's liberal democratic theory is committed first to the right to equal freedom for all and, within the framework of such equal freedom, to assisting those most in need. Michael Sandel argues that any adequate moral theory must be built on convictions about the fullness of the human good, convictions that are formed and sustained only in communities shaped by friendship, tradition, and shared vision. For Sandel, therefore, any notion of justice that seeks to circumvent the differences of tradition and vision of the good among historical communities is necessarily limited and even flawed. Michael Walzer contends that equality is at the root of the meaning of justice. But for Walzer equality is a complex concept, with a meaning that is partly the same and partly different in different spheres of life, such as the polity, the workplace, the system of merit and status, and the family.[19]

This welter of competing presuppositions for a theory of justice could easily be seen as vindication of MacIntyre and Hauerwas. On the contrary, I want to interpret it as a source of hope. We are witnessing, I want to contend, a movement from sheer confusion about the meaning of justice to genuine argument about it. The basic consensus of a public philosophy is far from achieved, but the outlines of a framework for real debate are taking shape. And if we could agree on this framework a lot of the fog would lift. It would not move us into the light of noonday, or raise us totally out of Plato's cave into the blinding brightness of the pure good, but it would surely help us figure out a better way to understand the complementarity of all the fragments of human wisdom and Christian religious conviction.

I do not intend to offer some grand synthesis of Rawls, Nozick, Sandel, Walzer, and the others who are part of the current American argument about the meaning of justice. In fact one of my chief points is that there is not *one* meaning of justice in some univocal sense. All of the interlocutors in the current disputation have got their hands on some part of the reality we are in search of. Socrates knew this phenomenon well: dialectic, that is argument, is a process of sorting through a host of opinions to discern what is true in each, in search of that which is most true, most good. The argument about what justice means is as old as Western civilization. The quality of the argument today may well determine whether this civilization has a future, or whether its future will be in any sense civilized. In the face of these high stakes, I think that the sectarian retreat of MacIntyre and Hauerwas is ultimately, if unwittingly, a failure of nerve. It fails to appreciate new possibilities present today for expressing love of one's neighbor by engaging in the long march of cultural transformation.

Dialogue with Political Philosophy

So then, what do I propose? Let me start with two central theses from the participants in the present American philosophical debate. John Rawls has proposed a theory of "justice as fairness." This is not based on any commitment about what is ultimately *good* in human life. Justice-as-fairness, Rawls states, has no metaphysical presuppositions about human purpose, human ends, or what finally makes people happy. On ultimate ends and the full human good we must be free to disagree. In a recent essay Rawls argues that all we need to get the concept of justice off the ground is a mutual desire to work out "a fair system of cooperation between free and equal persons."[20] He thinks that such a basis can be laid down without decreeing an end to pluralism among our various visions of the good. Nor does justice-as-fairness want to abolish the commitments people have to goods greater than fairness. In addition, justice-as-fairness does not depend on the belief that individual autonomy is an end in itself. But it does presuppose that free choice regarding ultimate ends and personal goals must be politically protected in a just political community. Further, within a context of a primary commitment to free choice, justice-as-fairness seeks to identify "the kernel of overlapping consensus" among the various ideas of the full human good that different persons and groups hold, a consensus which "when worked up into a political conception of justice turn out to be sufficient to underwrite a just constitutional regime. This is the most we can expect, nor do we need more."[21]

Justice-as-fairness turns out, then, to be a vision of a tolerant society that respects freedom and wants to aid those in need as long as this aid is compatible with the freedom of people to disagree about their personal definition of happiness.

Is this really enough? I think not. And the most cogent argument to express my disagreement is drawn from Michael Walzer. Walzer, too, wants to respect differences. But his definition of the differences that count is quite different from Rawls's. Walzer knows that people do not achieve happiness or full lives apart from friendship, kinship, and many other particular, nonuniversal relationships. But note: for Walzer *relationship* is key. Who is in positive relationship with me determines whom

I have certain obligations of justice toward. And the *kind* of obligation I have depends on the *kind* of relationship it is: political, familial, economic, ecclesial, etc.

Thus for Walzer the diverse kinds of communities we belong to are the source of diverse "spheres of justice," where the big word *justice* gets differentiated into smaller parts. But this does not mean that it gets blown apart into utterly incompatible fragments. The key to Walzer's argument about the unity among the different spheres of justice is his concept of "membership."

Let me outline his main thesis. In arguing about justice we are arguing about who gets what, and on what basis they get it. We are also arguing about who gives what, and on what basis they give it. We are arguing about the criteria that should govern sharing in the creation and distribution of the goods of some kind of community, whether it be an economic, political, honorific, or familial community, or even a community of grace. Thus, the bottom-line question in arguments about justice is this: *who counts* when we talk about sharing in the goods that come from being part of a particular kind of community?

This means that fairness is not simply a matter of the *size* of the slices of the pie being distributed. More basic than the arguments about the size of the slices is the one about who should be at the table in the first place. The answer to this question differs in different spheres of human existence. If I am an employer distributing wages then I have obligations to my employees that I do not have to nonemployees. If a community is bestowing honor and praise, it should go to honorable and praiseworthy people. Nobel prizes should go to peacemakers and eminent scientists, not warmakers and charlatans. In family life, parents face the awesome task of both loving each of their children equally while acknowledging and encouraging their different gifts. And though family members have very important obligations to those outside the bonds of kinship, they don't have the same *kind* of obligations to people down the block or halfway around the world that they do to spouses, children, or parents. A central question in disputes about justice, therefore, is that of specifying the set of relationships or particular kind of community we are talking about when urging a particular standard of justice. In short, who is a member of the club to which the standard of justice is to apply? In Walzer's words:

> The primary good we distribute to one another is membership in some human community. And what we do with regard to membership structures all our other distributive choices: it determines with whom we make choices, and from whom we require obedience and collect taxes, to whom we allocate goods and services.[22]

The criteria of membership, of course, are different for different kinds of communities, and therefore the criteria of justice will vary from one zone of life to another. Justice has a plurality of meanings because we have many kinds of relationships in our lives. In some of them, such as the political community, a standard of strict equality applies. One person, one vote. In others the criterion of merit is relevant. Grading exams is a case in point. In still other areas need is the relevant measure. Parents do not do justice to their children if they treat one who is handicapped in an identical way with one who is not.

Respect for the richness of social life, therefore, calls for a nuanced and differentiated understanding of the meaning of justice. A single criterion, such as need or merit, administered by a single institution, such as the government or the market, betrays the rich and complex reality of social existence. On this key point, the tradition of Catholic social ethics is remarkably close to Walzer. In line with this tradition, the bishops' letter makes a distinction between the state and society. Society is the more inclusive reality, composed of many subcommunities of various types: families, neighborhoods, labor unions, small businesses, giant corporations, farm cooperatives, a host of voluntary associations, and the churches. Respect for this pluralism of communities rests on the fact that justice is not the concern of the political community alone, nor is it to be administered solely by the state. The freedom of these other forms of human community to exist and to operate according to the kinds of communities they are must be protected. This is the substance of what Catholic thought calls the principle of subsidiarity. Note, however, that these other communities are not purely *private* bodies. They are parts of *society*, ways in which persons come to participate in social life.

This way of formulating an approach to the meaning of justice is an important point of intersection between the bishops' letter and the contemporary philosophical argument. For example, in a statement that is at least in tension with his contractarian presuppositions, Rawls has recently stressed the notion of membership as key to his understanding of civic life.

> Since Greek times, both in philosophy and law, the concept of the person has been understood as the concept of someone who can take part in, or who can play a role in, social life, and hence exercise and respect its various rights and duties. Thus we say that a person is someone who can be a citizen, that is *a fully cooperating member of society over a complete life*. We add the phrase "over a complete life" because a society is viewed as a more or less complete and self-sufficient scheme of cooperation, making room within itself for all the necessities and activities of life, from birth to death.

> A society is not an association for more limited purposes; citizens do not join society voluntarily but are born into it, where, for our aims here, we assume they are to lead their lives.[23]

To be a person is to be a *member* of society, active within it in many ways through diverse sets of relationships. The key question that the bishops would place on the national agenda rests on the premise that the meaning of justice rises from this link between personhood and social participation.

Participation, Marginalization, and Basic Justice

It is in this framework that the bishops' letter most directly challenges American economic and cultural life today. They state the challenge this way: "*Basic justice demands the establishment of minimum levels of participation in the life of the human community for all persons.* The ultimate injustice is for a person or group to be actively treated or passively abandoned as if they were nonmembers of the human race."[24] The antithesis of such participation is called "marginalization" by the pastoral letter—exclusion from active membership in the human community.

Unjust exclusion can take many forms, as justice can take many forms. There is political marginalization: the denial of the vote, restriction of free speech, the tyrannical concentration of power in the hands of a ruling elite, or straightforward totalitarianism. It can also be economic in nature. Where persons are unable to find work even after searching for many months or where they are thrown out of work by decisions they are powerless to influence, they are effectively marginalized. They are implicitly told by the community: "We don't need your talent, we don't need your initiative, we don't need *you*."[25] If society acquiesces in this situation when remedial steps could be taken, injustice is being done. One can hardly think of a more effective way to deny people any active participation in the economic life of society than to cause or allow them to remain unemployed. Similarly, persons who face hunger, homelessness, and the extremes of poverty when society possesses the resources to meet their needs are treated as nonmembers. As Walzer puts it:

> Men and women who appropriate vast sums of money for themselves, while needs are unmet, act like tyrants, dominating and distorting the distribution of security and welfare. . . . The indifference of Britain's rulers during the Irish potato famine of the 1840s is a sure sign that Ireland was a colony, a conquered land, no real part of Great Britain.[26]

In the same way, the hungry and homeless people in this nation today are no part of anything worthy of being called a commonwealth. The extent of their suffering shows how far we are from being a community of persons.

The bishops' general normative perspective is made concrete by their survey of the extent to which people are excluded or left behind in the economic life of the nation and throughout the world today. Over eight million people are looking for work in this country but unable to find it. Thirty-three million Americans are below the official poverty line. One out of every four children under six and one out of every two black children live in poverty. One-third of all female-headed families are poor. And from 1968 to 1978 one-fourth of all Americans fell into poverty during at least one year. Beyond our borders at least eight hundred million persons live in absolute poverty and nearly half a billion persons are chronically hungry. This despite fruitful harvests world-wide, and a food surplus in the U.S. that is driving down prices and causing bankruptcy for large numbers of American farmers.

In the face of these realities we have to ask: is being born into the human race any guarantee that one will be treated as a person in Rawls's terms: "a fully cooperating member of society over a complete life"? Even raising the question is an invitation to cynicism. The chief problem in explicating an adequate concept of justice in our society today is not the different conceptions Americans have of what makes for full happiness or what private "life-plans" are worth pursuing. The problem is that many would prefer not to reflect on what it means to say that these marginalized people are members of the human community and we have a duty to treat them as such.

On the basis of their biblical faith and their tradition's emphasis on civic obligations to the common good, the bishops are unable to ignore this problem as our culture seems tempted to do. On the basis of their conviction about the complementarity of Christian faith and human understanding, they are seeking to stimulate genuine argument and debate about the meaning of justice in this pluralistic society through arguments parallel to those I have made here. They state that "no one may claim the name Christian and be comfortable in the face of the hunger, homelessness, insecurity, and injustice found in this country and the world."[27] I would add no one may claim to be genuinely human and remain at ease with these problems. That, I believe, is at least the beginning of a consensus or public philosophy. Within the framework of such a public philosophy we can argue about how to overcome these injustices and about which public policies will most effectively help us to do so. There can, however, be no legitimate debate in a truly civilized society on whether we have a duty to overcome them.

Part Three

Human Rights in a Divided World

Chapter 6

Global Human Rights: An Interpretation of the Contemporary Catholic Understanding

The emergence of human rights as a central concern for contemporary Roman Catholicism is a remarkable historical development. From some points of view it is even an astonishing development. The Catholic church was a vigorous opponent of both the democratic and socialist revolutions that were the chief proponents of the civil and social rights enshrined in twentieth-century human-rights declarations.[1] In recent years, however, various groups within the Catholic church have become highly visible on the global horizon as advocates of respect for the full range of human rights.[2] Also, the central institutional organ of the Catholic church, the Holy See, has adopted the cause of human rights as a prime focus of its ethical teaching and pastoral strategy in the domain of international justice and peace. This rapid change in the Catholic church's stance toward global human rights is a crucial fact that must be taken into account in any effort to understand current church theory and practice in the rights field.

The interpretation presented here is just that: an interpretation. The Catholic church is a highly differentiated community, composed of sub-communities divided from one another along regional, cultural, economic, and educational lines. This interpretation attempts to grasp the predominant understanding of human rights in the Catholic church, i.e., the one that is setting the course on which the church as a whole seems presently embarked. Therefore, in addition to providing a descriptive account of the prevailing understanding of human rights in the church, what is said here contains an element of prediction. The uncertainty of such an approach may be counterbalanced by the interest it sparks.

The first part of the chapter argues that the impetus for the rapid development of the Catholic understanding of the church's role in the human-rights field came from a major event in the modern history of Catholicism: the Second Vatican Council and the pontificate of Pope John XXIII. This part tries to show that it was not only the developments in theology that occurred at the council that brought about this change. Rather, under the leadership of John XXIII, Vatican II was the occasion of a fundamental shift in the church's understanding of its social and institutional place in a pluralistic world. The effort to respond to this newly understood social location in global society caused a rapid development in the church's normative stance toward human rights. The second part of the chapter will then outline the content of this development and show its relationship to the central elements of previous Catholic social thought. It will show how a major and unexpected development was legitimated by appeals to tradition. Finally, the concluding section will make some suggestions about the contribution that the newly developed Catholic understanding of human rights can make to current discussions. Also, some of the questions about human rights that remain unanswered in Catholic thinking will be highlighted.

The Context for Development: A Transnational Church in a Pluralistic World

Perhaps the single most significant statement contained in the collection of decrees, constitutions, and declarations of the Second Vatican Council is the following apparently innocuous sentence from the first article of *Dignitatis humanae*, the Declaration on Religious Freedom: "This sacred Synod intends to develop the doctrine of recent Popes on the inviolable rights of the human person and on the constitutional order of society."[3] In fact, the statement is far from innocuous, for it represents an acknowledgment on the highest level of church teaching that Catholic doctrine can develop, can change. The importance of this assertion has been noted by the theologian who was chiefly responsible for the drafting of the declaration: "In no other conciliar document is it so explicitly stated that the intention of the Council is to 'develop' Catholic doctrine."[4]

In its immediate context the statement was a prelude to the unambiguous affirmation of the fundamental right of every person to religious freedom. In earlier Catholic teaching this right had been variously qualified and even denied. It is remarkable enough to find a reversal of the explicit content of church teaching coming from as traditionalist a body as the world-wide episcopacy of the Catholic church assembled in council.

In the context of the overall influence of the council on the church's life, however, the statement is even more noteworthy. It suggests that the development in question touches the basic structure of the church's understanding of human rights and constitutional order. The fact that the need for such development is acknowledged most directly in the religious freedom declaration provides a clue for interpreting the fundamental shift in the Catholic understanding of rights that occurred at the council. The reorganization of the normative foundations of the Catholic understanding of human rights was produced by the same social force that precipitated the Declaration on Religious Freedom, namely the reality of pluralism. At the council the modern Catholic church for the first time was compelled to come to grips in an official way with the realities of the religious, cultural, social, economic, political, and ideological pluralism of the contemporary world. The most obvious effect of this acknowledgment of pluralism was the council's movement from the kind of unitary model of church-state relationships that prevailed through almost all of previous church history to a pluralistic model based on the right of all persons to religious liberty.

The new experience of the reality of pluralism, however, was not limited to the religious sphere in conciliar discussions. The diversity of political and economic systems and the conflicting social ideologies present in contemporary global society were also central concerns. These concerns were underlying themes of the council's Pastoral Constitution on the Church in the Modern World. In the council's view, the diversity of political, social, economic, and ideological systems is a threat to peace and an obstacle to justice. The depth of disagreement among fundamental social and ideological visions prevailing around the globe leads to disagreement about the meaning of peace itself and justice itself. This basic conflict between interpretations of the central normative foundations of social order was one of the "signs of the times" that inspired the council's examination of the place of the church in the world today.

Had the council followed the lead of past Catholic tradition in formulating its response to the reality of contemporary pluralism and conflict, it would have proposed a normative model of social structure and political order chosen from among those available on the basis of compatibility with Catholic tradition and faith. Such an approach would have been roughly parallel to past Catholic solutions to the problem of religious pluralism—the proposal of a single ideal religious order in which Catholicism would hold a privileged place. But just as the option of a single normative social/religious system was rejected as the Catholic ideal in *Dignitatis humanae*, so also conciliar and postconciliar Catholic teaching has rejected the ideal of a single, normative model of political and economic order. This parallelism is also evident in the kind of solution actually proposed for dealing with pluralism and conflict. In the religious sector the council did not abandon Catholic commitment to the truth of the Christian religion. Far from it. Rather it asserted that a Christian understanding of the human person, rooted both in the Christian tradition and the tradition of reason, demands that human dignity be respected through the civil guarantee of religious freedom. Similarly, conciliar response to social and ideological pluralism did not take the form of a retreat by the church from the effort to establish justice and peace in global society. Rather, it affirmed that there are basic rights in the social, economic, political, and cultural fields that all systems and all ideologies are bound to respect. These are the basic rights of the human person, derivative from the fundamental dignity of the person.

In the midst of Vatican II, Pope John XXIII issued his encyclical letter *Pacem in terris* in which he sought to move the council toward this new perspective. In his words:

> Any human society, if it is to be well ordered and productive, must lay down as a foundation this principle, namely, that every human being is a person, that is, his nature is endowed with intelligence and free will. Indeed, precisely because he is a person he has rights and obligations flowing directly and simultaneously from his very nature. And as these rights are universal and inviolable so they cannot in any way be surrendered.[5]

Following John XXIII's lead, the council affirmed the full array of human rights spelled out in *Pacem in terris* as the norms to which every society is accountable no matter what its political, economic, or ideological system, and to which the international order itself can be held accountable. These rights include both the civil and political rights generally associated with Western democracies and the social and economic rights emphasized in socialist societies. In following John XXIII, the council did not propose a single model of society or nostalgically seek the elimination of pluralism. It adopted a normative framework for a pluralistic world.

This move amounts to a shift from a social ethic that proposed a concrete model of the structure of society as a necessary exigency of natural law to a social ethic in which all social models and structures are held accountable to the standards of human rights. The difference between the two perspectives is the acceptance of social, political, and ideological pluralism as an inescapable fact in the contemporary world. Human-rights norms do not lead to the prescription of any single economic, political, or ideological system. Rather basic human rights set limits and establish obligations for all systems and ideologies, leaving the precise form in which these systems will be organized undefined. In making this somewhat more modest claim, conciliar and postconciliar Catholicism has actually increased its capacity to make a critical and creative contribution in the social life of a pluralistic global society.

How did this substantial shift in the foundation of Catholic social thought come about? There were a variety of intellectual and theological currents operating in the church in the two decades immediately preceding the council that prepared the way for the change. From the viewpoint of social rather than intellectual history, however, an equally important cause can be discerned. As an event in the social history of the church the council had an impact on Catholic thought similar to the influence that the founding of the United Nations exerted on the content of secular political thought in general. Both events gathered representatives from all regions of the globe, persons with vastly different cultural backgrounds, from countries with enormously different levels of economic development and wealth, from societies with opposed political and ideological systems. Though the events leading to the creation of the United Nations and those which transpired at the Vatican Council had evidently different purposes, they had a common concern with the problem of the unity of the human community and the task of finding norms and structures for world peace in the face of ideological pluralism and conflict. It is true that Westerners had the largest voice both in the founding of the U.N. and at the Second Vatican Council. But in both assemblies the conflicts between East and West, between Western and non-Western culture, and between rich nations and poor nations were conflicts *internal* to the two assemblies themselves. The need to find consensus on a normative basis for international justice and peace without suppressing the legitimate differences among regions and social systems led both bodies to a human-rights focus. The early years of the U.N. saw the first really significant efforts at the elaboration of a fundamental set of internationally accepted standards for a pluralist globe. The Second Vatican Council attempted the same task for a church newly aware of itself as a transnational, transcultural community.

Theologian Karl Rahner has suggested that the most fundamental significance of the Second Vatican Council lies in the qualitative difference between broad representation of non-European regional subunits of the church that occurred at the council and the Europocentrism of the history of Catholicism since the days of the Apostle Paul. In Rahner's view the Second Vatican Council marked the beginning of Catholicism as a self-consciously world-wide community. At Vatican II, "a world Church as such begins to act through the reciprocal influence exerted by all its components."[6] In other words, at the council the Catholic church became, at least incipiently, a genuinely transnational body rather than a European one with missionary outposts.[7] Though the council was obviously a Christian assembly, the forms of Christianity represented were culturally diverse and had been shaped by very different economic, political, and ideological contexts. At Vatican II these diverse contexts were brought into direct contact with one another. It should, therefore, have been almost predictable that a new emphasis on the full range of human rights, both civil/political and social/economic, would develop once the decision had been reached to convoke a council of the transnational Catholic church.

Since the Second World War nongovernmental organizations, like the International Commission of Jurists and Amnesty International, which are both transnational and also advocates for international justice and peace, have increasingly employed the perspective of human rights as the normative basis for their activities. In a world that is simultaneously pluralistic and interdependent, human-rights norms have gained a central place because they attempt to articulate the immunities and entitlements that are due every person "simply by virtue of being a human person, irrespective of his or her social status, cultural accomplishments, moral merits, religious beliefs, class memberships, or contractual relationships."[8] This quality of universality and the status of human rights as "moral claims that human persons can make independently of and prior to their acknowledgment by particular societies"[9] are especially important for groups that aim to contribute to the development of a transnational ethic for a pluralist world order.

The impetus for the rapid development of a human-rights ethic in the Catholic church came in large part from the non-European regions of the transnational church (from the poor countries of the Third World in the area of social/economic rights and from the United States in the area of civil/political rights, especially the right to religious freedom). The recent systematic elaboration of the normative human-rights framework of contemporary Catholicism, however, was initiated principally at the center, namely at the transnational assembly of all the Catholic bishops in council under the leadership of the chief transnational agent of the church, the pope. Thus the exigencies of regional and ideological pluralism combined with need for unity at the center to produce a fundamental reorientation in the church's understanding of the appropriate normative foundation for global politics and economy.

All this was only incipient at the council. But as Rahner insists, the process of developing a transnational human-rights ethic and pastoral strategy was definitively begun at the Second Vatican Council. Since the council the normative framework has been developed in greater detail. The postconciliar period has also seen the development of local, national, regional, and transnational institutional structures within the church for the implementation of this new normative human-rights perspective. This process of implementation has been hesitant, conflicted, and at times self-contradictory. Nevertheless, the understanding of rights that has been developing since the council in normative Catholic social thought in response to its newly discovered transnational context is the chief explanation of the new visibility of the church in the human-rights struggle.[10]

The Normative Understanding: An Integral Theory of Rights

The fact that the Catholic church pursues both its religious mission and its pastoral role in nearly all the regions of the globe has brought it into contact with all the major forms of human-rights violations and with the chief ideological interpretations of human rights. In its attempt to formulate an understanding of human rights appropriate to its transnational existence the church has inevitably had to face the arguments about the central focus of human-rights theory that divide the Western democracies from the Eastern socialist bloc. In the liberal tradition of the West the civil and political freedoms of speech, worship, assembly, press, and the juridical guarantees of habeas corpus and due process are at the center of human-rights thinking. Human rights are rooted in the liberty of the individual person. In Marxist socialism, on the other hand, the rights to work, to minimum levels of nutrition, and to active participation in the process of creating a socialist society are central. These rights are grounded by the conviction that personal freedom is an abstraction unless it is viewed in the economic and social context that conditions it.[11] A similar though not identical polarity characterizes the debate between the industrial powers of the North and the less developed countries of the South. In general, the Northern societies argue for an effort to meet human needs within the context of a social system based on a prior commitment to political and economic liberty. In the countries of the South the emphasis is often inverted. Political and economic freedoms are regarded as obtainable for the vast majority of the population of these countries only in the context of policies aimed at meeting basic needs for food, clothing, shelter, and minimum education.[12]

These divergent emphases in thinking about human rights have all had an impact on the content of the contemporary Roman Catholic understanding of rights. It is one of the deep biases of the Catholic tradition to respond to basic intellectual and social choices by saying both/and rather than either/or. John XXIII's *Pacem in terris* includes all the rights emphasized on each side of these East/West and North/South debates. It includes all the rights enumerated in the U.N. Universal Declaration and its two accompanying covenants. It affirms the rights to life, bodily integrity, food, clothing, shelter, rest, medical care, and the social services necessary to protect these rights. It includes the rights to freedom of communication (speech, press), to information, and to education. In the area of religious activity it affirms the right to honor God in accord with one's conscience and to practice religion in private and in public. In the area of family life the rights to marry, to procreate, and to the economic and social conditions necessary for the support of family life are all included. Economic rights include the rights to work, to humane working conditions, to a just wage, to appropriate participation in the management of economic enterprises, and to the ownership of private property within limits established by social duties. The rights of assembly, association, and the right to organize are also affirmed, as are the rights to freedom of movement and to internal and external migration. Finally, the encyclical asserts the political right to participate in public affairs and the juridical right to constitutional protection of all other rights, including habeas corpus and due process.[13]

The appeal of this comprehensive list of human rights is certainly a powerful one, as the enthusiastic reception that *Pacem in terris* received in many parts of the world testifies. Several questions must be raised, however, about such an all-inclusive understanding of rights. The strengths of such a universal and integrative approach to rights may also be a weakness. In seeking to incorporate the emphases of both East and West, of North and South, the church's understanding of human rights may be in danger of rising above the actual conflicts of global society that generate human-rights violations. It can be asked whether some more recent statements from the Holy See do not show unmistakable signs of using abstract comprehensiveness as a substitute for concrete choice and action in the midst of conflict. For example, Pope Paul VI, after an analysis of capitalism, socialism, liberalism, and Marxism, affirmed that the foundation of Christian engagement in political action "is above and sometimes opposed to the ideologies," and is "beyond every system."[14] At their Third General Conference held in Puebla, Mexico, in 1979, the Latin American episcopate expressed ambivalence about how the commitment of the church to human rights should be related to the major ideologies that currently motivate political action in Latin America.[15]

A response to this question involves three points. The first concerns the ultimate foundation of the Catholic rights theory. The second deals with the historical background of the theory in modern Catholic thought. And the third addresses once again its relationship to the current context for the protection and violation of human rights in global society.

First, then, the foundational principle of the theory must be distinguished from an abstractly inclusive harmonization of the rights emphasized by the various competing ideologies. The fundamental value that undergirds it is neither simply the liberty of the individual person stressed in the liberal democracies nor simply the social participation and economic well-being stressed in various ways by Marxism and socialism. Rather the theory maintains that respect for freedom, the meeting of basic needs, and participation in community and social relationships are all essential aspects of the human dignity that is the foundation of all rights. The institutional protection of personal freedom is emphasized by liberal democracy. The fulfillment of human needs is stressed by the developing "basic-needs" strategies at the center of the North-South debate. And the restructuring of the social and economic order in a way that allows genuine communal participation in the corporate life of society is the program of socialist thought. Each of these ideologies links its fundamental understanding of human rights with a particular structural obstacle to the realization of human dignity. The contemporary Catholic understanding, however, refuses to tie its notion of human dignity to only one of these three spheres of life in which persons can be either violated or protected by the structure of the social order. As John XXIII put it, "The cardinal point of this teaching is that individual persons are necessarily the foundation, cause, and end of all social institutions. We are referring to human beings, insofar as they are social by nature, and raised to an order of existence which transcends and subdues nature."[16] Any political, economic, or social system that is to be morally legitimate must provide respect for these spheres of freedom, need, and relationship. Thus the foundational norm of human dignity does not claim to be an ideological principle of social organization but rather a principle of moral and political legitimacy.

The Catholic tradition offers two warrants for the validity of the foundational principle. The imperative arising from human dignity is based on the indicative of the person's transcendence over the world of things. The ability of persons to think and to choose, their hopes which always outrun the historical moment, and the experienced call to discriminate between good and evil actions—all these indicate that persons are more than things. This warrant for the foundational principle of Catholic rights theory is held to be accessible and plausible apart from the particularist doctrines of the Christian faith. The Christian faith does provide, however, a second explicitly Christian warrant for the principle of human dignity. The beliefs that all persons are created in the image of God, that they are redeemed by Jesus Christ, and that they are summoned by God to a destiny beyond history serve both to support and to interpret the fundamental significance of human existence. The theological doctrines both illuminate general human experience and are themselves illuminated by such experience. With this as the basic relationship between theological and philosophical approaches to the norm of human dignity, the Catholic tradition does not hesitate to claim a universal validity for the way it seeks to ground human rights in the dignity of the person rather than in convictions about institutional and structural means for the protection of this dignity.[17]

A full response to the charge that this notion of human dignity is the result of a false abstraction from the realities of social conflict and the need for choice leads to the consideration of a second point. As a norm of political legitimacy the standard of respect for human dignity affirms that political and economic institutions are to serve human persons as free, needy, and relational beings. The primary referent of the term is not abstract and conceptual but concrete and existential: actually existing human beings. At the same time, however, the notion of human dignity is nearly empty of meaning. Unless it is further specified, the notion of human dignity lacks all reference to particular freedoms, needs, and relationships. Therefore, unless the relationship between the transcendental worth of persons and particular human freedoms, needs, and relationships can be specified in greater detail, the notion of dignity will remain an empty notion.[18]

The task of determining the concrete political and economic conditions that are in fact required to protect human freedom, meet human needs, and support human relationships is a historical one. The move from the affirmation of the worth of persons to the proposal of *specific* rights that may legitimately be claimed from society is mediated by historical experience and historically accumulated understanding.[19] Historical memory and continuing historical experience are thus the only means by which the notion of dignity gains enough concrete content to support particular rights and claims. Therefore every theory of rights that claims human dignity as its foundation necessarily presupposes a tradition of historical memory about the human effects of different kinds of social and political systems in the past. It also presupposes an understanding of the human effects of present patterns of social organization.

Over the past hundred years the Catholic ethical tradition has been self-consciously engaged in a protracted effort to determine more precisely just what conditions *are* necessary if human persons are to be protected in their dignity. During the years of Leo XIII's pontificate two of these conditions were brought to the fore. The first was the indispensability of minimum economic levels for all, in the form of adequate wages and broad distribution of property. Second, in the political realm it was recognized that the freedom of the majority in a democracy or of the ruling powers in other forms of polity must be limited by their obligation to serve the common good of the whole society. This is a principle of the limited state, a principle that places a check on all forms of state absolutism by making government accountable to the basic rights and liberties of all citizens. These two principles are respectively the bases of social/economic rights and civil/political rights.

The history of the church's understanding of these principles has followed a circuitous path through the past century. Opposition to anticlerical interpretations of religious liberty led to a limited understanding of the way persons would be protected in their dignity by a constitutional guarantee for civil liberties and political rights. Also resistance to the totalitarianism and programmatic opposition to religion in the Soviet Union led to a narrowed understanding of the potential human benefits of other kinds of socialist models.[20]

Despite the hesitant movement of Catholic understanding of the concrete exigencies of dignity, however, one basic insight was ingrained in the historical memory of the church by its efforts in this area: the conviction that dignity would be violated by any system that denied political freedom in the name of economic rights or that appealed to the primacy of individual liberty as justification for its failure to meet basic human needs. This insight was often expressed in the form of proposals for a "third way" between capitalism and socialism. This middle path was variously elaborated in the social models known as corporatism, solidarism, and Christian democracy. All of these models were based on the assumption that respect for civil and political rights could be combined with protection of social and economic rights in a harmonious, nonconflictual social order. The supposition that this inclusive vision of human dignity could be protected concretely without the continuing presence of social conflict was the chief reason why Catholic concern has often been one step removed from the actual sources of conflict and rights violations. The reluctance to address the reality of conflict often cut the nerve of action that leads to social change. Thus the predominant Catholic disposition to seek resolution of the problem of the pluralism of ideologies and diversity of social systems by direct appeal to social harmony was linked with a reluctance to deal with the realities of power and conflict. This negative side of Catholic human-rights thought was, however, directly linked with its experience and memory of the indispensability of both civil/political and social/economic rights.

The shift in appreciation of the reality of ideological and social pluralism that was begun by Vatican II is the focus of the third point to be considered in discussing the charge of abstractness leveled against the current Catholic approach to rights. The transnational and transcultural institutional self-consciousness of the church has reinforced its historic bias against opting for one of the competing ideologies or social models that shape the context in which the church exists. The beginning of the legitimation of pluralism that occurred at the council, however, has freed the church to approach the issue of conflict in a new way. Though this development is still incipient, the postconciliar church has begun to look for the realization of the fullness of human dignity in the midst of political and economic conflict. Rather than proposing a model of social organization that claims to protect human dignity in every nation or culture, recent statements from Rome have emphasized the ways that the interconnected package of civil/political and social/economic rights is today threatened by a variety of oppressive power configurations. The normative postconciliar church's statements have increasingly argued that civil/political and social/economic rights are interconnected and that respect for one set of rights is dependent on respect for the other. The historical memory of the church is combining with its present historical experience as a community to produce what amounts to a transnational human-rights ideology. The elements of this new ideology are a respect for social pluralism, a conviction that all human rights are interconnected, and a willingness to stand for the rights of those who are simultaneously denied their political and economic rights against those whose disproportionate political and economic power is the cause of this denial.

The basis of this new "human-rights ideology" was particularly evident at the 1971 Synod of Bishops, an assembly which, significantly, was a transnational one. The interconnection of all rights was highlighted in the synod's assertion of the "right to development." This right was defined as "the dynamic interpenetration of all those fundamental human rights upon which the aspirations of individuals and nations are based."[21] It is also evident in the assertion of the "right to participation"—a right which is to be applied in the economic and in the social field.[22] Both the "right to development" and the "right to participation" are shorthand ways of affirming the interconnected rights of those deprived of development and excluded from economic and political participation. These two "synthetic" rights are in the best tradition of the Catholic bias to say: *both* political liberty *and* basic human needs. The *both/and* that is lodged in the Catholic historical memory has new relevance in the context of an interdependent and pluralistic world.

Implications: The Rights of the Oppressed

Several conclusions about the implications of the contemporary Catholic church's understanding of human rights can be drawn from the generalizations proposed in this essay.[23] If the historical memory and present transnational experience of the Catholic community is in any way accurate it would seem that the argument between those who say "bread first" and those who say "freedom first" has reached a dead end. People who lack bread also usually lack political freedom. And increasingly those without political freedom and access to political power seem to end up without bread. The interconnection of rights has become evident not only in theory but in practice. As J. P. Pronk, Minister for Development Cooperation from the Netherlands, put it:

> In Latin America and elsewhere we see in a dramatic way how people set about achieving social justice, how they need to exercise political freedoms to do this, and how they are oppressed and become the victims of inhuman tortures. The link between the different categories [of rights] is shown clearly not only in the preambles to treaties but also in the practical exercise of human rights.[24]

If such an interpretation of the situation is correct then the charge of "abstractness" and indecisiveness against the inclusive Catholic approach to rights is unfounded. The same can be said about similar charges against the U.N. Universal Declaration.

Those who would learn from the mistakes of the past, however, should realize that this inclusiveness of Catholic rights theory has hindered the church's capacity for action and frequently fostered a reactionary stance. The condition for translating an inclusive theory of rights into a strategy for action and policy is the recognition that pluralism is inevitably accompanied by conflict. Defense and support of the full range of rights for every person under current patterns of economic and political conflict, therefore, calls for a choice. This choice is one that will orient policy toward preferential concern for the rights of those who have neither bread nor freedom. It means that the rights of the oppressed, those denied both political and economic power, should take priority in policy over privileged forms of influence and wealth.

The contemporary Catholic understanding of human rights has just begun to move in this direction. But the leaders of both liberal and authoritarian governments and of capitalist and socialist economies have something to learn from transnational organizations like the Catholic church. It may even be that a community with as long a memory and as pragmatic a style as the Catholic church has something unique to contribute to a global understanding of a new human-rights ideology. The potential for such a contribution will become an actuality if and only if the church continues on the course charted by Vatican II.

Chapter 7

Religious Freedom and Economic Rights: A Note on an Unfinished Argument

John Courtney Murray's contributions to Christian life and thought indubitably qualify him to be called the most outstanding theologian in the history of American Catholicism. His greatest achievement was a critical reappropriation of the Catholic tradition on church-state relations, a reappropriation that enabled him to make a creative American contribution to the renewal of the world-wide church. For a time he fell under the suspicion of churchmen ill at ease with thoughts either critical or creative. But in the end the deep fidelity and sheer power of his arguments enabled the Second Vatican Council to proclaim boldly: "This sacred Synod intends to develop the doctrine of recent Popes on the inviolable rights of the human person and on the constitutional order of society."[1]

The development of doctrine effected by the council, of course, concerned the matter of religious freedom. The shift is made vividly clear when Gregory XVI's 1832 teaching that liberty of opinion and separation of church from state are rooted in "crazed absurdity" *(deliramentum)* is compared with the council's unambiguous declaration that "the right to religious freedom has its foundation in the very dignity of the human person, as this dignity is known through the revealed word of God and by reason itself."[2] The council's declaration is fortunately taken for granted today. If the broader significance of the counciliar understanding of human rights and constitutional order is to be understood, however, it is important to follow Murray's example by understanding how the development came about.

The curial officials and theologians who opposed Murray's argument both before and during the council had a certain logic to their position. It can be displayed succinctly in the following syllogism:

- The Roman Catholic faith is the true religion.
- It is good for people to believe what is true.
- The state is obligated to promote the common good.
- Therefore, the state is bound to promote Catholic belief, and wherever possible to establish Catholicism as the religion of the state.

This reasoning sets forth the theological perspective known as "integralism." Granted the premises, the argument is unimpeachable. Thus anyone who would challenge the conclusion must modify one of the propositions on which it rests. Gregory XVI believed, with some good evidence to back him up, that continental advocates of religious freedom were denying the first premise. That is, they were rejecting the truth of Catholic Christianity. This the pope could hardly accept. Murray's integralist adversaries also believed that his views at least weakened the force of the first premise and would strengthen the currents of secularism and indifference running through modern Western culture.

Murray's knowledge of the dynamic nature of Christian tradition prevented him from adopting the view that *all* truth has been exhaustively enshrined once and for all in Catholic doctrine and teaching. He was too well schooled in history and too much aware of the wisdom to be gained from secular and ecumenical discourse for such a simplistic and static understanding of the truth of Catholicism. Nevertheless he was unambiguously committed to this truth, properly interpreted. His challenge to the position that establishment of Catholicism as the state religion is the "ideal" in church-state relations was directed against another element of the integralist position. His goal, in numerous articles written over several decades, became that of providing a more nuanced understanding of the role of government than that contained in the syllogism's third proposition.

As chapter one above pointed out, there were three levels to Murray's argument.[3] The first was theological: human existence has an end and value transcending the temporal and terrestrial. The spiritual dimension of human life is the concern of church, not the government. Indeed, government is fundamentally incompetent in matters touching the eternal destiny of human beings. Its sole role in matters ecclesiastical is to guarantee the freedom of the church to pursue its mission. The second level of the argument was political: the distinction between society and the state. Society is made up of many diverse communities and forms of association: families, voluntary associations, businesses, labor unions, corporations, the churches, as well as government on its various levels. The state is part of society, with a limited role within it. The denial of these limits, whether in principle or in fact, is what is meant by state absolutism, and it leads to totalitarianism. Good government is the servant of society, not *paterfamilias* to the nation, much less dictator. This is the core principle of constitutional government. The third plane of Murray's argument was juridical and ethical. It distinguishes between the common good of society, which all persons and communities that make up society are morally bound to pursue, and the narrower juridical notion of public order, which is the proper concern of government.

The common good includes all aspects of human living that make for human flourishing. It has both material and spiritual dimensions. The common good of society will be fully achieved when society's members attain, among other things, wisdom, knowledge, true belief, and faithful worship of God. The integralist argument is quite correct in its insistence that believing what is true is a human good that all are morally obligated to seek, and that this good is social in nature. It is wrong, however, when it asserts that government has charge of the enforcement of this obligation.

The power of government is limited to the protection of the basic prerequisites of communal life in society, prerequisites that Murray described as "necessary for the sheer coexistence of citizens within conditions of elemental social order."[4] There are four such prerequisites, which together define what is meant by public order: justice (which secures for people what is due them, that is, their fundamental human rights); public peace (which will only be genuine peace when it is built on justice); public morality (the minimum standards of public behavior on which consensus exists in society); and finally public prosperity (which makes possible the material welfare of the people).[5] Only when one or more of these fundamental prerequisites of social existence is violated should government intervene. Otherwise freedom is to prevail. These are the basic principles of a free society and constitutional government. They "require that the freedom of the human person be respected as far as possible, and curtailed only when and in so far as necessary."[6]

The linchpin in Murray's argument for religious freedom, therefore, was his theological, political, juridical, and ethical defense of constitutional government. His argument was overwhelmingly persuasive to the bishops gathered at the council, and it became the backbone of the conciliar declaration. By surfacing the deep structure of the Catholic tradition's understanding of the freedom of the church and the limits of the state, and by showing that this was compatible with American political institutions, Murray helped bring about the council's development of doctrine "on the inviolable rights of the human person and on the constitutional order of society."

As Murray was fond of observing, however, important arguments are never finished. They always have a "growing end." The debate about the role of the churches in public life has been vigorous in the United States during the past few years. The question of *whether* religious communities should raise their voices in the public square, however, is hardly the growing end in the Catholic theological discussion today. As the council declared: "It comes within the meaning of religious freedom that religious bodies should not be prohibited from freely undertaking to show the special value of their doctrine in what concerns the organization of society and the inspiration of the whole of human activity."[7] The entrance of the U.S. bishops into the public debates about abortion, U.S. defense policy, and the economy are good examples of the kind of exercise of religious freedom to which the council referred in this passage. The chief point in the argument today is not *whether* the voice of the bishops, for example, should be raised, but rather *what* should be said when it is.

A case in point that is important in this context is Michael Novak's forceful objection to the notion that human beings have economic rights to such goods as food, housing, and employment as well as civil and political rights such as free speech and religious freedom. Novak is particularly disturbed that this idea is present in the bishops' pastoral on the economy, and he implies that the writings of certain Catholic scholars, including the present author, have seriously misled the bishops into adopting this erroneous view. Novak believes that the argument for the existence of economic rights is a betrayal of the legacy of John Courtney Murray in that it fails to appreciate the limits on government action and the concept of natural rights that establish these limits. This is a serious charge, and it deserves a response.

The brunt of Novak's argument is that the notion of economic rights is necessarily embedded in an ideological framework that confers massive power on the state and denies the limits of constitutional government. Guaranteeing adequate nutrition, housing, and employment for people will of necessity involve massive governmental intrusion into the workings of the economy. Therefore, he concludes that "the extensive effort underway to commit the church to 'economic rights' has the potential to become an error of classic magnitude. It might well position the Catholic Church in a 'preferential option for the state' that will more than rival that of the Constantinian period."[8]

If Novak's analysis is correct, he is right to be agitated. But is it correct?

In order to answer this we need to step back a pace or two to acquire perspective. Novak's argument against economic rights has two strands, one moral and the other institutional. These are of necessity closely interwoven, but for purposes of clarity they need to be considered separately, at least initially.

His moral argument affirms that we have an obligation in justice, not just charity, to come to the assistance of those in need. This is undeniable from the perspective of biblical faith and the natural-law tradition, as Novak fully acknowledges. However, at this point a confusion enters his argument. For he states that food, shelter, a job, etc., are "goods indispensable to a *full* human life" (emphasis added), not rights inhering in the nature of human persons. As a *moral* argument I find this difficult to understand. Let me state that I completely reject the often heard contention that bread is a more basic human value than freedom. This is wrong not only because goods of the spirit are more noble than material goods, but also because the denial of freedom almost always means that the poor and powerless lose out. Nevertheless, I find it impossible to see how one could reasonably say, from a moral point of view, that the avoidance of hunger, homelessness, and chronic unemployment is part of a "full human life" while democratic freedoms are somehow more basic. From my perspective they both look equally fundamental.

To be fair to Novak, it appears that the institutional or political/juridical aspect of his argument overlaps with his moral argument at this point. He wants to maintain that food, shelter, and employment should be provided out of a sense of justice but not as human rights, because if they are rights then the state will become far too involved in the economy. To use the language of Murray and the council, Novak suggests that provision of basic economic necessities is part of the obligation to promote the common good (the fullness of human flourishing), but not part of the obligation to protect public order (the minimal conditions for social coexistence). It is on the strength of this distinction that Novak's brief against economic rights rises or falls. He will hardly be surprised to learn that I think it falls.

It must be admitted that John Courtney Murray had little to say of an analytical nature about issues of economic justice. On several occasions he pointed out the many highly praiseworthy achievements of the U.S. economy. Novak has cited Murray's words on these achievements in several of his own writings. It is also quite true that Murray stressed the great value of freedom and initiative in the economic sphere. Such matters are not in any way disputed by advocates of economic rights, and certainly not by the bishops' pastoral letter. What *is* at stake is the proper role of *limited* government in securing economic necessities for its vulnerable citizens.

Murray noted that Pope Leo XIII drew the distinctions between society and state and between the common good and public order most clearly in the encyclical *Rerum novarum*. This was precisely in the context of an argument for the legitimacy of governmental intervention on behalf of the "wretched multitude" when no other alternatives were available for securing their dignity. Such intervention is not a form of paternalism, as if "the government were somehow to become Father of the Poor."[9] It is not a paternal but a properly political function of government, a matter of protecting the foundation of civil society: justice and public peace.

In other words, Leo XIII called for intervention in the economy to secure basic necessities for the poor on the basis of the demands of public order. This is an order in which the rights of all are secure. Thus, following the thread of both Leo XIII's and John Courtney Murray's arguments, minimum economic resources are due people *by right*, and not simply as a desirable part of the full common good. This is the case because persons can be just as effectively excluded or left out of the life of the human community by long-term unemployment or homelessness as by the denial of the vote or freedom of speech.

Both Leo XIII and Murray insisted, of course, that securing economic necessities for all is not, in the first instance, the responsibility of government. Individuals, families, and a variety of mediating institutions in society have an obligation to see to it that people do not go hungry, homeless, or jobless. Nevertheless, when the problem exceeds the power of these persons and groups, government can and should intervene in ways carefully guided by political prudence. This is the meaning of the principle of subsidiarity so often stated in Catholic social teaching. Novak admits this also, but is reluctant to follow through on its implications. If government's proper sphere is public order and not the common good, and if, as Novak appears to believe, the provision of basic economic resources is part of the full common good rather than the more basic conditions of public order, then it makes no sense to sanction any intervention at all. Novak's refusal to go this far shows that there is a basic flaw in his argument. And that flaw is his refusal to admit that economic rights exist.

This argument about economic rights in a constitutional commonwealth goes beyond the concerns that preoccupied Murray during his lifetime. It is an unfinished argument, and this essay has dealt with only the tip of a much larger iceberg. It would be helpful in the future if opponents of economic rights would refrain from suggesting that idea of these rights is somehow un-American, undemocratic, and unfaithful to the legacy of Murray and the council. Within the context of a serious engagement with the intellectual issues the Catholic tradition on the role of limited government will continue to grow. And with this, I think, John Courtney Murray would have been pleased.

Chapter 8

Human Rights in the Middle East: The Impact of Religious Diversity

This chapter will address an additional aspect of the continuing argument about the foundation and meaning of human rights: the conflict between the universality of human-rights standards and the particularity of moral perspectives rooted in religious traditions. The modern charter of human rights, formulated by the United Nations in 1948, is called the Universal Declaration of Human Rights. One philosopher has defined human rights as those rights that are "held equally by all human beings."[1] That is, they are rights which exist and should be respected universally, wherever human beings exist, independent of the economic, social, political, cultural, or religious context in which they live. In other words, as the theologian Jürgen Moltmann has put it, "human rights point to a universal community in which alone they can be realized."[2] It is true that most of the nations of the world are in formal agreement with the list of rights proposed in the Universal Declaration, and many have ratified the two U.N. covenants that seek to translate this declaration into binding legal standards. It is not at all clear, however, that those who give formal assent to the Universal Declaration understand these rights in the same way, nor that they would rank these rights in the same order of priority.

This question has surfaced in recent discussions among philosophers and social scientists about the foundation and meaning of human-rights standards when these are looked at from an international, transcultural perspective.[3] It has been examined by social scientists concerned with the influence of diverse cultural contexts on the interpretation of human rights and with the political implementation of rights policies.[4] And most significantly for the actual development of U.S. foreign policy, some recent government officials have been strongly critical of efforts to base strategy and diplomacy directly on universally accepted human-rights norms. For example, the former U.S. ambassador to the United Nations, Jeane Kirkpatrick, has argued that an adequate foreign policy must "abandon the globalist approach which denies the realities of [diversity in] culture, character, geography, economics, and history in favor of a vague, abstract universalism."[5]

The Political Impact of Religion

The conflict between globalist universalism and the particularities of cultural and ideologically distinctive moral standards is most intense when the particularism in question is religious in nature. Historian of religion Wilfred Cantwell Smith has pointed out the particularly divisive character that has marked the history of religious communities—the "fissiparous quality of religious life."[6] Bloody conflicts between religious communities rooted in particular traditions of belief and the universal civil community assumed in human-rights discussions are in part a result of a betrayal and misuse of religiously rooted moral norms. But this is not the whole story. In Smith's view, conflict is not simply an aberrant result of the distortion of religious ideals. "It is inherent in them, a function of them, central to them . . . for a virtue of our religious faith is that it binds persons together into partial wholes."[7] The great strength of religious faith as a social force is also its great danger. It creates deep loyalties and powerful loves that bind persons not only to God but also to one another. These communities of loyalty are partial communities, however, for the symbols and beliefs that create them are not universally shared by all persons. Hindus and Muslims in Pakistan and India, Christians, Jews, and Muslims in the Middle East, Catholics and Protestants in Northern Ireland may all espouse the importance of human rights. But how these rights are interpreted, whose rights are of primary concern, and which kinds of rights are given priority are all significantly influenced by particularist loyalties of the religious communities involved. If respect for human rights in a religiously pluralistic world is to be enhanced, then the relation between distinctive moral communities and their traditions and the universal civil community that transcends these distinctions needs much deeper exploration than we have seen up to now.

The need for such exploration is not a new idea. As chairman of a 1947 UNESCO conference, Jacques Maritain argued that the United Nations could reasonably expect practical agreement on the rights to be included in the Universal Declaration. He judged the possibility of such agreement to be a major milestone in human history. But he also noted that such practical agreement is only the first step toward the creation of a true civil community in which human rights are both interpreted in roughly the same way by all and universally attributed to all. In his words:

> Where the difficulties and arguments begin is in the determination of the scale of values governing the exercise and concrete integration of these various rights. Here we are no longer dealing with the mere enumeration of human rights, but with the principle of dynamic unification whereby they are brought into play, with the tone scale, with the specific key in which different kinds of music are played on the same keyboard, music which in the event is in tune with, or harmful to human dignity.[8]

Richard McKeon's comments at that same UNESCO conference were similar to those of Maritain. He noted that the most significant difficulties in the attempt to secure human rights for all do not arise from disagreements over which rights are to go on the universally accepted list. In McKeon's view,

> . . . the differences are found rather in what is meant by these rights, and these differences of meanings depend on divergent basic assumptions, which in turn lend plausibility to and are justified by contradictory interpretations of the economic and social situation, and finally lead to opposed recommendations concerning the implementation required for a world declaration of human rights.[9]

Among the most significant sources of disagreement about the "scale of values" and "basic assumptions" that influence the interpretations and priorities given to human rights are the divergent traditions of religious belief and forms of religious community prevalent in the world. The issue that this fact brings into focus can be stated bluntly: are the traditions of belief and particularist loyalties of these religious communities compatible with the commitment to the universal community and civil discourse presupposed by the Universal Declaration? This question is in part historical, in part sociological, in part philosophical, and in part theological. In what follows the theological aspect of the issue will be addressed. This focus is a necessary one because the final locus for the answer to this question is the religious traditions and communities themselves. A positive answer to the question of the relation between religious faith and universal human rights must be a religious and theological answer. If believers within a particular religious tradition and community do not recognize a proposed response to this question as a legitimate expression of their faith, then answers from other quarters will be nugatory.

The task of a Christian theologian is not to prescribe the way this question should be answered by other faith communities. The primary concern of a Christian theologian is to develop the components of a Christian response to the relation between the particularity of Christian norms and the normative standards of global civil community presupposed in human-rights standards. Nevertheless, in order to identify the components of such a Christian answer, attention to the shape of the issue in other faith communities is necessary. The discussion will be restricted to the problems and possibilities that arise in the mind of a Christian theologian examining the relationship between major faith communities of the Middle East and the human-rights situation in this conflict-ridden region.

The problem has three levels. First, some of the sources within each of the traditions that can serve to legitimate and encourage participation in a universal civil community based on respect for human rights will be identified. Second, some of the elements within each tradition that conflict with or retard such participation will be discussed. Third, the actual historical experience of the relations between the three communities as this experience is imprinted in the living memories of believers will be sketched. Against this background several suggestions will be made about how the religious communities might contribute more effectively to the enhancement of a global civil community in which human rights are respected.

Sources of the Problem and Elements of a Solution

First, then, there are resources within the traditions of Judaism, Christianity, and Islam that can and often do contribute to the formation of a sense of universal community. These religious beliefs counteract the tendency of communal particularity to undercut the sense of universal civil community that is essential to the protection of human rights. In each of the three religions the true object of faith is not the community of believers but the one, transcendent God who is the Creator and Lord of all. In the Jewish *Shema* ("Hear, O Israel: the Lord our God is one God" (Deut 6:14), in the first article of the Christian Creed ("We believe in one God, the Father Almighty, creator of heaven and earth"), and in the first phrase of the Muslim *Shahadah* ("There is no God but God") the one, unique God of all the universe is proclaimed as the only reality worthy of ultimate loyalty and devotion. Belief in the transcendent unity and uniqueness of God provides an internal critique of all tendencies to absolutize the faith community itself.

In addition, the loyalty owed to God implies loyalty to and responsibility toward every human being. Judaism and Christianity share the common belief that every person is created "in the image of God" (Gen 1:27). Muslims are guided by a *Hadith* (normative tradition) which states that "God created Adam upon his own form." In the Qur'an Allah declared that each human being is worthy of reverence: "When I have shaped him, and breathed My spirit in him, fall you down, bowing before him!" (Sura XV, 29). These religious statements about the nature of the human person legitimate and enhance each tradition's support for universal community.

The same can be said of the way the three religions emphasize the universal inclusiveness of God's love and compassion. In Talmudic and Rabbinic Judaism discussions of the Noachic covenant between God and all creatures, symbolized by the rainbow that arcs the earth from horizon to horizon, provided theological basis for the discovery of a common moral ground on which Jews, Christians, and Muslims could stand together.[10] The Hebrew Bible also calls upon Jews to respect and care for the alien in their midst as well as for fellow Jews, just as God cared for the Jews when they were aliens in Egypt. "The stranger who sojourns with you shall be to you as the native among you, and you shall love him as yourself" (Lev 19:34). For Christians, Jesus' response to the question "Who is my neighbor?" in the parable of the good samaritan vividly portrays a form of love that responds to human need wherever it is found. Like God's love, the love that Christians are called to show toward their neighbors must not be constrained by the dynamics of in-group/out-group relations. The Qur'an teaches that the diversity of peoples must be viewed in the light of the more fundamental fact that they are all creatures of the one God. Racial and ethnic pluralism should lead to mutual understanding rather than opposition and strife: "O mankind, We have created you male and female, and appointed you races and tribes, that you may know one another" (Sura XLIX, 12).

Each of the three religions, therefore, contains normative principles that emphasize the religious and ethical relationship that binds all persons together in a universal moral community. On the basis of such principles theologians within each tradition have developed a link between the primary symbols and doctrines of their faiths and the notions of the universal dignity of every person and of the universal human community that undergird modern understandings of human rights. When these symbolic resources are emphasized, religious belief can become an ally of universal moral community and human rights rather than a threat to them.

It would be a serious mistake, however, to regard the problem as solved once a general affinity between these universalist aspects of each of the religions and the moral foundations of the contemporary understanding of human rights has been identified. Despite the religious bases for universal moral community in each of the traditions, the language of human rights in the Universal Declaration is not the language of the Hebrew Bible, the Christian scriptures or the Muslim Qur'an. It is not the language that any of the three holy books uses to speak of the universal moral community of all persons. The notion that religious language and human-rights language can be translated into each other without distortion is highly doubtful. That they can be so translated without remainder is certainly false. And this remainder is the central factor that makes Judaism, Christianity, and Islam religions rather than secular moral value systems and gives them their unique power to generate loyalty.

The Universal Declaration was adopted by the United Nations specifically in order to advocate a moral code that prescinds from the cultural, ideological, and religious differences of the peoples of the world. The language in which this code is expressed is universal because it is abstract and ahistorical. By contrast the vocabularies of the moral codes of Judaism, Christianity, and Islam are symbolic, concrete, and historical. The Hebrew Bible, the Christian scriptures and the Qur'an each tells the story of God's dealings with a particular people. In setting out a vision of the kind of moral responsibility that people have toward one another, the three holy books use proper names, preeminently those of Moses, Jesus, and Muhammad. They describe specific historical events: the exodus and giving of the law on Sinai, the death and resurrection of Jesus, the "recitation" and Hijrah of Muhammad. The universality of God's relation to humanity is affirmed. But the story of this universal relation is but one chapter in the book that tells the story of a particular people and the faith of this people. The very universalism of each of the three religions is set forward in particularist terms.

The language of rights in the Universal Declaration works the opposite way. It subsumes the particularities of persons, nations, and historical events under norms of universal human dignity and universal community. It subsumes the concrete particularities of specific religions under the universal by affirming the right to religious freedom as a universal right.

Because of the universal, nonhistorical quality of the language of the Universal Declaration, however, it is easy to forget that there is in fact a human-rights *story* that is itself historical. The declaration as formulated in the early years of the United Nations gave expression to world-wide moral outrage at the atrocities of Hitler and the carnage of the Second World War. Lockean liberalism and Marxist socialism are perhaps the most obvious sources of the civil/political and social/economic rights enshrined in the declaration at the urging of the major powers of the postwar period. The roots of the modern notion of human rights, however, go deeper than these more immediate modern sources. These roots are buried in the history of the relation between Christianity and the political and social institutions of Western Europe.

First, the long history of struggle between the Christian church and the kings and emperors of medieval Europe effectively established the notion of limited government as both a principle of Western political thought and as norm of Christian theology. It also established the principle that government can be held accountable to the fundamental norms of justice and morality (the natural law). The church saw itself as the chief guardian and interpreter of these norms. Thus in the medieval model, the principles of Christian religion and those of social and political life were institutionally differentiated but normatively correlated.

Second, the reality of religious pluralism emerged as a central theme in the consciousness of Western Europe at the time of the Reformation. Protection of the right to religious freedom became an urgent political necessity. As Christopher Dawson put it, "the modern liberal secular state emerged as the solution to the problem of religious disunity which had plunged the peoples of Europe into civil war."[11] The same necessity gradually became evident to Christian theologians as well as to politicians, though this occurred more rapidly in some branches of Western Christianity than in others. The right to religious freedom came to be seen as a necessary condition both for remaining faithful to one's Christian beliefs and at the same time continuing to show the kind of universal respect for one's neighbor that Christianity demands. Thus, Western Christians have been able to affirm the right to religious liberty as a political correlate of Christian faith in a pluralistic world, and not (as some secularist thinkers would have it) as a political correlate of agnosticism or religious indifference. In this way the right to religious freedom became the leading edge of a political and religious development that has made the freedom and rights of the person into foundation stones of Western European political thought, institutional life, and religious conviction. For Christians, the institutional differentiation and normative correlation of faith and politics of the medieval period has been maintained but transformed to respond to the realities of pluralism. It has come to be enshrined in a synthesis that is both continuous with the past and genuinely new: the modern theory of the rights of the individual human person.

This, of course, is hardly the whole story of the development of the contemporary understanding of human rights expressed in the Universal Declaration. It does show, however, why contemporary Western Christians in general find the language of human rights so congenial. For example, the Second Vatican Council, recent popes, the World Council of Churches, the World Alliance of Reformed Churches, and the Lutheran World Federation have all made major declarations on the social responsibility of Christians which are formulated in human-rights terms. This is not because there can be a direct deduction of human-rights principles from the symbolic and doctrinal content of Christian faith. Rather, to paraphrase John Courtney Murray, in the practical syllogism that leads from biblical faith and Christian theology to an ethical and constitutional theory of human rights, the middle term is history.[12] More precisely, it is their common history that has enabled both Western political thought and Christianity to *develop* and *grow into* a common agreement on the fundamental rights of the person.

This conclusion provides an important clue in the effort to understand why Christianity, Judaism, and Islam have difficulty interpreting the language of human rights in the same way. It also suggests a reason why Western Christians have such difficulty understanding what is going on at the interface between religion and human rights in the Middle East. Neither Jews nor Muslims fully share the history of Western Europe as their own history. Nor, for that matter, do Eastern Christians. Thus, even though the Judaism, Christianity, and Islam of the Middle East espouse religious norms that support commitment to the universal moral community essential for the protection of human rights, their understandings of the appropriate way of expressing this commitment are significantly different from those of both Western Christians and Western secular thinkers.

In Judaism, the mode of commitment to universal moral community places much greater emphasis on the preservation of distinctive communal values and structures than is the case in more individualist Western approaches. Generalizations about the religious and political views of contemporary Jews are hazardous at best. But both the symbolic structure of Jewish biblical faith and the historical experience of the Jewish people have made the protection of communal distinctiveness a key element in the Jewish understanding of human rights.

The importance of communal particularity is evident in the central biblical symbols of Jewish faith: the covenant with Israel, the permanent bond between the people of Israel and the land, and the gift of the Torah. It is precisely in its distinctiveness as a people bound both to a specific land and a distinctive law that Israel is related to the God who is Creator and Lord of all the earth. These biblical symbols have permanently shaped the cultural identity of the Jewish people and continue to determine the content of Jewish faith in the one God. This identity and faith are privileged causes for communal pride and communal responsibility.

"What great nation is there that has a god so near to it as the Lord our God is to us, whenever we call upon him? And what great nation is there that has statutes and ordinances so righteous as all this law which I set before you this day?" (Deut 4:78).

In the biblical vision, the covenantal relation between God and the people of Israel, its land and its law, gives communal identity a status that has its Christian equivalent only in the foreshadowing of the universal kingdom of God in the church. But while in Christianity the expectation of the coming of this universal kingdom has provided the motivation for missionary activity, Jewish covenantal faith has viewed its task as that of remaining faithful to the distinctive identity conferred on it by God. By remaining faithful to this distinctiveness, Israel will serve God's purposes among all the peoples. "I will give you as a light to the nations, that my salvation may reach to the end of the earth" (Isa 49:6). As Krister Stendahl has noted, this way of conceiving the relation between the particular religious community and the universal community of all persons can be called a "witness model" rather than a "missionary conquest model. . . . It is a model for a distinct minority, without expectations of becoming a majority."[13] This model, rooted in the structure of Jewish biblical faith, has made deep respect for the communal distinctiveness of peoples, both Jewish and Gentile, an important aspect of the Jewish understanding of human rights.

This strand of Jewish biblical faith has been intensified and transformed by the social experience of the Jewish people through history. For millennia the small Jewish minority has been colonized, isolated in ghettoes, subjected to pogroms, and finally almost exterminated. Protection of the right of Jews to exist as a people and their right to the preservation of their communal and religious identity have been central Jewish concerns throughout this whole history. The emergence of secular liberal thought in Europe during the eighteenth century and of a variety of European nationalisms in the nineteenth century gave these traditional concerns a new urgency. Zionism in its different religious and secular forms can only be understood as an affirmation by the Jewish people that they were unwilling to buy civic emancipation and equal individual rights if the cost were to be the submersion of Jewish communal identity in the rising tide of liberal and nationalist movements in Europe.

The distinctive symbols of Jewish faith thus interacted with the emerging patterns of modern European society to produce the Zionist program.[14] The goal of this program was to translate Jewish insistence on distinctive identity into an active social and political force. During the modern period the European Christian majority was gradually able to develop an explicit correlation between the symbols of Christian faith and the notion of universal human rights of the person. For the Jewish minority the same historical context called forth a new linkage between Jewish religion and the right to national and cultural self-determination.[15] Zionism, in both its religious and secular forms, translated the Jewish experience of the importance of communal particularity into a foundational principle for its understanding of rights of all people. As Uriel Tal has put it, "Jewry in the state of Israel today and much of Diaspora Jewry both refuse—with a stubbornness which is not always admired by the Christian world—to accept the interpretation of equality in terms of uniformity. Equality, in the Jewish interpretation, means the equal right to maintain socioreligious selfhood amidst human unity. . . . It is precisely this stiff-necked insistence upon being itself that makes Judaism aware of the universal equal right to be different."[16]

Contemporary Judaism, therefore, has synthesized its religious symbols with the notion of universal rights in a distinctive way. The universalist aspects of Judaism demand that rights be acknowledged and respected universally. This universality, however, must incorporate within itself a genuine respect for the particularities of communal identity, nation, and religion. The "right to be oneself," and "the right to be different" occupy a central place in Israeli discussions of universal human rights. The human race is conceived of as a "community of communities" rather than as an undifferentiated whole composed of identical individuals. This very emphasis on communal difference, however, puts contemporary Judaism in normative disagreement with Christianity and Islam. It is one of the sources of the unresolved tension in the interpretation of human rights in the Middle East.

The relation between Islam and the normative foundations of contemporary Western human-rights theory has its own story that also contributes to a distinctive interpretation of these rights. Like Christianity and Judaism, Islam has strong scriptural foundations for a commitment to the creation of universal community. Islam, however, rejects both the modern Western solutions to the problem of pluralism (the secular state) and the Jewish willingness to make the "right to be different" into a universal political norm for nation-states. Islam's solution to the tension between universal community and religious particularism begins with the audacious statement that its political ideal is a universal, world-wide Islamic state. It then affirms that the rights of non-Muslims will be protected *within* the Islamic state. This is possible because the norms of Islam are regarded as identical with the fundamental norms of justice. In the view of most Muslims, both traditionalist and modernist, Islam itself is the single strongest guarantee for the protection of human rights available. Traditionalist Muslims frequently argue that the Shari'ah -eceded the United

Nations by fourteen hundred years in setting forth the true rights of the human person. The more modernist Ahmad Zaki Yamani, a lawyer and former Saudi petroleum minister, has written in a similar vein: "The universal ideology I envisage, and which shall come into existence someday, is very similar to the system brought about by Islam fourteen centuries ago."[17]

Convictions such as these are shaped by Qur'anic faith and have been reinforced by the historical experience of the Islamic world. The Qur'an brooks absolutely no deviation from its uncompromising monotheism and vigorously asserts the unity of all aspects of life under the one God. The one God is the focus of every aspect of human life, both "secular" and "religious," both personal and political. Setting up any value in competition with God, or even associating any creature with God *(shirk)* is the cardinal violation of Islamic faith. Thus the whole of creation is to be integrated in a single unity *(tawhid)* focused on the one transcendent God. This fundamental principle has a dramatic effect on the Muslim concept of social order. As the Shi'ite scholar Seyyed Hossein Nasr has put it: "Every manifestation of human existence should be organically related to the Shahadah, *La ilaha ill' Allah* (there is no God but God) which is the most universal way of expressing unity. . . . The political ideal of a single Muslim government, with all the ups and downs it has experienced over the centuries, is based on the central metaphysical doctrine of unity."[18] The unity of God, the unity of the entire human community and the unity of the world-wide Islamic state are all variations on the same fundamental Islamic theme.

The Qur'anic religious/political principle of unity has been closely related to the historical experience of Muslims from the very beginning. Up to the time of Muhammad the Arabian peninsula was a fragmented tribal society, characterized by perpetual blood feuds, inequality, and the subordination of the worth of the individual to the life of family and tribe. The prophet's message of unity responded to a need for the social integration that was sorely lacking. It gave the individual person a value no longer subordinate to clan and tribe and no longer threatened by feuds, raids, and exploitation. Thus the identification of the Islamic religiopolitical system with the fundamental principles of justice and human dignity has had a genuine social plausibility for Muslim peoples from the days of Muhammad himself. This plausibility was reinforced by the astonishing expansion of Islam in its early centuries. Islam's early history convinced Muslims not only that their faith was true but also that it would work as a social system. The violence done to Muslim peoples during the time of the Crusades and the subjugation that they suffered under Western colonial powers in modern times have further intensified commitment to the necessity of an Islamic state and social order. These experiences have supported the conviction that the Western model of the relation between religion and politics is inherently unjust. Opposition to belief in the particular chosenness of the Jewish people and, more recently, the Arab/Israeli conflict have led many contemporary Muslims to a similar conclusion about Israel and Zionism. Today, not only in Iran but throughout the Middle East, an increasing number of Muslims refer both to Western Christians and to Jews simply as "the imperialists." Thus the establishment of the Islamic state has become a primary goal of the Islamic resurgence. In the eyes of most Muslims the achievement of this goal will simultaneously protect true religion, establish justice, and guarantee human rights.

Islam is not without a response to the charge that this goal is incompatible with the rights of non-Muslims. The relation between Muhammad and the Jews and Christians of the Arabian peninsula led him to a complex attitude toward religious differences. On the one hand, the Qur'an regards the "people of the book" as genuine believers in the one God and as recipients of genuine revelation from God through their prophets. At the same time, Jews and Christians have introduced errors into this revelation and corrupted true faith, respectively through their beliefs in a special, nonuniversal covenant and in the divinity of Jesus. Thus, Jews and Christians were to be protected and respected by the Islamic state. This protection, however, was to be conditional upon their willingness to accept the correctness and legitimacy of the Islamic foundation of the state that has undertaken the task of protecting their rights. This arrangement was later extended to other religious communities as Islam expanded to the East. The protected communities *(dhimmis)* were both guaranteed the right to exercise their own religious faith and assured the benefits of the other aspects of Islamic justice.

This kind of arrangement is fundamentally one of religious tolerance rather than religious freedom. It is foreign to the contemporary Western and Christian consensus on the nature of the right to religious freedom. Western Christians would do well, however, to recognize that such a system has been characteristic of Christianity throughout most of its history. Roman Catholicism, for example, officially abandoned it only in 1965 at the Second Vatican Council. Also, it is important to note that the historical record of Islam in its treatment of non-Muslim minorities in Muslim lands has been notably better than the record of Christianity in the same regard. This is due in large part to the fact that the Qur'an makes explicit, legal provision for a limited protection of non-Muslim rights. The New Testament contains no such specific provisions because the earliest Christians never faced the problems associated with holding responsibility for government. Contemporary Muslims frequently cite the historical records of the two communities in arguing for the superiority of the Islamic approach. For example, the Pakistani thinker Abul 'Ala Maudoodi has insisted that "the establishment of an ideological Islamic state is the greatest guarantee for non-Muslims in Pakistan."[19] Thus though Muslims argue strongly that their faith provides a firm basis for the protection of human rights, including the rights of religious minorities, there can be no doubt that they interpret these rights in a way that is significantly different from the contemporary Western view. The differences are also evident in their discussions of the rights of women and the rights of those convicted of crime. But in these cases the source of disagreement is the same as in the case of religious freedom. In other words, the Qur'an's teachings on the universality of human dignity and the cultural and political history of the Muslim people have been synthesized in a way that could not possibly be the same as the European/Christian synthesis.

Conclusions

In the face of these divergent interpretations of the relation of civil community and religious traditions by Christians, Jews, and Muslims, what conclusions can be drawn about the future of human rights in the Middle East? Several responses that readily suggest themselves are in fact quite inadequate. First, the evident tension and conflict between loyalty to a religious community and commitment to the equal protection of the rights of all persons could lead one to conclude that religious loyalty should be rooted out as systematically as possible. Not only the states but the cultures of the Middle East as well should be thoroughly secularized. The mere statement of this suggestion is enough to show its unacceptability. An attempt to enhance human rights by directly attacking the most fundamental communal relationships of a people would not only be the height of arrogance, but quite evidently self-contradictory. As the Iranian experience under the Shah has shown, even an "enlightened" attempt of this sort could only be pursued by repressive, authoritarian, and violent means. Iran also suggests that enforced modernization as the path to greater respect for human rights is unlikely to succeed. The Arab-Israeli conflict provides another illustration of the counterproductive effects of refusal to take a religious community's self-definition seriously. The tendency of most Muslims and many Christians flatly to deny the validity of all aspects of Zionism has heightened conflict and led to increased human-rights violations. Here Westerners, both Christian and secular, and Muslims, both traditionalist and modernist, have something very important to learn from the Jewish insistence on the "right to be different."

A second conclusion that might be drawn from this analysis of the Middle East situation is that the very notion of universal human rights is built on sand and is ultimately impractical. As ideological conflict, cultural antagonisms, and superpower interests in the Middle East have intensified in recent years, there has been an increase in this kind of talk. Cultural relativism and the strategic use of power threaten to displace human-rights considerations from the political agenda. Two facts make this tendency extremely dangerous. On the one hand, none of the religious communities in the region is prepared to replace its normative system with a relativistic, strategic calculus. On the other hand, it was precisely the absence of an accepted standard of the rights of other peoples and nations that led to the horrors of the Second World War. Political strategists and theorists on all sides of the Middle East conflict need especially sharp memories of this recent history, for the potential for a world conflict is nowhere greater than in the region. Advocacy of human rights can never be a substitute for the art of politics and statecraft. But political calculation devoid of concern for human rights is at least as dangerous as religious loyalty and particularist understandings of rights.

Third, one might conclude that since the notion of universal human rights is a product of Western political, religious, and cultural history, it will have concrete influence in the Middle East only when that part of the world is thoroughly Westernized. If this means the construction of political institutions and cultural norms identical with those of Western Europe and North America, the proposal is naive. For these institutions and norms have evolved out of the religious and secular experience of the Western Christian majority. By definition neither Jews nor Muslims fully share this historical experience. This history cannot be rewritten by fiat. However, if Westernization means the development of institutions and norms that are compatible with the fact of religious pluralism in the Middle East, the proposal has evident plausibility.

This suggests the direction in which we must look if we are to find a solution to the problem of the conflict between religion and human rights in the Middle East. The task is that of developing what might be called indigenous pluralism. Each of the three religious communities examined here has a normative theory of how it should relate to members of the other faiths. These theories have been developed out of the interaction of their normative religious beliefs and symbols with the trajectory of their historical experience. Thus their interpretations of the rights of others are different and in conflict. An opportunity for a greater convergence of these interpretations has arisen because for the first time the three religious communities are beginning to share a common history. Though the three religions have interacted vigorously in the past, the interaction has never been based on each having an equal stake in finding a way to respect the rights of the others. Just as Europe discovered the right to religious freedom as a result of religious wars, so the three religions of the Middle East are challenged by the conflicts there to discover a common understanding of human rights that is concrete and living rather than formal and abstract.

This challenge is fundamentally religious and theological in nature. The reality of an emerging common history and equal stake in peace is factual. But the task of relating normative symbols and deeply held religious beliefs to the new situation has yet to be carried out. Only when Jews, Christians, and Muslims have discovered *in their own beliefs* a better way to respect one another will the "fissiparous quality of religious life" be transformed. The universalist aspect of each tradition is a key factor in this process. Taken alone, however, it is insufficient. In addition, each community must find a basis for respecting the distinctiveness of the other communities within the structure of its own belief. The task, then, is not the homogenization of the religious faiths but of their *development* in a new direction. For each faith, this development will entail a new respect for and understanding of the distinctive religious faith of the others.

Thus the development must be more than a replication of the development of the notion of religious freedom in Europe. Western Christians cannot rest content with the fact that a strong affinity already exists between their religious self-understanding and the Universal Declaration. As the history of European Jewry sadly shows, the development of a theory of religious liberty and the secular state correlated with Christian symbols and experience alone was insufficient to guarantee the rights of Jews. One of the missing components was the ability of Christians *as such* to acknowledge the rights of Jews *as such.* In the Middle East, the same kind of problem exists today writ large. Christians, Jews, and Muslims are confronted with the urgent necessity of developing a religious and theological understanding of one another. This task will perhaps be easiest for Jews because of their nonmissionary and particularist beliefs. It will perhaps be most difficult for Muslims because of their unitary understanding of religion and society. It is, however, most onerous for Christians because of the way Christianity has dominated Jews and Muslims through history, thus intensifying the adversarial relations among all three. The present inability of most Western Christians to comprehend even the rudiments of what the Islamic resurgence is all about suggests that our Western religiohistorical synthesis is an insufficient basis for guaranteeing the rights of Muslims. The development of a genuine global civil community in which human rights are respected calls for something quite different from an intensified process of global secularization. It calls for religious development in new, positive directions. Believers and theologians are not on the fringes of this process, but rather close to its center.

This suggestion may appear to be a counsel of despair, for it can only be regarded as an utterly long-range task, one which likely will only be accomplished at the "end of days." Though the vast scope of what is proposed is undeniable, despair is not necessarily the consequence. The very acceptance of such a need for religious and theological development by these religious communities would *already* constitute an incipient commitment to the rights of the other communities and their members. Commitment to the task of such a religious and theological development of itself breaks through the most dangerous aspects of in-group religious loyalties. The language of universal human rights remains a different tongue from that of Judaism, Christianity, or Islam. But if believers can learn to speak their own language in a new way, they will also be able to speak the language of universal human rights more fluently. If they can reconceive the relation between their own faith communities and the other faith communities of the world, then universal civil community will become a concrete possibility rather than an abstract and formal ideal. And this new way of speaking their own tongue will develop when Jews, Christians, and Muslims learn to talk to one another *as believers*. To the extent that this happens, religious faith will become an ally of universal human rights rather than a threat to them. The engagement in such religious interaction and dialogue is a key contribution Christian theologians can make to the development of a global civil community in which the dignity of every person is genuinely respected. A failure of Christians to enter into this interaction would not only be a failure of civility but a failure of Christian commitment as well.

Part Four

Peace and War in the Nuclear Age

Chapter 9

Nuclear Weapons and Nuclear War: The Shape of the Catholic Debate

Argument about nuclear policy has been a fact of public life in the West since the awesome power at the heart of matter was first unleashed during the Second World War. This debate has assumed a number of distinct forms, which have been influenced by the political climate prevailing between the superpowers, by the state of relations between members of the Atlantic Alliance, by the development of new technological capacities, by the proliferation of nuclear weapons, and by the level of public awareness and understanding of nuclear-policy questions.[1]

The 1980s have been a time of increased public awareness of the nuclear threat and of heightened public debate about the moral dimensions of nuclear policy. These developments have set the context for a new engagement by the churches in the nuclear debate. In particular, the Roman Catholic church in the United States has embarked on a course that has thrust it into public argument on a central matter of government policy in a way that is almost certainly unique in its history. The U.S. Catholic bishops' pastoral letter, *The Challenge of Peace*, has become a standard point of reference in arguments about ethics and strategic policy even for those who do not agree with all of its recommendations. The uniqueness of this level of involvement makes it imperative that Christians become as clear as possible about the relation between the central realities of the Christian faith and the host of complex issues that swirl through the clouds of public discussion.

As background for understanding the U.S. bishops' pastoral letter, this chapter will sketch some of the major issues that have emerged in Christian ethical discussion of these questions. The following chapter will look at the pastoral letter in greater detail. Here the effort will be to identify the reasons—theological, political, and military—that account for the different conclusions drawn about the ethics of nuclear policy. A basic theological approach to the moral issues will also be proposed for consideration and further debate. The focus will be on developments within the Catholic community, although these developments will be set against the horizon of the larger theological and secular argument.

The analysis will proceed in three steps: (1) the question whether the gospel of Jesus Christ demands total renunciation of violent force; (2) the moral debate about the use of nuclear weapons; (3) the moral ambiguities of deterrence policies. I conclude with a word about the church's task in the continuing discussion.

Theology, Pacifism, and Just-War Theory

The emergence of a visible and articulate pacifist movement within the American Catholic community in recent years is one of the most significant forces shaping the moral argument about nuclear policies within the Catholic church today. To understand this development, it is worth noting that the complete renunciation of the use of violence has been present in one strand of Catholic tradition from the time of Jesus to the present day. Relatively few Christians in the first several centuries participated in the military forces of the Roman Empire.[2] Also during this period there is no evidence that the patristic authors ever presented theological justification for such participation. After Constantine, however, as Christianity moved from the status of a persecuted minority to the official religion of the Empire and Christians became responsible for the governance and administration of society, their participation in the military became much more general. This social development was accompanied by the beginning of an elaboration of moral norms setting limits to legitimate warfare and to Christian participation in warfare. These norms have gradually been refined into what has come to be known as the just-war theory or the just-war tradition.

Just-war thinking, however, did not completely replace the earlier pacifism of the Christian community. Rather, this pacifist commitment became the particular evangelical witness and vocation of monks and clerics.[3] The rapid growth of monastic life in the post-Constantinian period was in part the result of the conviction among numbers of Christians that the teachings of the gospel were being compromised by the growing engagement of the church in the affairs of "the world."[4] The monastic response was withdrawal from participation in the prevailing institutions of economic, familial, and political life and positive commitment to the evangelical counsels of poverty, chastity, and obedience lived in community. The nonparticipation of monks in military activity was one aspect of this effort to embody the teaching and example of Jesus in a concrete sociological form. As Roland Bainton has put it, "The prime transmitters of the nonmilitary tradition of the early church were the monks."[5] Thus contemporary pacifist Christians who have become major participants in the debate within the church on the nuclear question are heirs to a tradition which has been consistently alive through the history of the church.

It is also evident that since the fourth century this Christian pacifist heritage has been largely overshadowed by the just-war tradition's understanding of the limited legitimacy of the use of force. Just as the early monks regarded the increasing engagement of Christians and the church in the affairs of the world as the great betrayal of the teachings and example of Jesus, so today there are those in the Christian community who regard Christian reliance on just-war thinking as unfaithfulness to the gospel. James W. Douglass has stated this position straightforwardly:

> Inasmuch as war's central action of *inflicting* suffering and death is directly opposed to the example of Christ in *enduring* these same realities, the church has reason for repentance in having allowed herself to become involved since the age of Constantine in an ethic which would justify what conflicts with the essence of the gospel.[6]

This statement must be taken with the greatest seriousness in the current debate within the church, for it makes a claim about the essence of the gospel. It was this claim that led the early monks to take a stand over against the posture of the established church of post-Constantinian Christendom. It is the same claim that underlies one of Aquinas's arguments for the nonparticipation of clerics in military activity:

> All the clerical orders are directed to the ministry of the altar, on which the passion of Christ is represented sacramentally, according to 1 Cor xi.26: "As often as you shall eat this bread, and drink this chalice, you shall show the death of the Lord, until He come." Wherefore it is unbecoming for them to slay or shed blood, and it is more fitting that they should be ready to shed their own blood for Christ, so as to imitate in deed what they portray in their ministry.[7]

Though neither the early monks nor Aquinas rejected the participation of *all* Christians in warfare, it is important that they did see an intrinsic connection between nonviolence, the passion of Christ, and the church's ministry of word and sacrament. Today, following the Second Vatican Council's teaching that the fullness of holiness is the vocation of every

Christian (layperson, religious, and cleric alike),[8] and in light of the theological recovery of the fact that the church's ministry to the world is rooted in the baptism common to all Christians, the pacifist challenge to the just-war tradition has become central for the church as a whole. One must ask: If there is indeed a fundamental congruence between the passion of Christ and the renunciation of violent force, should not the church as a whole "imitate in deed" what it portrays in the baptismal and eucharistic life in which all Christians participate?

We will seriously misunderstand the theological basis of the just-war theory if we do not accept the full weight of this question. There can be no doubt that the New Testament proclaims a message of peace and calls those who would be Jesus' disciples to a nonviolent way of living. This proclamation and call are evident in Jesus' teachings on love of neighbor and love of enemy.[9] They are embodied in Jesus' renunciation of the revolutionary tactics of the Zealots, who proposed resistance to the oppressive Roman occupation of Palestine through violent means.[10] Most centrally, the death of Jesus on the cross was an unjust execution of an innocent man. Though the full meaning of the crucifixion cannot be reduced to its ethical significance, it is impossible for Christian theology to avoid the challenge of nonviolence that the crucifix presents. As Stanley Hauerwas has put it, the cross of Jesus reveals to us "the kind of suffering that is to be expected when the power of nonresistant love challenges the powers that rule this world by violence."[11]

An ethical analysis of war and peace that seeks its roots in the central religious identity of Christianity must acknowledge, therefore, that the values of peace and nonviolence make urgent demands upon the Christian conscience. That the just-war tradition, when it is rightly interpreted, begins from such an acknowledgment is evident from a consideration of what James Turner Johnson has called "the original just-war question." On the basis of his extensive studies of the history of just-war thinking, Johnson has shown that this question "arises again and again in patristic and medieval writers concerned with Christian participation in violence. Put generally, it is the query, 'May a Christian ever morally take part in violence?' "[12] The treatment of warfare in Aquinas's classic discussion of the topic puts the question even more strongly than does Johnson. The *quaestio* with which Thomas begins his reflection is this: "Is it *always* a sin to fight in war?"[13] The just-war theory, properly understood, rests on the conviction that violent warfare should be presumed to be morally unacceptable and even sinful.

It is both theologically inaccurate and culturally disastrous if this presupposition is forgotten. In Johnson's view, such a loss of historical memory is exactly what has happened in recent centuries in discussions of the just-war tradition.

> It is one of the sad ironies of history that this origin of the just war tradition has been so badly remembered as to turn it inside out: rather than a sign of a reluctance to justify violence for Christians, the tradition has come to be regarded, and not only by pacifists, as an attempt to declare the need to justify Christian resort to violence a non-question, a question that has already been answered. . . . An attempt to recollect again, in and for the Christian community, what this original just war question was about leads to the somewhat startling discovery that pacifist and non-pacifist just war Christians have something profoundly in common: a searching distrust of violence.[14]

The original just-war question thus implies that nonviolence is the Christian norm and that the use of force can only be moral by way of exception, if at all. Violent force should be *presumed* to be incompatible with a fundamental Christian moral orientation. Only under the most stringently defined circumstances can this presupposition be overridden.

James Childress has made this same point in the language of contemporary moral philosophy. In his reading, the just-war theory rests on the conviction that we have a prima facie obligation not to harm or kill other human beings. A prima facie obligation is a genuine moral duty intrinsically binding on our consciences. It is to be distinguished from an absolute obligation, however, for it may conflict with another equally important and binding obligation.[15] For example, I have an obligation to keep the promises I have made. If, however, taking time to stop and assist a person injured in an automobile accident were to cause me to leave unfulfilled a promise to meet a friend for dinner, the more important obligation should take precedence. The logic of just-war theory has a similar structure. It rests on the supposition that the imperative not to harm or kill other human beings can in some circumstances tragically conflict with other equally important obligations, such as the defense of innocent lives, the preservation of basic freedoms and human rights in the face of aggression, or the liberation of persons from situations of degrading poverty and political repression. The *jus ad bellum* norms of just-war theory provide a carefully wrought rational framework for determining whether such an exception to the prima facie duty of noninjury and nonviolence is justified in a given situation. Similarly, the *jus in bello* norms of the tradition further tighten the structure of the moral basis for exceptions to the duty of nonviolence by placing limits on the means that can be morally used even in a justified war.

Johnson and Childress throw considerable light on the historical and philosophical basis of the relation of pacifism and just-war theory. By extrapolation they can also be extremely useful in helping to clarify the fundamental theological roots of the pacifist/just-war debate so central in the nuclear discussion in the church today. Their essays point to several fundamental issues that are at the heart of the debate.

First, in a biblical and theological frame of reference, we must ask: Can there ever be an obligation that is weighty enough to override the call to nonviolence? In other words, in a Christian perspective, is it legitimate to conclude, as do Johnson and Childress, that the challenge to nonviolence contained in the gospel is a prima facie rather than an absolute imperative? There are grounds for saying that just-war theory has not answered this question in an entirely satisfactory way.

The obvious candidate for a duty or fundamental value that might be judged equal to or even more stringent than the duty of nonviolence is justice. Just-war theory has been willing to argue that under tightly limited conditions the defense of justice can sometimes provide the basis for an exception to the general norm of nonviolence. If justice and nonviolence should not be simultaneously realizable, just-war theory is willing to grant priority to justice within the narrow boundaries of the *jus ad bellum* and *jus in bello* norms.

In just-war thinking, justice is regarded as a precondition for genuine peace, and thus the pursuit of justice by limited force can take priority over nonviolence. As John Paul II put it in his 1982 World Day of Peace message:

> Peace can develop only where the elementary requirements of justice are safeguarded. . . . This is why Christians, even as they strive to resist and prevent every form of warfare, have no hesitation in recalling that, in the name of the elementary requirement of justice, peoples have a right and even a duty to protect their existence and freedom by proportionate means against an unjust aggressor.[16]

Theologically, this argument rests on the affirmation that conflicts between justice and nonviolence are possible in a sinful world. It presupposes that the nonviolent teaching and example of Jesus must be supplemented by a full consideration of the biblical and theological centrality of the Christian commitment to justice if a *comprehensive* Christian answer to the question of warfare is to be developed. It further assumes that peace as understood biblically and theologically includes justice as one of its essential dimensions[17] and that a commitment to peace that does not rest on an active struggle for justice will produce neither peace nor justice.

This theological argument possesses genuine plausibility. It does not account, however, for one of the central aspects of the New Testament witness, namely, the fact that Jesus did not resort to violent force in self-defense against unjust attack. Nor did Jesus counsel the use of violence in the defense of justice for the Jewish people in the face of Roman oppression. The theology underlying the pacifist stance on warfare appeals to these aspects of Jesus' life and death to argue for the religious and ethical priority of the duty of nonviolence over the duty to establish justice. This posture is well expressed in the statement of an American advocate of nonviolence, A. J. Muste: "There is no way to peace. Peace is the way."[18] The priority assigned to justice as a precondition of genuine peace by the just-war theory is reversed in the ethics of nonviolence.

This pacifist posture is not unconcerned with the pursuit of justice. Activist advocates of nonviolent resistance to injustice are as deeply convinced that nonviolence is the only path to true justice as are just-war theorists that a commitment to the pursuit of justice, even by force, is the only path to true peace. The examples of Gandhi, Martin Luther King, and a host of other nonviolent activists provide strong evidence that the commitment to the priority of nonviolence is neither passive nor ineffective in the face of injustice. Theologians such as Yoder and Douglass have argued that the commitment to a nonviolent ethic is the only hope humans have of breaking the "spiral of violence" that breeds further injustice. In their view, to take up arms in the cause of justice is self-defeating. Further, it contradicts the strategy for the pursuit of the kingdom of God exemplified in the life of Jesus. As Edward Schillebeeckx has interpreted the scriptures on this question, God's kingdom cannot be brought about by arms; the force of arms is a sinful obstacle to its coming.

> The messianic coming of God, before which evil yields, is not a coming in power, which will shatter evil with nationalistic and messianic force of arms. It works through *metanoia*, repentance. It is a victory over evil through obedience to God, and not through human force. For anyone who seeks to achieve a kingdom of peace-without-tears by means of human force calls Jesus 'a Satan' (Mark 8:27-33 par.; see also Matt 4:1-11; Luke 4:1-13; Mark 1:13). Jesus espouses the cause of redemptive and liberating love, which while not itself disarming and bringing to repentance—on the contrary—nevertheless eventually proves victorious over force. That Beelzebub cannot be driven out by Beelzebub also applies here. . . . What applies to Jesus in the New Testament applies to all Christians: to follow Jesus to the point of suffering.[19]

In the final analysis, however, the religious-theological commitment to nonviolence as an absolute imperative of the gospel does not base its case on its effectiveness in the pursuit of justice within history. Though Yoder and Douglass are activists in the cause of justice, both acknowledge that effectiveness cannot be the ultimate reason for the absolute priority of nonviolence. Yoder acknowledges the possibility of a conflict between nonviolence and justice that can be resolved only outside of history. When such a conflict occurs, Christians are called to acknowledge that it is God, not they, who holds the ultimate responsibility for establishing the fullness of justice and peace.

This is the deepest meaning of Jesus' willingness to accept an unjust execution rather than take up arms to resist it. As Yoder puts it:

> The choice that [Jesus] made in rejecting the crown and accepting the cross was the commitment to such a degree of faithfulness of divine love that he was willing for its sake to sacrifice "effectiveness." Usually it can be argued that from some other perspective or in some long view this renunciation of effectiveness was in fact a very effective thing to do. "If a man will lose his . . . life he shall find it." But this paradoxical possibility does not change the initially solid fact that Jesus thereby excluded any normative concern for any capacity to make sure that things would turn out right.[20]

In other words, the cross of Jesus implies that making things "turn out right" (justice) is subordinate to trust in the God who is the only truly "legitimate authority" in these matters of the ultimate outcome of human history and politics. Gordon Zahn's conclusions about the implications of the Beatitudes and the Sermon on the Mount echo Yoder's understanding of the meaning of the cross:

> These, taken in context with the workings of grace and the power of God (which, as Scripture tells us, is made perfect in infirmity), combine to produce an "otherworldly" perspective in which the practice of statecraft becomes at best a secondary consideration. After all, if it avails us not to gain the whole world at the cost of our immortal souls, it might follow that the salvation of our souls could require us to be prepared to suffer the loss of the political and spiritual freedoms we prize where the only alternative is to commit sin.[21]

Zahn, like Yoder and Douglass, is a strong advocate of creative nonviolent action in the defense of these freedoms. Nevertheless, his theology, like pacifist theology in general, is prepared to tolerate injustice in the limit situation where justice cannot be attained by nonviolent means.

The debate between pacifism and just-war theory thus presses us to some very fundamental theological questions. What is the ethical significance of the death of Jesus? Does the commandment to love one's neighbor imply that the incarnation of love in a just social order should take priority over the love of enemies that is expressed in nonviolence? Does the victory of Christ over sin and death in his resurrection imply that Christians are now empowered by God to participate in the shaping of a new and more just earthly society, or is its primary meaning the bestowal of the grace to follow Jesus Christ in the way of the suffering servant?

These are basic theological issues that need to be explored at greater depth and in direct relation to the urgent questions of war and peace. My own approach to them takes the following general form. The fullness of God's love revealed in the death and resurrection of Jesus is both model and cause of Christian action for peace and justice. The kingdom of God, inaugurated by the paschal mystery of Christ, is a kingdom in which love, justice, and the abolition of all violence will be accomplished. In the words of the Psalmist, it is a kingdom in which "kindness and truth shall meet, justice and peace shall kiss" (Ps 85:11, NAB). It is the paschal mystery as a single unified event, however, that is the basis of Christian hope for the full realization of both justice and peace. Neither the crucifixion alone nor the resurrection alone adequately represents the content of Christian conviction. The death of Christ on the cross is one aspect of the coming kingdom. The Father's act of raising him from the dead and inaugurating the kingdom of justice is a second and equally significant aspect of the paschal event. In shaping their lives in history, Christians are therefore compelled to look back to Jesus' nonviolent death and to see in it a demand to practice nonviolence. At the same time, Christians are compelled to look forward to the kingdom whose realization will establish the fullness of love and justice in the relations between all persons and God. This hope and anticipation of the kingdom are as important for a Christian theology of peace as is the historical memory of the crucifixion.

The tension between this memory and this hope can never be fully overcome within history. Both the pacifist tradition's commitment to nonviolence as the way to justice and the just-war tradition's commitment to justice as the way to peace are therefore partial embodiments of the memory and hope that are the bases of Christian faith and Christian love. The total reconciliation of justice and peace is an eschatological reality. Within time the imperatives of justice and the demands of nonviolence can and sometimes do conflict. I would conclude, therefore, that both the pacifist ethic and the just-war ethic are legitimate expressions of Christian faith. Each of them, however, is incomplete by itself and neither can claim to be the only Christian response to the relation of peace and justice. As Childress has put it, "Pacifists and proponents of just-war theories really need each other."[22] This conclusion should not be interpreted as the expression of a desire not to offend either camp. It is intended as a theological statement about the reality of Christian life "between the times" of the inauguration of the kingdom and its eschatological fulfillment. A pluralism of responses to the question whether nonviolence or justice is primary in a Christian ethic is a theological necessity, not just a sociological fact.

This conclusion needs considerably more support than has been provided here. A few remarks will suffice to show its implications for the sections to come. Those who use just-war theory in addressing the nuclear question need the pacifist witness to the centrality of nonviolence. They need this to prevent them from losing their memory of the original just-war question as they engage in the intricate analyses of the relation between just-war norms and the complexities of current policy debates. Similarly, pacifists need the refined categories of moral analysis and reasoning about conflicting values that just-war theory provides. Without these categories they risk removing themselves from the policy debate. Though on some questions Christians might be justified in withdrawing from careful debate about the intricacies of public policy, this can surely not be the case where hundreds of millions of lives are at stake. Pacifists need just-war thinkers to keep the Christian community engaged in shaping these policies in accord with the demands of both justice and peace.[23]

The Moral Debate on the Use of Nuclear Weapons

Both pacifists and just-war theorists are in agreement that the dawning of the nuclear age has brought with it a qualitatively new potential for both murderous violence and profound injustice. The growth of pacifism within the church in recent years has in large measure been a response to the ominous threat posed by nuclear weapons. In discussing this threat in his encyclical *Pacem in terris*, John XXIII stated that "in an age such as ours, which prides itself on its atomic energy, it is contrary to reason to hold that war is now a suitable way to restore rights which have been violated."[24] In the context of a similar discussion, Vatican II referred to "the massive and indiscriminate destruction" that modern scientific weapons are capable of inflicting.[25] The council then went on to state: "All these considerations compel us to undertake an evaluation of war with an entirely new attitude."[26] The theme of the morally problematic character of warfare in the nuclear age was reiterated most recently by John Paul II in his homily at Coventry Cathedral in Great Britain: "Today, the scale and the horror of modern warfare—whether nuclear or not—makes it totally unacceptable as a means of settling differences between nations. War should belong to the tragic past, to history; it should find no place on humanity's agenda for the future."[27]

J. Bryan Hehir has pointed out that papal and conciliar statements such as these are open to various interpretations when placed in the context from which they have been drawn.[28] Douglass appears to believe that the nuclear age is leading the church to a pacifist position through a two-step evolution of thought which is not yet complete. First, he acknowledges that the prime concern of just-war theory is the pursuit of justice, not the legitimation of war. He argues, however, that in the nuclear age it is becoming apparent that violent force is not in fact compatible with the attainment of justice:

> Always implicit [in just-war theory] is the assumption that the waging of war can sometimes be consistent with the attainment of such justice. If, as a result of weapons developments which St. Augustine could hardly have foreseen, war and justice should be seen to have reached an absolute conflict, war as the physical factor in the theory must give way to justice as the ruling moral principle.[29]

This conflict between modern war and justice is the basis of the contemporary argument that even on just-war grounds Christians are obligated to adopt a stance of nuclear pacifism. The nuclear pacifist maintains that all use of nuclear weapons fails the test of the just-war criteria or, in stronger form, that in a nuclear-armed world no war can withstand scrutiny according to these norms.

The second step in the evolution that Douglass believes is underway in church teachings on warfare is a move from nuclear pacifism to a recovery of the early church's commitment to nonviolence. He believes that this step was implicitly taken by John XXIII in *Pacem in terris* and is the logical outcome of Vatican II's call to "undertake an evaluation of war with an entirely new attitude."[30]

As Hehir has observed, Douglass's argument for the presence of these twin developments in church teaching goes beyond the evidence. Vatican II and John Paul II have both reiterated the existence of "the right to legitimate defense once every means of peaceful settlement has been exhausted."[31] Also, as has been argued above, it would seem that an *exclusive* commitment by the church to nonviolence would go beyond the theological possibilities of our existence "between the times."

The question whether the use of *nuclear* weapons can ever be a genuine instrument of justice is less clearly addressed in recent church documents.

This question has thus become one of the chief foci in the continuing discussion of the morality of warfare in the church today. For the pacifist the issue is clear: since all use of force is judged incompatible with the gospel, then this is true *a fortiori* of nuclear weapons. For just-war theory the issue cannot be resolved in this clear-cut manner. A reasoned argument about the possibility or impossibility of just use of nuclear weapons under the concrete contemporary historical circumstances is a prerequisite. The important challenge that the pacifist tradition brings into this just-war debate is its reminder that nonviolence is a prima facie obligation. In light of the "original just-war question," the use of nuclear weapons or of any other form of violent force must be presumed unjustified until strong reasons to the contrary are produced.

The just-war tradition has developed a refined set of moral categories for reasoning about the possible justification of violence in the pursuit of justice. These categories have been formulated in different ways during different phases of the tradition, but in this context they can be summarized briefly. The criteria fall into two broad groups. *Jus ad bellum* criteria determine whether the alleged grounds for the initiation of armed hostilities are sufficiently grave to override the prima facie obligation of nonviolence. *Jus in bello* norms govern the judgment regarding the use of particular means within war.

Ad bellum norms include the following: (1) legitimate authority, i.e., the authority to resort to force is subject to the general criteria of political legitimacy; (2) just cause, i.e., defense against injustice; (3) last resort, i.e., all peaceful alternatives to the use of force in securing justice have been exhausted; (4) a declaration of war—in effect, a way of insuring that resort to arms is indeed a last resort; (5) reasonable hope of success, i.e., if the values of justice on which the overriding of the duty of nonviolence depends are unlikely to be achieved, then the prima facie obligation to nonviolence remains in effect; (6) proportionality, i.e., the values of life, freedom, and justice which are achieved must be greater than the death, suffering, and social upheaval that the war will produce; (7) right intention, i.e., the war must be conducted with the intention of achieving justice and ultimate peace, not out of hatred, desire for revenge, or in a quest for dominance over others.

The *in bello* criteria for the judgment of the morality of the use of particular means (i.e., certain strategies or tactics, particular types of weapons, etc.) are two: (1) discrimination, i.e., noncombatants must be immune from direct attack; (2) proportionality, i.e., the values sought by the use of particular military means must outweigh the harm caused by these means.[32]

These norms embody the culturally accumulated wisdom of the Christian and humanist traditions. They encapsulate the historical experience of the West about the restrictions that must be placed on the use of force if force is to be limited to the protection of justice as the basis of a genuine peace.[33] The question that cries out for an answer is this: Can the use of nuclear weapons ever be a reasonable means to the attainment of justice?

This question actually concerns a number of different but related issues, for there are a variety of ways in which nuclear weapons could conceivably be used in warfare and a variety of strategic doctrines concerning their use. The most horrendous of these possibilities, a direct nuclear attack upon population centers of another nation, patently fails to meet the just-war criteria. Such an attack involves the intended killing of vast numbers of noncombatants. It therefore falls under Vatican II's often-quoted condemnation of indiscriminate bombing: "Any act of war aimed indiscriminately at the destruction of entire cities or of extensive areas along with their population is a crime against God and humanity itself. It merits unequivocal and unhesitating condemnation."[34] This *in bello* norm of discrimination applies to countercity attacks whether they be first-strike or in retaliation. This conclusion is reinforced by other just-war criteria, particularly that of proportionality, for countercity warfare, once begun, is very likely to lead to an all-out exchange resulting in the destruction of all those values that might make more limited forms of warfare sometimes marginally justifiable.

The contemporary debates about nuclear policy raise several other considerations about the use of nuclear weapons that call for a more complex form of reflection than that required by countercity warfare. Some U.S. defense analysts advocate policies that envision the limited use of strategic nuclear weapons against the military forces, command-control-and-communication systems, political and bureaucratic leadership, and key economic resources of the Soviet Union. Proposals of such limited "war-fighting" and "war-winning" strategies are accompanied by the contention that they represent a moral improvement over policies that threaten and prepare for countercity warfare.[35]

These strategies give the appearance of coming closer to meeting the *in bello* criteria of discrimination and proportionality. However, this appearance is deceptive for two reasons. First, these counterforce war-fighting strategies do not eliminate the technical means for countercity warfare. They also leave open the strategic option of resorting to massive attacks on population centers, should limited war fail to achieve its goals. Second, the actual effects of a counterforce attack by one superpower against the other will be difficult to distinguish from an attack on population centers. Both the collateral damage to population centers and the likely loss of command-control-and-communication systems in counterforce nuclear war will make it exceedingly difficult for national leaders to know what the adversary's intentions and actions really are. Collateral damage and command-control-and-communication vulnerability thus exert powerful pressure for escalation to mutual destruction. As Spurgeon Keeny and Wolfgang Panofsky have remarked, there is an "almost inevitable link between any use of nuclear weapons and the grim 'mutual hostage' realities of the MAD world."[36] The use of any strategic nuclear weapons, therefore, increases the likelihood of massive countercity attacks.

Thus a key element in the dispute over whether strategic counterforce war-fighting strategies are morally less objectionable than are strategies that envision the destruction of cities is the prudential military-political judgment about whether the limitation of nuclear war can indeed be predicted with reasonable confidence. U.S. Department of Defense policy statements acknowledge that any employment of strategic nuclear weapons by one superpower against the other can be expected to rapidly escalate into an all-out war.[37] No one can be sure of the outcome of an attempt to conduct limited nuclear war directed against the military and political structure of a nation that itself possesses nuclear weapons. But the bulk of the strategic literature on this question, as well as most of the public statements of the national leaders of the countries involved, imply that it is highly unlikely that such limits would be respected.

The *ad bellum* criterion of reasonable hope of success becomes the relevant moral norm in this debate. In my view, the hope that any use of strategic weapons can be kept limited exceeds the bounds of reasonable judgment. A policy that aims at the actual use of strategic weapons against the other superpower's forces must thus be judged unacceptable as an instrument for the pursuit of goals which are themselves just. In my judgment, this conclusion applies not only to the initiation of a limited nuclear exchange but also in retaliation. To respond to a nuclear attack on one's own military forces by launching strategic nuclear weapons against the forces of the attacking nation increases the probability of escalation to the point of mass slaughter. Therefore the use of strategic nuclear weapons even in would-be limited wars must be judged morally unjustifiable on the grounds of both *ad bellum* and *in bello* norms. This conclusion goes beyond the explicit teachings of the Holy See, though it has been supported by a number of individual bishops' statements.[38] I believe it should become a firm judgment in all future church teaching on warfare.

The current debate on nuclear strategy has also focused on the possibility of another form of limited nuclear war: the use of intermediate-range or tactical nuclear weapons in defense of West Europe. Here again the moral judgment about such scenarios is dependent upon a military-political judgment about the actual likelihood of keeping such use limited. An important debate on this point was stimulated by an essay by McGeorge Bundy, George Kennan, Robert McNamara, and Gerard Smith. They urge NATO to adopt a policy of "no first use" of nuclear weapons. In order to make such a policy feasible they also call for a reexamination of the overall structure of NATO defense and deterrence strategy. In the course of their discussion of this complex area, they affirm that the profusion of nuclear-weapons systems in Europe on both sides of the East/West boundary "has made it more difficult than ever to construct rational plans for any first use of these weapons by anyone."[39] They go on to state an even stronger conclusion:

> It is time to recognize that no one has ever succeeded in advancing any persuasive reason to believe that any use of nuclear weapons, even on the smallest scale, could reliably be expected to remain limited. Every serious analysis and every military exercise, for over 25 years, has demonstrated that even the most restrained battlefield use would be enormously destructive to civilian life and property. There is no way for anyone to have any confidence that such a nuclear action will not lead to further and more devastating exchanges. Any use of nuclear weapons in Europe, by the Alliance or against it, carries with it a high and inescapable risk of escalation into the general nuclear war which would bring ruin to all and victory to none.[40]

A number of the published responses to the Bundy-Kennan-McNamara-Smith essay have been critical of their proposal.[41] All these critical responses base their objections on the grounds that a no-first-use policy would weaken the Western deterrent against Warsaw Pact aggression. I shall deal with the deterrence issue in the next section. In the context of the present discussion on the morality of the use of nuclear weapons, it is important to note that the critics of the proposal made by Bundy et al. do not respond to the fundamental assertion that it is highly improbable that a nuclear exchange could actually be kept limited once any use had in fact occurred. The authors of the original essay have taken note of this fact:

> In all the comment and criticism our essay has received, there has not been one concrete suggestion as to just how a first use of nuclear weapons would be carried out—in which numbers and with what targets. We think there is a reason for this reticence. All the specific proposals we have encountered over the years, and they have been many, look unacceptably dangerous in the context of the forces now deployed on both sides.[42]

The dangers of first use that are emphasized here are also present in the case of retaliatory use of nuclear weapons in the European theater. The likelihood of escalation to general nuclear war which attends *any* use of nuclear weapons in Europe makes such use an irrational means to the pursuit even of such legitimate values as freedom and justice. I would therefore again conclude, on the basis of a combination of the *in bello* criteria of discrimination and proportionality and the *ad bellum* criterion of reasonable hope of success, that no nuclear-weapons use in Europe can be justified.

An additional consideration about the moral aspects of strategies for fighting limited nuclear wars concerns the moral legitimacy of collateral damage to civilian populations that would accompany nuclear attacks on military targets. The traditional *in bello* criterion of discrimination rules out direct attacks on noncombatants. Consequently some participants in the current public argument have concluded that the deaths of civilians indirectly caused by nuclear attacks on military targets do not violate the norm of discrimination.

In contemporary Catholic moral theology there has been an intense dispute about the significance of the direct/indirect distinction.[43] This debate is important in itself, and the way it is resolved is relevant to the way one reasons about the morality of collateral damage to civilian populations. Nevertheless, I believe that proponents of the different positions in this debate should reach the same conclusion about the issue at hand.

One view holds that the directly intended object in such an attack is the destruction of a military target and that civilian deaths are unintended indirect consequences. According to this view, one is still bound, by the traditional interpretation of the principle of double effect, to weigh the evil consequences that indirectly accompany the attack against the good effects that flow from it. Here all the considerations discussed above regarding the likely outcomes of counterforce nuclear war between the superpowers become relevant. Even if, therefore, one argues that collateral damage to civilian populations is indirectly voluntary, the judgment about proportionality between the two effects must be negative.

The other school of moral theologians in the debate about the direct-indirect distinction takes a different approach in its treatment of intention. This school argues that one cannot determine what an agent intends to do without taking all the foreseen consequences into account. If the agent chooses to perform an action whose good consequences are proportionately greater than are the evil consequences, this school would judge that the evil consequences are not the object of direct intention. If, on the other hand, the foreseen evil consequences are proportionately greater, then the direct object of intention is evil. In other words, for the second school the direct intention cannot be determined apart from a judgment of proportionality. Both schools, therefore, must evaluate the morality of collateral damage by assessing the proportionality between the evils of loss of life plus possible escalation and the goal of defending justice. This assessment, I believe, should lead to a negative moral judgment on attacks that will cause significant damage to population centers. All nuclear attacks in Europe fall under this judgment. The two schools, however, will reach this conclusion by different routes.[44]

From all these considerations one conclusion must be drawn: the use of nuclear weapons can never be morally justified in any realistically foreseeable conflict between the superpowers and their allies in Europe. This conclusion follows from a judgment at once normative and prudential. Normatively, it rests on the just-war theory's insistence that there are limits both to the legitimacy of the resort to force in the pursuit of justice and to the means that can be legitimately employed even in justified conflict. Prudentially, the conclusion arises from a judgment about the course of events that can be expected to follow on the use of nuclear weapons in a variety of different contexts. A prudential judgment, by definition, is not subject to logically certain demonstration. And in the case of nuclear war, the practical experience that is the ordinary source of prudence is fortunately unavailable. But the strong weight of the evidence from strategic studies is on the side of the argument advanced here.

Thus, on the question of the use of nuclear weapons, the pacifist and the just-war traditions converge. We can modify Douglass's statement quoted above as follows: nuclear war and justice can be seen to have reached an absolute conflict. Therefore both the pursuit of justice and the commitment to peace demand the rejection of the use of nuclear weapons. I believe that this nuclear pacifist conclusion should be placed at the foundations of future church initiatives for justice and peace.

Moral Responses to the Ambiguities of Deterrence

The conclusion that nuclear weapons can never be used morally leaves unresolved the central question of how to prevent such use from occurring. Here we must enter the paradoxical world of deterrence theory. Agreement on the unacceptability of any use of nuclear weapons can and does coexist with disagreement about the morality of the possession of and threat to use nuclear weapons for purposes of deterrence. The moral legitimacy of strategic doctrines designed to deter an adversary from the use of military force through the threat to use nuclear weapons against that adversary has become the most controverted question in the nuclear debate today.

Indeed, the moral issues in the debate about deterrence must be faced even by those who do not share the conclusion that no use of nuclear weapons can ever be justified. Those who argue that some extremely limited use of nuclear force could be morally legitimate generally do so as part of a larger argument about deterrence. For example, proponents of policies that threaten and prepare to use tactical and intermediate-range nuclear weapons in the defense of Europe argue that these policies are the most effective way to deter both nuclear and conventional aggression by the Warsaw Pact against NATO.[45] The same is true of those who support policies that project the limited use of strategic nuclear force by the superpowers against each other's homelands. They argue for such policies as the best means for preventing precisely such horrible events from occurring.[46] Pacifists too must face the paradoxes inherent in the moral debate about deterrence doctrines. Those committed to an ethic of nonviolence reject the just-war criteria as an appropriate basis for the conclusion we have reached about the moral illegitimacy of nuclear-weapons use. However, they hold to the conclusion itself at least as tenaciously as do Christians who rely on the just-war tradition. They are therefore faced with the challenge of advancing their own views of the best means for the prevention of nuclear war. Pacifists argue that there are forms of nonviolent action that can be effective in resisting unjust aggression. The pacifist branch of the Christian community, however, must ask the question whether the forms of nonviolent resistance developed by Gandhi and Martin Luther King can in fact successfully deter the use of nuclear weapons by an adversary. Theologians such as Yoder and Zahn argue that "effectiveness" and "statecraft" are at best secondary considerations in a Christian theological perspective. If their primary commitment is to the protection of all human life, however, they cannot consistently support actions that would make nuclear war more likely. Therefore they cannot logically refuse to enter into the debate about the best way to prevent such warfare from occurring. Pacifists may rightly conclude that the possession of and threat to use nuclear weapons is itself immoral. But the rightness of such a conclusion will depend on the cogency of their argument about the best means of preventing war in the nuclear age.

Thus just-war thinkers who reach the nuclear pacifist conclusion advocated here, those whose strategies include preparations for the possibility of limited nuclear war, and those who reason from a pacifist starting point must all face the paradoxes and ambiguities inherent in nuclear deterrence. Though the rhetoric employed by national leaders and defense analysts is sometimes overheated and even bellicose, it is not reasonable to believe that any sane person wants to set the nuclear juggernaut in motion. The policy debate about deterrence is not a debate between those in favor of nuclear war and those against it. It is a debate between persons with differing perspectives and convictions on how to prevent nuclear violence. The moral ambiguity inherent in deterrence strategy is reflected in the fact that persons who share fundamentally similar goals reach such different conclusions about the way to attain them.

The moral ambiguity of deterrence strategies is also reflected in recent church teachings. Vatican II took note of the fact that the theory of deterrence is advocated as a way of preventing nuclear war. On the basis of the theological and strategic thinking at its disposal, the council did not reach a firm conclusion on the moral legitimacy of the possession of and threat to use nuclear weapons for purposes of deterrence.

> This accumulation of arms, which increases every year, also serves, in a way heretofore unknown, as a deterrent to possible enemy attack. Many regard this state of affairs as the most effective way by which peace of a sort can be maintained at the present time. Whatever be the case with this method of deterrence, all people should be convinced that the arms race in which so many countries are engaged is not a safe way to preserve a steady peace.[47]

The care and caution evident here are the result of the inherent paradox of deterrence in a nuclear world. In following the logic of deterrence theory in such a world, nations threaten and prepare to undertake actions that we have concluded can never be justified. At the same time, the intention that leads to such threats and preparations is the intention to prevent nuclear war. The paradox of deterrence is rooted in the fact that intention (nuclear-war prevention) and action (the preparation and threat to unleash nuclear war) move in opposite directions.

Discussions of the issue within the U.S. Catholic community during the years immediately preceding the issuance of the bishops' pastoral letter in 1983 show that this paradox is agonizing to the Christian conscience. Several different efforts have been made to come to grips with it. The pacifist approach that predominates among Catholics affiliated with groups such as Pax Christi moves in a straightforward way from an objection to all violence, to a condemnation of the use of nuclear weapons, to a rejection of the threat to use them, to a delegitimation of their possession and production.[48] In an earlier pastoral letter of 1976, the American bishops did not adopt this line of reasoning fully, but they did condemn both the use and the threat to use nuclear weapons against noncombatants. "As possessors of a vast nuclear arsenal, we must be aware that not only is it wrong to attack civilian populations, but it is also wrong to threaten to attack them as part of a strategy of deterrence."[49]

In testimony on behalf of the United States Catholic Conference before the Foreign Relations Committee of the Senate in 1979, Cardinal John Krol repeated this earlier judgment about the threat to use nuclear weapons against noncombatants. He carried the argument a step further by distinguishing between threatening with these weapons and simply possessing them.[50] He used this distinction in an argument that has been repeated in a number of subsequent statements by individual bishops and was incorporated into the first draft of the NCCB pastoral letter on war and peace. He stated that the possession of nuclear weapons could be tolerated as the lesser of two evils provided that negotiations toward the reduction and elimination of nuclear weapons are proceeding in a meaningful way.

This argument rests on three presuppositions. First, it assumes that it is possible to make a morally significant distinction between the possession of nuclear weapons and the threat to use them. Second, the conclusion that the possession of nuclear weapons is the lesser of two evils in the present situation presupposes a judgment that unilateral nuclear disarmament by the U.S. could increase the possibility of Soviet nuclear aggression against the Atlantic Alliance. Third, it appears to imply that if arms-control negotiations are not leading to meaningful reductions in force levels, the church would be compelled to challenge the moral legitimacy of deterrence as such.

The reasoning of the Krol testimony has been challenged from both flanks. The presupposition that one can distinguish between possession of nuclear weapons and the threat to use them has been denied both by those who reject possession and by those who contend that there can be no deterrent without a genuine threat of use.[51] Catholic moral theology has always maintained that it is immoral to intend to do that which is itself immoral. The Krol testimony accepts the conclusion that any use of nuclear weapons is immoral. It sees the *threat* to use them as an indication of the presence of an *intention* to do so. It assumes, however, that the *possession* of these weapons is compatible with an intention *not* to employ them. But it also assumes that mere possession can serve as a deterrent, for unilateral disarmament is implicitly rejected on the grounds that it might well invite Soviet aggression. Thus possession must at least be *perceived* as a threat by potential adversaries.

The involuted quality of this argument is ground for suspecting that something has gone awry in the way its approach to the morality of deterrence has been structured. The reformulation of two aspects of this argument would be of considerable help in clarifying what is at stake.

First, the actual content of the intention that guides the formulation of deterrence policy must be made explicit. Second, a reconsideration of the notion of toleration as used in the Krol testimony is needed.

The relation between intention and action in deterrence strategy has several different levels which must be carefully distinguished. Were the intention that of using nuclear weapons and the action their actual use, there would be no question that both intention and action should be declared morally illegitimate if the conclusion of the previous section of this essay is accepted. Deterrence policies, however, are formulated with the explicit purpose of preventing the outbreak of nuclear war. The actions implementing these intentions are not the actual use of nuclear weapons but military and political steps that attempt to prevent nuclear conflict. One must distinguish, therefore, between the intent to use nuclear weapons and the intent to deter their use. No simple logical argument can be made from the illegitimacy of use to the moral evaluation of the intentions involved in deterrence.

Nevertheless, this does not mean that any and every strategic doctrine or weapons system proposed in the name of deterrence is morally acceptable. Quite the contrary. The factor that makes the intention behind a deterrence policy distinguishable from an intention to employ nuclear force is a reasoned judgment that the policy in question will actually prevent use. One must be able to make a solid judgment that the policy in question will decrease the likelihood of nuclear war if the policy is to be regarded as a true deterrent policy. To go ahead with the implementation of a policy that increases the likelihood of the use of these weapons is to *intend* this outcome. But to pursue policies that can be reasonably projected to make nuclear war less likely, even if these policies involve implicit or explicit threats, is to *intend* the avoidance of war. The moral judgment on the intention behind deterrence policies is therefore inseparable from an evaluation of the reasonably predictable outcomes of diverse policy choices.

In other words, it is impossible to reach a moral judgment about the morality of nuclear deterrence as a general concept. The real question for moral judgment is whether a concrete strategic option will actually make the world more secure from nuclear disaster or less so. There is no such thing as deterrence in the abstract. Rather, there are only specific defense postures involving diverse weapons systems, targeting doctrines, procurement programs, and strategic master concepts. It is these that must be subjected to ethical scrutiny, not some abstract notion of deterrence or intention. As there is a wide diversity of ways that nuclear weapons might conceivably be used, so an equally large number of policies are advanced in the name of deterrence. In the question both of use and of deterrence, the moral conclusion will depend on a complex form of reasoning involving the concrete options from a simultaneously normative and prudential point of view.

This fact is implicit in the Krol testimony, but I believe it is obscured by the way the questions of intention and threat are handled. It is also implicit in the cardinal's statement that the moral legitimacy of a deterrence policy is contingent upon genuine progress in arms control and reduction. To make the legitimacy of deterrence contingent upon "meaningful and continuing reductions in nuclear stockpiles"[52] is another way of saying that a particular strategic policy must truly make nuclear war less likely if this policy is to be ethically legitimate. But the Krol argument moves back to the abstract level again when it concludes that if the hope of arms reduction were to disappear, then "the moral attitude of the Catholic church would almost certainly have to shift to one of uncompromising condemnation of both use *and* possession of such weapons."[53] Rather than calling for a shift to a generalized condemnation of use and possession, a breakdown of arms-control and reduction negotiations would rather be cause for moral objection to the specific policies that have caused such a breakdown. Such a response would more accurately reflect the fact that the real moral judgment concerns concrete policies, not abstract ideas about use and possession. It would also avoid the unfortunate outcome of removing the church from the policy argument precisely at a time when its participation in this argument is most urgently needed.

The second issue in the deterrence debate raised by the Krol testimony that needs reconsideration is the *toleration* of the possession of nuclear weapons as long as arms-reduction negotiations are moving forward effectively. The intention of the testimony is to acknowledge that the risks entailed by the existence of nuclear weapons make their possession by the United States a genuine evil. This evil is judged tolerable if two conditions are simultaneously present: (1) the Soviet threat continues to exist, making unilateral disarmament even more dangerous than continued possession; (2) this risk is being decreased through effective arms reduction rather than increased through a continuing arms race.

The logic of this position is essentially correct, but it can be formulated in a way that will provide much clearer guidance in the effort to reach decisions about actual policy choices. The point of the argument would be more evident if the conditions under which specific deterrence policies are justified were more explicitly stated. These conditions are two. First, any new policy proposal must make nuclear war less likely than the policies presently in effect rather than more likely. Second, any new policy proposal must increase the possibility of arms reduction rather than decrease this possibility.

These two principles have the advantage of acknowledging that the moral judgment about deterrence is fundamentally a judgment about the direction in which we are moving. There is an intrinsic link between the direction of a particular deterrence policy and its legitimacy or illegitimacy. One cannot reach a moral judgment about such policies in a nonhistorical way. The possession of nuclear weapons is indeed an evil because of the inevitable risk of use which such possession carries with it. But the judgment of moral rightness or wrongness concerns the way human agents respond to the existence of this evil in their actual policy choices. The twin principles of reduction of the probability of nuclear war and increase in the possibility of arms reduction can provide more help in guiding such choices than can the general concept of toleration.[54]

The moral issue in the debate about deterrence strategy can be stated simply: Are the policies being advocated really deterrents or not? If they increase the probability of nuclear war or if they make arms control and reduction more difficult to achieve, they are not. Pacifists, nuclear pacifists, and even those who envision some forms of strictly limited use of nuclear weapons should be able to reach consensus on these two principles for the evaluation of deterrence policies. The great danger in the present moment is that moral judgments about the use of nuclear weapons will be adjusted to fit the logic of a favored deterrence posture. This appears to be happening in scenarios for limited intercontinental nuclear war, for tactical nuclear war in Europe, and in the rationales that are proposed for a variety of new weapons systems. Such developments turn on its head the structure of reasoning that is the only possible basis for just deterrence. The urgent task of the church in the current debate is to keep this moral inversion from gaining popular acceptance. It will do so by focusing the debate over deterrence on the central values of war prevention and arms reduction and by continually scrutinizing concrete policies in light of these values.

Conclusion

This overview of the nuclear debate has attempted to survey the significant moral positions on the matter. It has reached three conclusions: both pacifist and just-war approaches to the morality of war must be represented within the church if it is to pursue its ministry of justice and peace adequately; no use of nuclear weapons in conflicts between the superpowers and their allies is justifiable in the circumstances of the present international political and military order; and concrete deterrence policies must be individually evaluated from the viewpoint of their contribution to war prevention and disarmament.

The first conclusion is theological and ethical; the second and third are ethical and prudential. Because these last two conclusions rest in part on nontheological judgments about the likely outcomes of certain military and political activities, it is likely that there will be more disagreement with them than with the first conclusion. It must be recognized, however, that even the first principle, with its legitimation of some limited uses of force, rests on a prudential judgment about the means that may sometimes be necessary for the attainment of justice. If the Christian community had refused to make any corporate prudential judgments about the affairs of the political order, the just-war theory could never have emerged. Neither could judgments have emerged about intrinsic linkage between Christian faith and such secular institutions as limited government, the constitutional protection of the right to religious freedom, and the guarantee of a living wage.

In the nuclear debate the church is being invited to see a new link between Christian faith and the international politicomilitary order. It took centuries for the church to reach consensus on these other institutional correlates of Christian faith. The time left for reaching consensus on the questions of nuclear morality is short. But there is no more urgent task. The analysis and conclusions offered here are an attempt to contribute to the formation of this consensus. We will now turn to the 1983 pastoral letter of the U.S. bishops to examine its contribution to the church's understanding of these questions.

Chapter 10

The Challenge of Peace in the Context of Recent Church Teachings

In their pastoral letter on war and peace, *The Challenge of Peace: God's Promise and Our Response*, the American Catholic bishops address the urgent moral questions posed by the threat of nuclear war from the vantage point of Christian faith and the church's long tradition of ethical reflection. The two and a half years devoted to the preparation of the letter involved the bishops in all of the religious, philosophical, historical, political, and military issues discussed in the previous chapter. The significance and success of the outcome can therefore be evaluated from a number of perspectives. This essay will analyze and assess the letter from a single, somewhat limited point of view. It will situate the letter in the context of the official teachings of the Catholic church on war and peace since World War II and outline the distinctive contributions of the letter to developing Catholic thought.

Though the question of the relation between the views expressed in the letter and the official teachings of the church since 1945 is a limited one, it seems to have been very much on the minds of the drafters of the letter and the bishops conference as a whole. Several explicit discussions of this relation are contained in the document itself. For example, in outlining the basis on which the pastoral letter proposes guidance for Christian conscience and public policy, the bishops state that they draw heavily on Vatican II's Pastoral Constitution on the Church in the Modern World. They add that "for similar reasons we draw heavily upon the popes of the nuclear age, from Pope Pius XII through Pope John Paul II."[1]

They go on to add, however, that they intend to bring their own distinctive contribution to the debate rather than simply to reaffirm the conclusions of the council and recent popes.

> The teaching of popes and councils must be incarnated by each local church in a manner understandable to its culture. This allows each local church to bring its unique insights and experience to bear on the issues shaping our world. From 1966 to the present American bishops, individually and collectively, have issued numerous statements on the issues of peace and war, ranging from the Vietnam War to conscientious objection and the use of nuclear weapons. These statements reflect not only the concerns of the hierarchy, but also the voices of our people, who have increasingly expressed to us their alarm over the threat of war. In this letter we wish to continue and develop the teaching on peace and war which we have previously made and which reflects both the teaching of the universal church and the insights and experience of the Catholic community of the United States.[2]

The pastoral letter, then, sets out to interpret the recent teachings of councils and popes in light of American experience and insight.

That the bishops' decision to do more than reiterate conciliar and papal teaching was quite self-conscious is evident from a comparison of the above quoted paragraph from the final version of the document with the paragraph from Draft III which it replaced. Draft III described the relation between the bishops' teaching and that of recent Roman statements this way:

> We make our own their [the popes'] teaching and that of the council, while in consonance with such teaching we add observations born of the experience of the church in the United States.[3]

The differences between these two paragraphs is significant. They show that the final version of the pastoral letter acknowledges that it intends not only "to continue" but also "to develop" the recent teachings of the church on war and peace. The final document goes beyond "adding observations" related to the American experience to making a distinctive American contribution to the understanding of the church as a whole.

The contribution of the letter to such ecclesial understanding can be made more explicit by comparing it with conciliar and papal teaching since World War II on three points: its basic perspective toward the morality of war, the moral norms proposed concerning the use of nuclear weapons, and the complex question of the morality of deterrence policy.

Basic Perspective on the Morality of War and Peace

Pius XII was the first pope of the nuclear age and therefore the first to address the problem of warfare in light of the nuclear threat. Pius XII stood firmly in the just-war tradition that for centuries has been historically linked with the Catholic moral tradition. The advent of the new dangers posed by modern total warfare, including atomic, biological, and chemical warfare, did not lead Pius XII to question the just-war tradition's argument that the use of force could sometimes be a tragic necessity. Pius XII argued forcefully that Christians are called by both faith and reason to the pursuit of peace. But this peace must be firmly based on justice. Therefore the Christian commitment to peace does not imply an aquiescence in the perpetration of injustice by an aggressive nation. Governments have an obligation to protect their citizens against injustice by resisting such aggression, even by the use of force. The pastoral letter cites Pius XII's unambiguous words on this issue:

> A people threatened with an unjust aggression, or already its victim, may not remain passively indifferent, if it would think and act as befits a Christian. . . . Among [the] goods [of humanity] some are of such importance for society that it is perfectly lawful to defend them against unjust aggression. Their defense is even an obligation for the nations as a whole, who have a duty not to abandon a nation that is attacked.[4]

This right of self-defense was reiterated by the Second Vatican Council and was strongly reaffirmed by Pope John Paul II in his 1982 World Day of Peace message. The most notable point in the citation of Pius XII, however, is the insistance on the *duty* of states to resist aggression and the violation of basic human rights. The existence of such a duty was the basis of Pius XII's rejection of the legitimacy of conscientious objection to all war as a position open to Catholics.[5] For if states have a duty to resist aggression, and citizens have a duty to serve the common good of their country, then it is difficult to see how one can affirm a right to conscientious objection to all participation in warfare.

It is interesting, therefore, that the pastoral letter has drawn on this aspect of the teaching of Pius XII while at the same time affirming that conscientious objection is a legitimate position within the framework of Catholic teaching. The legitimacy of conscientious objection was affirmed by the Second Vatican Council and again by the American bishops' own 1968 pastoral letter, *Human Life in Our Day.* These earlier affirmations are cited with approval by *The Challenge of Peace.*[6] The bishops affirm both the duty to resist aggression and the right not to so resist.

One way to deal with this apparent contradiction is to note that the pastoral letter assigns the duty to resist evil to governments and the right to conscientious objection to individuals.[7] Also it is clearly and forcefully argued by the pastoral letter that armed force may be used to resist injustice only under the stringent conditions of the just-war norms and that nonviolent means must first have been exhausted. However, the pastoral letter has developed a perspective on the relation between just-war theory and nonviolence that goes beyond these distinctions between governmental duties and individual rights on the one hand and the last resort of force and the preferable option of nonviolent resistance on the other.

The most significant development contained in the letter's basic perspective on the morality of war and peace is its argument that the just-war ethic and the ethic of nonviolence are interrelated approaches and are not simply to be juxtaposed as contradictory alternatives. In affirming this the bishops state that they are putting forward "Catholic teaching":

> Catholic teaching sees these two distinct moral responses as having a complementary relationship in the sense that they both seek to serve the common good. They differ in their perception of how the common good is to be defended most effectively, but both responses testify to the Christian conviction that peace must be pursued and rights defended within moral restraints and in the context of defining other basic human values.[8]

It is certainly true that the Catholic social tradition, which the pastoral letter sees as "a mix of biblical, theological, and philosophical elements which are brought to bear upon the concrete problems of the day," will sustain this conclusion.[9] However, it is clear that the pastoral's position on the complementarity of the just-war ethic and the ethic of nonviolence had not been affirmed previously in these explicit terms in the conciliar and papal teaching since World War II.

The United States bishops are aware that they are breaking new ground in affirming this interdependence of just-war and pacifist perspectives in the contemporary situation. The impetus for such development comes from the conditions of the "new moment" in which we are located—a moment characterized by the massive destructive potential of nuclear weapons and by the new public perception of the dangers of these weapons.[10] In the face of both the threats and possibilities of the present situation the pastoral letter states:

> The task before us is not simply to repeat what we have said before; it is first to consider anew whether and how our religious-moral tradition can assess, direct, contain, and, we hope, help to eliminate the threat posed to the human family by the nuclear arsenals of the world.[11]

Here the bishops explicitly echo the call of the Second Vatican Council "to undertake a completely fresh reappraisal of war."[12] They go beyond the council, however, in proposing their own understanding of the basic moral perspectives to which such a fresh reappraisal should lead:

> While the just-war teaching has clearly been in possession for the past 1,500 years of Catholic thought, the "new moment" in which we find ourselves sees the just-war teaching and nonviolence as distinct but interdependent methods of evaluating warfare. They diverge on some specific conclusions, but they share a common presumption against the use of force as a means of settling disputes.
>
> Both find their roots in the Christian theological tradition; each contributes to the full moral vision we need in pursuit of a human peace. We believe the two perspectives support and complement one another, each preserving the other from distortion.[13]

It seems clear that the bishops have been led to this conclusion by the particular form that the nuclear debate has taken in the United States in recent years. Their letter argues the case for the mutual complementarity of just-war theory and pacifism within the church on both biblical and theological grounds. The need for both positions to be present within the church is the result of the tension between justice and peace in a world in which the kingdom of God has not yet been fully established.[14] But the American debate on the nuclear question has been the occasion of the emergence of a significant pacifist movement within the Catholic Church in the United States. The bishops' involvement in this debate has convinced them that the pacifist commitment to the nonviolent defense of justice should be granted new status as an expression of the deepest concerns of Catholic tradition.

The pastoral letter does limit the absolute rejection of the use of force to individuals and leaves open the limited right of governments to resort to arms. Nevertheless the complementarity of the two moral perspectives has had a significant impact on how the United States bishops formulate their understanding of the just-war theory itself. The link that binds the two perspectives together and prevents them from being simply contradictory is the common presumption they share against the use of force. This strong presumption against war is the central thread of the Christian tradition on the morality of warfare both for individuals and for governments. The bishops affirm that "the moral theory of the 'just-war' or 'limited-war' doctrine begins with the presumption that binds all Christians: We should do no harm to our neighbor; and the possibility of taking even one human life is a prospect we should consider in fear and trembling."[15] The suggestion that nonviolence is the norm and that the legitimacy of the resort to force must be seen as an exception to be justified in every case is an important new emphasis of a perspective that is at the heart of Catholic tradition. The "new moment" brought about by public understanding of the nuclear threat has led the bishops to make a significant contribution to the clarification and understanding of this tradition for the church as a whole.

Moral Norms Regarding the Use of Nuclear Weapons

In the papal and conciliar discussions of war and peace since World War II the catastrophic effects of the massive use of nuclear weapons have been a constant matter of deep concern. Denunciation of the arms race and appeals to turn back from the precipice of destruction is a central theme of this recent teaching. However, the post-Hiroshima teachings have been less detailed than one might expect in addressing the question of whether nuclear weapons might ever be legitimate means in the conduct of warfare.

Pius XII, for example, frequently referred to the grave dangers attendant on the use of these weapons. In 1953 he reaffirmed the just-war position that a nation would be called upon to "suffer injustice" if the only effective means of resistance would violate just-war norms.[16] In the same address, however, he left unresolved the question of whether all uses of nuclear weapons would come under this judgment.

> What we have just discussed applies especially to ABC warfare—atomic, biological, and chemical. As to the question of knowing whether it [ABC warfare] can become clearly necessary in self-defense against ABC warfare, let it suffice for Us to have posed it here.[17]

A year later Pius XII was somewhat more specific. He affirmed that the use of nuclear weapons without just cause is a "crime." This statement implies that there might possibly be circumstances in which such a just cause would justify use. However, the pope recognized that any use of nuclear weapons involving "such an extension of evil that it entirely escapes the control of man" must be rejected as immoral. Any use of these weapons that produces "the pure and simple annihilation of all human life within the radius of action . . . is not permitted for any reason whatsoever."[18]

In the writings of Pius XII we see foreshadowed an uncertainty about the morality of the use of nuclear weapons that has resurfaced in the debate leading up to and following the American bishops' pastoral. Relying on just-war norms, Pius XII condemned all forms of unlimited warfare, especially the indiscriminate use of nuclear, bacteriological, and chemical warfare. At the same time, the pope was hesitant to conclude that *every* use of nuclear weapons must be indiscriminate. This argument has become more heated and pointed with the development of a variety of tactical, intermediate-range, and precision-guided strategic nuclear weapons that are alleged to be discriminate enough to destroy military forces without falling under the condemnation of those uses of force that "entirely escape the control of man." The issue that Pius XII faced and was unable to answer was debated at length by the American bishops: can *any* use of nuclear weapons be reasonably expected to remain discriminate and limited?

Pope John XXIII approached this issue also, though with a similarly ambiguous result. In *Pacem in terris* he stated:

> In an age such as ours, which prides itself on its atomic energy, it is contrary to reason to hold that war is now a suitable way to restore rights which have been violated.[19]

This statement, taken literally, suggests that no use of force, let alone the use of nuclear weapons, could ever be justified in the nuclear age. From the body of John XXIII's writings, however, it is clear that this conclusion was not meant by him as an apodictic one. Nor did John XXIII enter into a detailed analysis of the morality of the use of nuclear weapons, the circumstances of such use, or the different kinds of nuclear weapons available for use in the arsenals of the world.

The most clear-cut statement on this question of use is that contained in Vatican II's *Gaudium et spes.* The council affirmed one of the strongest norms of the just-war theory—that of discrimination or noncombatant immunity from direct attack—in a way clearly relevant to the issue of the use of nuclear weapons.

> Any act of war aimed indiscriminately at the destruction of entire cities or of extensive areas along with their population is a crime against God and humanity itself. It merits unequivocal and unhesitating condemnation.[20]

This pronouncement was one of the few clear condemnations made by the council. It is a direct application of the just-war norm of discrimination. However, it does not settle the hard cases about nuclear-war fighting. Can there be a discriminate and proportionate use of nuclear weapons? Can there be a use of nuclear weapons that will succeed in achieving justice? Can there be a use of nuclear weapons that remains within human control and therefore satisfies the just-war demand that any marginally justifiable war must be limited and conducted by legitimate authority?

The pastoral letter makes its own the council's clear conclusion when it states that any use of nuclear weapons directly targeted against population centers—even in retaliation—must be condemned. The bishops personalize this position when they affirm that "No Christian can rightfully carry out orders or policies deliberately aimed at killing noncombatants."[21] The reference here to carrying out both "orders" and "policies" suggests that the bishops intend this conclusion to be carefully considered not only by soldiers and military personnel but also by Christians in governmental service at whatever level.

The recent teachings of popes and council, therefore, do not provide either comprehensive analysis or detailed moral guidance on the key debate today about the use of nuclear weapons: can use be discriminate and proportionate? John Paul II, in his sermon at Coventry Cathedral, stated:

> Today, the scale and horror of modern warfare—whether nuclear or not—makes it totally unacceptable as a means of settling differences between nations.[22]

Despite the ringing quality of this statement, it is clear from John Paul II's support of the right of self-defense that he did not mean it to be taken literally. John Paul's eloquent statements on these questions are more valuable for their hortatory than for their analytic emphasis.

The American bishops' letter is, in fact, the first official Catholic church analysis of the issue of the morality of the use of nuclear weapons that seeks to make careful distinctions between different ways these weapons might be used and to draw appropriate conclusions for public policy. *The Challenge of Peace* engages the public debate on three crucial points.

First, it resoundingly rejects the use of nuclear weapons against population centers. Here it is in continuity with the modern just-war theory, with Pius XII and Vatican II. *Second,* it strongly rejects any first use of nuclear weapons, no matter how just the cause or how careful the intent that such first use be kept limited within just-war norms. The bishops reach this conclusion on the basis of their judgment that "the danger of escalation is so great that it would be morally unjustifiable to initiate nuclear war in any form."[23] *Third,* they express their extreme skepticism about the possibility that *any* use of nuclear weapons can be kept limited.[24] Therefore, though they do not apodictically condemn all possible uses of nuclear weapons, they do state that the risk entailed by any such use is so great that there is "no moral justification for submitting the human community to this risk."[25] The pastoral letter, then, is a more nuanced and careful treatment of the issue of the use of nuclear weapons than can be found in other church teachings since World War II.

The American bishops' conclusions are not all of equal weight. In pre-Vatican II theology it was common to assign so-called "theological notes" to various positions contained within church teachings. Some positions were judged to be at the core of Christian belief, others to be important expressions of Christian faith in a particular social or cultural context. The "notes" attributed to different conclusions were an indication of their place on this scale of importance. I read the American bishops' letter as assigning the following notes to their conclusions on the various possible uses of nuclear weapons:

> Use against population centers, even in retaliation:
> *resoundingly rejected;*
> First use, even in a just cause: *strongly rejected;*
> Any use, even in defense of justice and human rights:
> regarded as an *unacceptable risk.*

In situating *The Challenge of Peace* in the context of recent church teaching, one thing becomes clear about its discussion of the use of nuclear weapons. It is at once more forceful and more nuanced than any of the documents produced by the popes or the council in the years since World War II. The care with which the actual dilemmas about the use of nuclear weapons has been approached is one of the most important results of the bishops' serious engagement in the current American debate.

The Morality of Deterrence Policy

There are two key statements that set the larger church context for the American bishops' discussion of the morality of deterrence: *Gaudium et spes* and the message of John Paul II to the Second Special Session of the United Nations General Assembly on Disarmament. The council acknowledged the dangers inherent in the possession of nuclear weapons for purposes of deterrence and appealed for a reversal of the arms race. It did not, however, reach a specific conclusion on the morality of deterrence as such.[26] John Paul II also spoke forcefully of the dangers of the arms race. Like the council he stopped short of condemning the possession of nuclear weapons for purposes of deterrence. Indeed his message to the United Nations Special Session went beyond the council in explicitly accepting the legitimacy of deterrence, provided such possession was in the context of serious efforts at disarmament.

> In current conditions "deterrence" based on balance, certainly not as an end in itself but as a step on the way toward a progressive disarmament, may still be judged morally acceptable. Nonetheless in order to ensure peace, it is indispensable not to be satisfied with this minimum which is always susceptible to the real danger of explosion.[27]

The difficulty faced by both the council and the pope in addressing deterrence can be stated simply. Nuclear-deterrence strategies rest on a threat to do something that is itself immoral or which runs an unreasonable risk of violating moral norms, i.e., a threat to use nuclear weapons. Catholic moral thought has always maintained that to intend an immoral act is itself immoral, even if the act is not in fact carried out. This would seem to imply that nuclear-deterrence strategies should be condemned. However, if one were to condemn deterrence and follow through with the implications of this condemnation, then one should also call for immediate nuclear disarmament, even unilateral nuclear disarmament. The fear that unilateral disarmament could occasion either the outbreak of war or the loss of freedom and human rights led both the council and John Paul II to stop short of such a condemnation. John Paul II went beyond Vatican II, however, in subjecting his "acceptance" of deterrence to a significant moral condition: it must be "a step on the way toward progressive disarmament."

The United States bishops faced this same dilemma. They accepted the basic structure of John Paul II's position. But they faced a further problem that had arisen in the context of the United States policy debate. A number of new weapons systems were being developed and deployed for the purpose of encouraging the U.S.S.R. to make concessions in arms-control negotiations. Thus the bishops were concerned that John Paul II's position, left as it stood, could provide legitimacy for an escalating arms race. This they clearly did not want to do, for some of these new weapons threaten to destabilize the nuclear balance and thus to increase the likelihood of nuclear war.

The pastoral letter goes beyond the position of John Paul II by entering into an analysis of different types of deterrence policies, together with the weapons-systems and targeting doctrines associated with these policies. Like the pope, the United States bishops are willing conditionally to accept the legitimacy of deterrence. But the conditions they set are considerably more detailed and stringent than are the pope's. The bishops state that "any claim by any government that it is pursuing a morally acceptable policy of deterrence must be scrutinized with the greatest care."[28] They enter into such a process of careful scrutiny of United States policy and apply John Paul II's basic position through their "own prudential judgments." The conditions they set down exclude so-called "war-fighting" strategies, the quest for superiority, and all weapons systems that make disarmament more difficult to achieve. This leads them to oppose first-strike weapons and strategies that lower the nuclear threshold.[29] These conditions provide considerably more guidance for the evaluation of the morality of deterrence than previous conciliar or papal statements. They represent another major contribution of the letter. They show just how marginal a Christian "acceptance" of deterrence must be.

Conclusion

One can conclude that the deepest significance of the way the American bishops have related Catholic teaching since World War II to the nuclear challenge is that they have in fact proposed a significant development in this tradition. They believe that this development is needed if Christians are to "assess, direct, contain, and, we hope, help to eliminate the threat posed to the human family."[30] The pastoral letter is therefore a genuinely prophetic document. And as in all prophetic speech that is rooted in concern for God's people rather than in self-righteousness, it is an appeal made both in humility and with the courage to present the reasons that support its challenging message. It is clear that not everyone, not even all Christians, are in agreement with all the conclusions of the pastoral letter. Some would like to see a greater willingness to accept present governmental strategies, while others would urge a complete rejection of all warfare and the entire system of nuclear deterrence. The American bishops state their openness to ongoing dialogue with these views. But their letter is no middle-of-the-road document that seeks to split the difference between the views found within the church today. It is a prophetic advance and a call to the whole church to a significant new development in its centuries-old tradition of moral-religious reflection and action.

Chapter 11

Ethics in Distress: Can There Be Just Wars in the Nuclear Age?

In the recent literature on the ethics of war, a vocabulary has come increasingly into use that provides a point of entry into the current debate on justice and war in the nuclear age. If an index of key words in the recent ecclesiastical pronouncements and scholarly analyses of the ethics of warfare were available, the references under *crisis, emergency, tension,* and *distress* would direct one to some of the most challenging passages of these documents. Every sane person knows, of course, that the employment of a significant number of the nuclear weapons deployed today would be a crisis or emergency for humanity of extreme magnitude. My interest in this vocabulary, however, has a different and less apocalyptic focus. These words are used in contexts that suggest not only that the realities of contemporary nuclear strategy may be in conflict with the traditions of Western and Christian ethical thought, but also that we may be faced with policy choices that are simply not analyzable in terms of traditional moral categories. If this is the case, we would be confronted not only with the possible crisis of an actual nuclear war, but also with a crisis of moral reason itself. Ethics would itself be in distress. It is my intention in this chapter to examine the reasons that have led to the emergence of this language of distress, to ask whether these reasons really imply a crisis of moral reason, and to explore what can be done about this situation.

The Situation of Distress

It will be useful to begin by pointing out some of the passages I have in mind in the recent literature. They occur principally in the context of the discussion of the morality of nuclear deterrence, especially those forms of deterrence that threaten to attack urban populations. For example, the Roman Catholic bishops of France, in their pastoral letter of November 8, 1983, were willing to justify the threat to use the French *force de frappe* as a means of deterring both nuclear blackmail and actual Warsaw Pact aggression against France. They argued that a smaller power like France can achieve a "deterrence of the strong by the weak" through possession and threat to use weapons capable of inflicting "intolerable damage upon a much more powerful aggressor."[1] The bishops acknowledge that the French strategy involves a threat to attack cities, and point out that such countercity attacks were "condemned, clearly and without appeal" by the Second Vatican Council.[2] They then note that "threat is not use" and reply to the question of whether the immorality of use makes the threat immoral with a rather vague response: "That is not evident."[3] They are pressed to this conclusion by what they call "a logic of distress."[4] Indeed, they state that their conclusion embodies an "ethic of distress."[5] Their exact meaning here is not spelled out, but it does seem to imply the existence of an inner moral tension in their conclusion. It may even contain a moral contradiction that is made tolerable only by the present lack of more acceptable alternatives and that must be overcome as soon as possible. A "situation of distress" makes bedfellows of moral purpose and the threat to do the immoral.

The Catholic bishops of West Germany have been led to a similar sort of conclusion. They characterize their temporary tolerance of a threat to do that which they judge to be immoral as acceptance of an "emergency system (*Notordnung*)" that is needed until we can find an alternative.[6] The realities of the conflict between East and West press them to adopt an "emergency set of ethics (*Notstandethik*)."[7] The emergency to which they refer is the "immense tension" at the heart of nuclear strategy. This cord of tension has two strands.

The first concerns the *goals* of policy. Nuclear strategy seeks to defend against "injustice, oppression and totalitarian extortion." It also seeks to prevent the "horror" that war, conventional or nuclear, between the superpowers would bring.[8] These twin goals of the protection of justice and the prevention of war cannot be considered a single unified objective. Indeed, a single-minded pursuit of one of them can threaten the other. The relation between the dual ends of justice and peace has been analyzed extensively through the history of the just-war tradition. The German bishops suggest, however, that the nuclear weapons deployed on both sides of the East-West divide have raised it to a level that deserves to be called an emergency.

The second strand of policy concerns the *means* employed in nuclear strategy. Here the tension is between the direction in which these means carry us and the ends that have pressed us to develop these means. Nuclear-force structures and targeting doctrines are designed to protect justice and secure peace. There is a serious danger, however, that these means could subvert one or both of the goals they seek to secure. In fact, present nuclear strategies are based on means that, if used, would violate both just-war norms and fundamental human rights. The emergency ethic of which the German bishops speak is based on an acknowledgment that such a subversion of the ends of strategy by its means is a distinct possibility in the nuclear age. Their toleration of the legitimacy of these means, despite the risks entailed, is anguished: "By virtue of this decision we are choosing from among various evils the one which, as far as it is humanly possible to tell, appears as the smallest."[9] Their dissatisfaction with this "emergency ethic" is evident in their repeated plea that some better arrangement must be created. Although they express a true Christian trust that "with God all things are possible," nevertheless, their optimism on the political level is not great:

> Those who rely on this will never be able to accept the existing conditions (cf. Mk 9:23). Such people are summoned to hope against hope (cf. Rom 4:18). . . . We know from the gospel that this emergency is not the final word in worldly wisdom, for God's wisdom is not our wisdom.[10]

Here the German bishops come close to saying that efforts to bring nuclear strategy under the direction of moral reason have not succeeded and that our only recourse is to a religious trust that God will extract us from this situation of distress. This response, though understandable, is a curious one, for although Roman Catholic theology has a very strong doctrine of divine providence, it has never viewed God's providence and human responsibility as antithetical to each other. As Thomas Aquinas stated, human beings are rational beings and, as such, "participate in providence by their own providing for themselves and others."[11] The problem that leads the German bishops to this transmoral religious *cri de coeur* is that it is far from clear just how we are to provide for ourselves and others under the nuclear shadow.

Michael Walzer has stated the problem in the most explicit and challenging terms. Walzer is no utilitarian and therefore strongly rejects most tendencies to collapse the moral criteria for the justice of warfare into the single norm of proportionality. He sees efforts to determine the morality of warfare solely on the basis of a comparative weighing of goods and evils as stumbling on the difficulty of weighing different kinds of incommensurable values against each other.[12] Further, the norm of proportionality is a "weak constraint,"[13] lacking the "creative power"[14] to set definite limits on war. It must therefore be supplemented, as the just-war tradition has long known, by a firm principle of noncombatant immunity from direct attack.

Walzer, however, is prepared to suspend this noncombatant immunity constraint in the situation he calls "supreme emergency." The phrase, borrowed from Churchill, refers to military-political circumstances where the fundamental values of civilization are in imminent danger of being destroyed or overthrown.[15] Walzer appealed to this line of reasoning to justify the initial instances of British saturation bombing of German cities during World War II. In his view, there was simply no alternative way to resist the massive evil being perpetrated by the Nazi regime. Walzer argued that this justification ceased as soon as other means for defending the fundamental values of civilization became available.

The status of the moral justification Walzer offers for these indiscriminate area bombings, however, remains ambiguous. On the one hand, he declares them to be legitimate. On the other hand, he states that those who ordered and carried out the bombings must be willing to "accept the burdens of criminality here and now."[16] This criminality is not only a violation of a legal code but also a transgression of moral norms:

> The deliberate killing of the innocent is murder. Sometimes, in conditions of extremity (which I have tried to define and delimit) commanders must commit murder or they must order others to commit it. And then they are murderers, though in a good cause.[17]

Walzer is fully aware that this conclusion is self-contradictory. Although not all killing is immoral according to just-war tradition, all murder surely is. Murder, by definition, is unjustified killing. To declare it morally legitimate is to make a nonsensical statement: this act is both justified and unjustified at the same time. It is to state, in Walzer's own words, "that what was necessary and right was also wrong."[18] Such a conclusion brings ethics itself into a state of emergency or distress, and Walzer's otherwise highly regarded study has been criticized for it.[19]

Coherent and consistent moral reasoning on the British decision to bomb German cities would, if just-war norms are really binding, press one to the conclusion that John C. Ford reached while the war was still being fought:

> If anyone were to declare that modern war is necessarily total, and necessarily involves direct attack on the life of innocent civilians and, therefore, that obliteration bombing is justified, my reply would be: So much the

> worse for modern war. If it necessarily includes such means it is necessarily immoral itself.[20]

Although Walzer does not believe that all modern war is necessarily total, his book seems to suggest that when the defense of truly fundamental values can only be achieved through the violation of moral norms, we should say "so much the worse for morality." Supreme emergency seems to provide temporary license to go "beyond good and evil"; that is, it grants license to commit immoral acts in the defense of the truly basic values of civilization. Supreme emergency confronts us with a fundamental moral antinomy or aporia in which we cannot seek justice without performing injustice, or in which we cannot remain just without allowing injustice to destroy the very foundations of a just society.

Walzer's position on the saturation bombing of World War II is consequently imbued with a deep sense of tragedy. He struggles mightily to hedge it around with stringent limits in an attempt to prevent the principle of noncombatant immunity from becoming another casualty of modern war. As Lawrence Freedman and others have pointed out, however, the doctrines that have governed plans for the use of nuclear weapons had their origins in the pre-Hiroshima theories on the strategic use of air power that led to bomber attacks on cities.[21] From a moral point of view, the key debate about the morality of the use of nuclear weapons through much of the nuclear age has a shape similar to that of the debate about the legitimacy of these bombardments of cities with conventional weapons. It is undoubtedly true that the advent of nuclear weapons in 1945 and their subsequent development must be regarded as a qualitative transition in the moral problem of warfare.[22] Nevertheless, the decision to resort to strategic bombardment during World War II provided a precedent for the development of strategies of counterpopulation nuclear warfare. In his critique of Walzer's argument from supreme emergency—a critique that is directed at Walzer because his position represents the most analytically precise version of a view held by a number of others—Stephen Lammers highlights the significance of this moral (or immoral) precedent:

> It is true that politics includes single, unrepeated acts, the effects of which are quite limited. Politics also includes policy decisions which are implemented over time and which, when implemented, take on a life of their own. . . . In politics, a policy decision may lead to the creation of a social practice which becomes part of political life in the future. The evil that was supposed to be done at a given time may live on long after the conditions which made the policy "necessary" are past. Thus an evil determinate in kind may become indeterminate in duration.[23]

In fact, this is just what has happened to the temporary suspension of the principle of noncombatant immunity since World War II. Although there have been repeated efforts to provide alternatives to counterpopulation threats, the ultimate threat to attack cities has remained a permanent feature of the plans and the strategies of the nuclear powers. It is indeed fortunate that these strategies have not yet been carried into action; nevertheless, the mainstream version of nuclear strategy has continued to rely on a threat to violate this basic principle of the just-war tradition.

The dilemma posed by these strategies is evident in the discussions of nuclear deterrence in the recent European bishops' statements. Once again, however, Walzer's writing has the advantage of making this dilemma more explicit than do either the French or German bishops. He argues forcefully that the threat to attack civilians is itself immoral, even when this threat is part of a strategy of deterrence. It embodies a "commitment to murder."[24] Although he acknowledges that the threat to kill the innocent and the carrying out of this threat are very different things, they are very close on the level of intention. Counterpopulation deterrence—mutual assured destruction, (MAD), for example—must therefore be judged morally perverted even if it succeeds in preventing the outbreak of war. Here, however, what Lammers is worried about becomes most relevant: once noncombatant immunity is set aside in a situation of supreme emergency, a social practice is legitimated that will be very difficult to delegitimate in the future. This is so because technological capacities and ideological rivalries have created social conditions in which the great nuclear adversaries of today feel supremely threatened, and this threat bodes to be of indeterminate duration. As Walzer puts it:

> Supreme emergency has become a permanent condition. Deterrence is a way of coping with that condition, and though it is a bad way, there may be no other that is practical in a world of sovereign and suspicious states. We threaten evil in order not to do it, and the doing of it would be so terrible that the threat seems in comparison to be morally defensible.[25]

Here the same questions must be put to Walzer's approach to the ethics of deterrence that were raised concerning his legitimation of the early saturation bombing attacks of World War II. Is it based on a utilitarian moral theory, or is it really a suspension of morality itself? If the former is the case, he must bid adieu to the principle of noncombatant immunity as a relevant moral criterion in the current nuclear debate. Such an outcome would undermine his entire project of rethinking and developing the just-war tradition as an expression of a human-rights ethic. If, on the other hand, he sees it as a suspension of morality, then there is little point in discussing the ethics of nuclear strategy at all. In either case, a wide chasm has been opened up between the traditional ethics of warfare and the contemporary policy arguments. Walzer sees no way out of this: "Nuclear weapons explode the theory of just war. They are the first of mankind's technological innovations that are simply not encompassable within the familiar moral world."[26] Unless an alternative can be found to this situation, ethics itself will succumb to the incubus of nuclear distress.

The Pacifist Alternative

There are two different kinds of possible response to this distressing analysis. Both call for recasting the presuppositions that lead Walzer and the European bishops to adopt this questionable emergency ethic. The first calls for an abandonment of the presupposition that moral responsibility necessarily demands the taking up of the burdens of political responsibility. This position is, broadly speaking, pacifist and sectarian. It is represented in the current debate by theologians such as John Howard Yoder and Stanley Hauerwas. The second alternative rests on the view that the situation of distress created by nuclear weapons can be transformed by replacing deterrence based on the threat to attack population centers with deterrence based on a credible, counterforce warfighting capacity. This alternative appears today in a variety of versions, represented by moral and strategic thinkers such as James Johnson, Albert Wohlstetter, and William O'Brien.

The pacifism of Hauerwas and Yoder is based on an interpretation of the religious foundations of Christianity in the story of the people of Israel and the life, teaching, death, and resurrection of Jesus Christ. No moral thought that claims to be Christian can have any other ultimate basis. It is clear, however, that Hauerwas's version of an ethic of nonviolence is also based on an interpretation of our contemporary social, intellectual, and political situation. It is this latter interpretation that has led him to the conclusion that it is quite literally *impossible* to embody the ethical meaning of the Christian story in the political institutions and cultural patterns of modern Western society.

Here Hauerwas relies heavily on the reading of the development of modern Western intellectual and social history proposed by Alasdair MacIntyre, a philosopher who shares a strong sensitivity to the traditions of Western religious thought. As noted above in chapter five, MacIntyre believes that the philosophical and cultural situation of modern society has made it impossible to provide a rational account of the basis of morality that will be intelligible to all persons. Morality has become a domain of perpetual dispute and disagreement, not convergence and consensus. There appears to be "no rational way of securing moral agreement in our culture."[27] As an example of moral disagreement for which there seems no terminus, MacIntyre cites the debate between those who regard the threat of nuclear war as a reason that we all ought to be pacifists today and those who argue that we must be prepared to fight nuclear war if we wish to maintain peace. The impossibility of adjudicating these disagreements is the result of the fact "that modern moral utterance and practice can only be understood as a series of fragmented survivals from an older past and that the insoluble problems which they have generated for modern moral theorists remain insoluble until this is well understood."[28]

MacIntyre regards the present situation as a kind of new "dark ages," and he prescribes a remedy that is analogous to the creation of monasticism and the revived emphasis on virtuous life in community during the dying years of the Roman Empire:

> What matters at this stage is the construction of local forms of community within which civility and the intellectual and moral life can be sustained through the new dark ages which are already upon us. And if the tradition of the virtues was able to survive the horrors of the last dark ages, we are not entirely without grounds for hope.[29]

Although the cogency of MacIntyre's interpretation of our intellectual and social history need not detain us here (in my view it has both strengths and weaknesses), it is clear why Hauerwas appeals to it as a secular, philosophical warrant for the revival of a form of Christian sectarian pacifism. The "explosion" of the just-war theory is the result of the head-on collision of the principle of noncombatant immunity, which is rooted in a theory of human rights, with the principle of proportionality, which calls for the comparative weighing of relative goods and evils. The collision is evident in Walzer's writings, where a human-rights–based just-war theory conflicts with a form of utilitarianism in the situation of supreme emergency. It has become impossible to reconcile these two principles as long as our world is one where threats against populations are deterred by proportionate counterthreats of the same sort. Discrimination and proportionality in the present circumstances are but "fragmented survivals" uprooted from the moral tradition in which they initially germinated by the force of modern political and military realities.

The tradition that gave rise to classical just-war theory shares a common presupposition with the pacifist perspective advocated by Hauerwas. The common ground on which just-war theory and pacifism stand is the conviction that survival—even the survival of the most fundamental of this-worldly values—is not an absolute value.[30] Both the biblical eschatology that sees the kingdom of God as the ultimate reference point for ethical choice and the Christianized version of the Aristotelian teleological ethic developed by Thomas Aquinas relativize intraworldly values. They envision the possibility that these values may sometimes have to be sacrificed. Fidelity to the call of the kingdom of God or to the teleological ordering of human nature to union with God can come into conflict with the political values of justice and human rights in ultimately tragic circumstances, and these later values must sometimes give way.

It is fair to say, I think, that neither social-contract theory nor utilitarianism shares this perspective. For example, a perpetual problem with social-contract theories has been the difficulty of providing reasons that the contract should be kept when doing so will subvert the reasons that support the obligations to adhere to the contract in the first place—that is, universal protection of freedom and enlightened self-interest, including my own.[31] At the same time, contract theory cannot advance cogent reasons why the contract should be broken, for to do so would also deny the universally normative rationality on which it rests. This bind is evident in Walzer's conclusion that the suspension of noncombatant immunity in the supreme emergency is both right and wrong at the same time.

This sort of problem inevitably arises when an ethic is based on universal, rational principles that lack an eschatological or teleological point of reference. Both contract theory and utilitarianism force us into antinomies where we simply cannot know what we ought to do, not because of a lack of social or political knowledge, but because of the limits of the moral theories themselves. The upshot is an increased fragmentation of the human moral community as diverse solutions are asserted from different quarters. Hauerwas concludes, therefore, that modern intellectual categories and social institutions make it impossible to develop an argument about the morality of nuclear strategy that has a chance of universal acceptance. He believes we must be prepared to accept the "dividedness" of the world, even on this fundamental moral level. He goes further than MacIntyre here, for it is not simply the loss of an Aristotelian teleological framework that has brought this dividedness about. From a Christian perspective, it must be this way, since the hope for a reconciled world is necessarily eschatological—it can be realized only beyond history. Therefore, the quest for a universal set of moral norms that can order a divided community in accord with reason is illusory.[32]

One can therefore interpret Hauerwas as implying that *all* contemporary normative ethical systems are in some sense sectarian. Or, better, there is no universal moral rationality to opt out of as the Troeltschian typology suggests "sect-type" religious groups are wont to do. All moral traditions are historybound and tied to the narratives and traditions of the communities that form them. Therefore, Christian pacifism cannot be charged with being morally deficient because it does not propose a political ethic capable of regulating the life of society as a whole on the basis of universal rational principles. In Hauerwas's view, all the competing normative visions available are subject to this charge as well. In addition, Christian pacifism has a distinct advantage over those systems that would justify violence for the enforcement of a partial ethical vision. It does not claim to be operating on the basis of universal rationality, but it acknowledges that it is shaped by a particular narrative tradition: the story of Israel and of Jesus Christ. It does not abandon the *hope* for universal reconciliation and the full achievement of justice and peace in society, but it regards this hope as eschatological and to be fulfilled by the action of God, not by human force of arms.

Neither does this sort of Christian pacifism believe that all normative visions are equally true. Rather, it holds that the ethics of nonviolence is in fact the true perspective, and that this truth is verified in the experience of the nonviolent community. Such a concrete historical experience of justice and peace in community is in fact the only basis for judging the truth or falsity of normative frameworks. Thus convincing those with other convictions to change their stance can only be done by inviting them to share this experience and providing an alternative community in which this experience is available to them. As Hauerwas puts it:

> We have no guarantee, of course, that others will accept such a way of life, but Christians must live with the confidence that others will find that such a life frees them from the fears that give birth to slavery and injustice. God has promised the church that if we are faithful our life will not be without effect. The church's task does not depend on nor is it sustained by such effectiveness, however; it is sustained by our experience that by living faithfully we do find God in the truth of our existence.[33]

This, I take it, is the sort of thing MacIntyre has in mind when he says that modern society, living under the threat of insoluble moral conflicts, is waiting not for Godot, but for a new St. Benedict.

I have discussed Hauerwas and MacIntyre at some length for two reasons. Their interrelated viewpoints are a relatively sophisticated reflection of an attitude that is increasingly present on the popular level of the nuclear debate—namely, that it is next to impossible consistently to relate moral norms to today's highly complex strategic arguments. For Hauerwas and MacIntyre, this is simply a particular case of the problem of relating moral norms to a form of rationality that has lost its teleological connection with ends and its religious connection with eschatological hope. On this level I am in full agreement with them. This is not to say that morality is impossible without religion (an issue that I prefer to leave to another occasion). Rather, it reflects a conviction that a loss of a sense of the historical possibilities for changing the present terms of the debate leads to an ethical dead end. Teleological and eschatological dimensions in ethics keep this from happening as neither social-contract theory nor utilitarianism can do. An ethic that starts and ends within the boundaries of the present conflict-ridden situation cannot fail to lead to insoluble puzzles. Ethics is meant to transform the human condition from what it is to what it could be, not simply to help us better understand the conflicting values of our world. For this reason I welcome the challenge from this quarter.

The second reason for considering this approach is to criticize it constructively in the hope of moving the debate on the relation of morality and nuclear policy to a more fruitful level. Despite Hauerwas's strong desire to move us out of the present bind by his appeal to an eschatological hope, he lacks principles that can guide policy in a historically incremental way. His view goes beyond an "ethics of distress" to the proclamation of the death of political ethics as this term is normally understood. This is because Hauerwas, in contrast to Augustine and Paul Ramsey, rejects the value of norms for distinguishing between more and less perfect forms of justice and peace in the earthly city.[34] He draws a stark contrast between the absolute peace and justice of the kingdom of God and the injustice and violence of the world of power politics. For Ramsey, following Augustine, the picture is considerably more complex than this.

In Augustine and Ramsey, the city of God and the earthly city cannot be identified with distinct communities in history—for example, the church and the Roman Empire or a contemporary pacifist community and the superpowers. The two "cities" coexist together in all things human, whether these be nation-states, churches, or even individuals. The ethical task, then, is transformation, not a division into sheep and goats. And it is the norms of the just-war tradition that guide us as we seek this transformation of a world that is a mixture of good and evil. This tradition situates conflict in a historical, developmental framework and demands that we seize every opportunity to further this transformation, while recognizing that it will always be incomplete within history. This Augustinian perspective, in other words, does not deny the moral tensions inherent in political life, but it does refuse to allow tension to become dualism or to explode into self-contradiction.

Ethics and Limited War

This transformationist Augustinian interpretation of political ethics and just-war theory may provide a clue to how we can move beyond the distressing state of the current debate on the relation of morality and nuclear war. The explosion of the just-war theory described by Walzer is the result of the presence of immoral intentions in MAD deterrence theories. The strategic debates of the 1960s had sought to find an alternative to this sort of deterrence by proposing a variety of counterforce strategies that could in fact serve as a credible deterrent without threatening to attack civilians directly. That debate, Walzer concludes, petered out in the mid-1960s when the extent of collateral damage to civilians by most imaginable counterforce attacks and the high likelihood of escalation of any superpower conflict to a catastrophic nuclear war became clear.[35] Walzer's conclusion in 1977 was similar to the one reached more recently by Lawrence Freedman:

> The position we have reached is one where stability depends on something that is more the antithesis of strategy than its apotheosis—on threats that things will get out of hand, that we might act irrationally, that possibly through inadvertance we could set in motion a process that in its development and conclusion would be beyond human control and comprehension.[36]

Nuclear strategy is a mixture of good intentions and evil threats. It is a construct of human rationality that only "works" because of our fear that human beings will act irrationally and immorally. Its consequences might be peace of a sort, a catastrophic war, or a long twilight struggle of uncertainty and doubt.

Nuclear strategy, we might say, is a quintessentially Augustinian phenomenon. It is virtually impossible to untangle the good and the evil elements in it. The good is an aspect of the evil, and the evil both the source and the possible outcome of the good it seeks to achieve. Just as the robber bands that Augustine described in the *City of God* had their own form of justice, so the darkness of nuclear strategy does contain a measure of rational purpose within it. But they *were* robbers, and the strategy *remains* full of demonic potential. We cannot simply accept it, nor can we simply reject it. The pacifist risks the loss of the good it can achieve by making aversion to the evil in it the sole basis of decision.

Walzer and the European bishops are more cautious, because their basic adherence to just-war tradition has given them a more Augustinian political sensibility. They recognize that rejection of deterrence could have a terrible price, and their acceptance of it is reluctant and even tortured. They call for the creation of alternatives to a system that seeks to "win the peace" by threatening civilian populations. But neither really says much about what these alternatives might be. This is understandable in Walzer's case, I believe, because the alternatives that are currently being proposed were still in gestation as he wrote his book. I am less willing to grant the French bishops this excuse, for when they wrote their letter in 1983 a wide array of alternatives to MAD not only were under discussion but were being translated into policy. As Stanley Hoffmann has noted, the French bishops seem insufficiently aware of the new technologies and strategic doctrines that make counterforce deterrence and defense the moral point at issue in the current debate.[37] By provisionally legitimating countervalue deterrence, they not only acquiesce in the explosion of the just-war theory, but also, because they do not take the newer strategic proposals into account, implicitly legitimate policies they seem not to have considered. The lack of attention to the specifics of these new strategic doctrines is also a problem with the German bishops' document, although I suspect the reasons for it were more political than in the case of the French.

The Augustinian view of political ethics should put us on guard against this sort of reluctance to take seriously the concrete possibilities of changing the dangerous situation we are in. Augustinian thinking does not expect to be able to untangle all the moral threads of political life. But it is equally insistent that history is an open system, capable of change and movement. The way we respond to the openings for the enhancement of justice and community among peoples and for the reduction of injustice and violence is an index of whether our polity is simply a band of murderers and robbers or something better than this. MAD seeks to establish a form of justice, but it is the justice of a murderous world. The issue is this: What can be done to transform it?

It is here that the various counterforce nuclear strategies under consideration today demand scrutiny from a moral perspective. I have argued in an earlier chapter that it is impossible to reach moral conclusions about nuclear deterrence and defense in the abstract. It is the abstraction from actual and concrete policy choices that induces the internal emergency or distress within ethics itself. If we fail to consider actual concrete alternatives to the morally self-contradictory strategy of MAD, we foreclose the possibility that ethical principles can transform the situation into one that is less dangerous and more just.

It is precisely this search for alternatives that can be found in contemporary discussions of whether there is a possibility of creating a strategy for the deterrence of war through a credible, counterforce threat that would itself meet the norms of discrimination and proportionality proposed by the just-war theory. The advocates of such limited nuclear-war strategies all admit that there is a grave level of uncertainty over whether these limits would in fact be respected should deterrence fail. They differ in how they actually conceive these limits. Albert Wohlstetter believes that targets should be limited to the military and that strict limits on collateral civilian damage are necessary.[38] Colin Gray would expand these limits to include the military and political leadership of the adversary, an expansion that renders a "decapitating" first strike at least imaginable.[39] William V. O'Brien stretches the limits even further, when he argues that strategic attacks on cities could conceivably be part of a "limited" war where they were carried out for purposes of intrawar deterrence—that is as a means of dissuading an adversary from taking further escalating steps that will likely lead to holocaust.[40]

In considering these proposals for moving away from MAD and toward a strategy that seeks to adhere to just-war norms, the problem is evident: the boundaries between counterforce and countervalue strategies are very tenuous indeed. We seem almost inevitably pushed to the conclusion, reached by Walzer and Freedman, that any sort of deterrence works only because of the fear that things will get out of control. In my view, the proposals of both Colin Gray and William O'Brien are virtually indistinguishable from MAD. If actually carried out, both seem certain to produce a form of spasmodic or indiscriminate response and counterresponse that would be impossible to distinguish from the failure of MAD. The danger of both proposals is increased by the fact that both Gray's decapitation strategies and O'Brien's limited-war proposals depend on the deployment of first-strike–capable weapons—a sure formula for making deterrence less stable. Therefore, neither of them, in my view, really represents the desired transformation of our political/military circumstances in accord with the Augustinian imperative. Both leave the situation of distress much as it was.

The case of Wohlstetter is more complex. His statement that we must "face up to evasions making 'murder respectable' in such chaste phrases as 'countervalue attacks' " seems clearly to rule out O'Brien's rather expansive version of the nature of limited war.[41] His view that Soviet leaders value military power as much as they do civilian populations has analogies with Colin Gray's emphasis on the value of political control in the Soviet system, a valuation that leads Gray to think that threat of decapitation will be such a strong deterrent to Soviet adventures. Wohlstetter does not seem to advocate this approach, but neither does he rule it out. His real concern is that MAD not only is an immoral strategy but is actually incredible as a deterrent, because it rests on an insane threat to commit suicide. His desire to develop a limited-war strategy as an alternative to MAD is supported by both moral and political reason. In this he is on solid Augustinian ground.

One of the chief problems with his approach, however, is his tendency to identify "minimum deterrence" with MAD. This use of language, which is not Wohlstetter's creation, introduces a conceptual confusion into the contemporary debate. It suggests that *increases in our war-fighting capacity* necessarily move us away from the specter of mutual destruction. This is not necessarily so. In fact, it may have the opposite effect, depending on *what kind* of war-fighting capacities are developed. For example, the Scowcroft commission proposed the development and deployment of both the MX and single-warhead mobile missiles. These two systems are both war-fighting weapons, designed for deterrence through a credible threat. But the threat posed by the two weapons to an adversary is significantly different. In my view, the replacement of MIRVed Minuteman missiles with the single-warhead mobile missile would be a step toward a "more minimal" deterrent than the one we now have, whereas MX is a move toward a "more maximal" one, if *minimal* and *maximal* are used to refer to the dangers they present. This would still entail a severe danger that nuclear war could occur. But the danger would be less than under the present arrangement and much less than in the world of vulnerable first-strike weapons we are moving into. Wohlstetter's polemic against minimal deterrence needs to be refined by distinctions like these. One can also ask: do not such distinctions enable us to imagine ways that large numbers of currently deployed nuclear weapons in our supposedly minimal deterrent could be replaced by conventional forces, including conventionally armed precision-guided missiles. Wohlstetter himself suggests this, but I would be much happier if he had more carefully explored the possible meanings of minimal deterrence before accepting the convention of identifying the idea with MAD. Such an exploration could open the way for us to seize opportunities to transform the grossly murderous logic of present strategy into something that is at least less murderous if not truly pacific.

In my opinion, this is the avenue that the U.S. Catholic bishops have taken in the pastoral letter *The Challenge of Peace*. This is not the place for a detailed analysis of this complex document.[42] One point, however, is notable in the context of this discussion. The U.S. bishops do not advocate minimal deterrence in the sense presupposed by Wohlstetter—that is, MAD. Indeed, they oppose it vigorously: "It is not morally acceptable to intend to kill the innocent as part of a strategy of deterring nuclear war."[43] At the same time they argue against forms of deterrence that will increase the danger of nuclear war or that target military forces in ways that are likely to produce disproportionate collateral damage:

> While we welcome any effort to protect civilian populations, we do not want to legitimize or encourage moves which extend deterrence beyond the specific objectives of preventing the use of nuclear weapons or other actions which could lead directly to a nuclear exchange.[44]

With these criteria as background, they consider specific alternatives to MAD and their implications for the quest for the goals of nuclear-war prevention and the defense of justice and human rights.

Their specific conclusions are an attempt to direct policy into avenues that are less dangerous than some of the war-fighting strategies being proposed (for example, that of Colin Gray); less open-ended than others (for example, those of Wohlstetter); and less inconsistent with just-war norms than a third type of limited-war doctrine (for example, those of O'Brien). The conclusions they draw are largely negative: no hard-target kill weapons, no protracted war scenarios, no quest for superiority, no systems which make disarmament more difficult to achieve.[45] They also make a number of positive recommendations, largely in the areas of the need for negotiated arms-control treaties; removal of nuclear forces from forward-based positions in Europe; and improved command, control, and communication systems.[46]

Some have argued that the U.S. bishops have moved to a level of specificity that goes beyond their competence as moral teachers in making recommendations of this sort. On the contrary, attending to the actual proposals being made today is really the *only* way to reach conclusions about the relation of morality to nuclear strategy. To argue against this level of specificity in addressing nuclear questions would be analogous to saying that moral teachers should speak about the morality of medicine but should never discuss any specific medical procedure. This would be absurd, for there is no such thing as the morality of medicine as such. One could say, of course, that if there had never been a fall from grace by Adam and Eve, there would be no sickness and death in our world, as Genesis, St. Paul, and the Christian tradition have long taught. But in a fallen and divided world, sickness exists, doctors are needed, and ethical perspectives on their practice are a legitimate concern of theologians, philosophers, and bishops, not just of the physicians themselves. The same can be said of the ethics of warfare. It depends on an analysis of the pathways that are open to us for healing political conflict and avoiding actions that make the illness worse.

In my view, the U.S. bishops have done as good a job as anyone has in synthesizing the religious, philosophical, political, and military dimensions of the nuclear issue. There are, however, limits to their achievement. In particular, I think more needs to be said about defensive systems and the various types of weapons proposed as replacements for MIRVed missiles. Can any of these serve the purposes of minimal deterrence as the term has been redefined here—that is, as minimally dangerous? Despite these limits, the U.S. bishops' letter serves as an example of moral reasoning that seeks to avoid the self-contradiction of the "ethics of distress." As good practitioners of Augustinian moral theory, they seek to transform and redeem a broken polis by seizing those opportunities for peace, order, and justice that history has given us today. Although their work hardly closes the debate, it does provide a model for avoiding some of the dead ends into which we have wandered.

Part Five

Social Ethics and the Church's Pastoral Life

Chapter 12

A Prophetic Church and the Sacramental Imagination

A central question in the effort to clarify the role of Christians in a pluralistic society concerns the social role of the church precisely as a corporate community. The Second Vatican Council strongly emphasized the communitarian nature of Christian existence:

> At all times and among every people, God has given welcome to whosoever fears him and does what is right (cf. Acts 10:35). It has pleased God, however, to make men and women holy and save them not merely as individuals without any mutual bonds, but by making them into a single people, a people which acknowledges him in truth and serves him in holiness.[1]

Though Christian faith is an eminently personal act that relates the believer to God, it is never the act of an individual apart from the church as a community of faith. Thus it is evident that the Christian vocation to work for greater justice and peace in society must be a communal undertaking. At the same time, however, the Christian community's role in society is different from that of a political party or an organized special-interest group. This chapter will explore several dimensions of the distinctively communal aspects of the Christian social mission and suggest that they have important implications for the whole of its life and ministry.

The first part of the chapter outlines some of the ambiguities that make the question of the corporate role of the church in society so confusing to many today. These ambiguities have their roots in the tensions between the sacred and secular dimensions of human existence. The second section will review some recent theological proposals concerning the scope and limits of the corporate role of the church in the social sphere. This review leads to the conclusion that recent discussions have given insufficient attention to the power of shared religious experience as a base of communal social action. In the third and concluding section, the sacramental character of distinctively Catholic forms of religious experience will be explored as an energizing and directing source of common Christian action. More specifically, it will argue that the Catholic sacramental imagination can be a rich resource for prophetic action of the church in the social and political spheres.

Sources of Ambiguity

Illumination of the corporate dimensions of the action of Christians in the spheres of social and political justice has been in scarce supply in the writings of recent theologians. Theological opinions are plentiful, but they conflict with one another or emphasize only a single aspect of the problem. The cause of the relatively confused state of theological reflection in this area is twofold.

First, the question of the proper scope of communal Christian action in the social sphere contains within itself a number of other extremely thorny theological questions that are urgently being debated within the church today. A partial list of these other issues includes the following: the scope and limits of pluralism with the church; the role of the teaching office; the internal structures of participation and decision-making; the distinction of various ministries in the church; the relation between universal Christian beliefs and the particularities of diverse cultures; the relation of general moral rules and individual conscience, and the relevance of the social sciences to the development of Christian ethics. All of these problems converge in the discussion of the church's role in the promotion of justice.

The second source of the present uncertainty about the communal and institutional dimensions of the contribution of faith to the realization of justice is the result of structural and historical factors in modern Western society. For the past several hundred years, approximately since the Enlightenment, the assumption that Christian faith is the primary integrating and organizing principle for Western social institutions has been gradually losing its plausibility. The activities and patterns of thinking necessary to keep our society running have become progressively more specialized and differentiated from one another. Max Weber has called this differentiation a process of "rationalization" leading to the "disenchantment of the world." It is a process by which "the ultimate and most sublime values have retreated from public life either into the transcendental realm of mystic life or into the brotherliness of direct and personal human relations."[2] One of the consequences of increasing specialization in both thought and action has been the differentiation of corporate religious associations from the political and economic spheres. This is most evident in the demise of Christendom and the separation of church and state, though this political phenomenon is but the tip of a much larger social, economic, and cultural iceberg.

The differentiation of the institutional church from other areas of social organization creates problems that must be addressed positively if Christianity is to fulfill its mission of justice. Secularization, in Karl Rahner's words, signifies "the growing influence of 'world' (as the outcome of human ingenuity) and the process by which it becomes increasingly autonomous and separates itself more and more from the church considered as a social entity in the world."[3] The legitimate autonomy of the political arena, expressed in the principles of religious liberty and separation of church and state, raises serious questions about the possibility of common Christian action for justice. If common action is to be effective in a bureaucratic society it must be organized action. There is a strong cultural bias present in our society that results in the misinterpretation of any public or political activity by the church as a violation of the separation of church and state. Thus the secularization of the state, the economy, and the broader sphere of culture can be read as a powerful source of the privatization of religious belief—the withdrawal of religious experience into the spheres of personal salvation and the immediate interpersonal relationships of the family and the primary group. Cultural pressure to keep the Christian community's action in society noninstitutionalized also leads to the fragmentation of Christian efforts to bring greater justice to social organizations. It often leads to the view that religiously motivated actions by individuals are legitimate expressions of religious liberty while such actions by organized groups or churches are attempts at reestablishment. Thus both of these tendencies of the contemporary Western structural relation between religion and society—the privatization and the fragmentation of religious influence in society—seem undesirable if one is convinced of the essentially communal nature of Christian faith and its internal demand for the promotion of justice in society.

Recent attempts to find a way around these tendencies toward privatization and fragmentation without moving back to a kind of neo-Christendom tend in two directions.[4] The first emphasizes commonly shared ethical principles and universalizable imperatives. It views the public role of the church as a prophetic one, and describes the content of the prophecy as both general ethical principles and specific social imperatives derived from a combination of theological and social analysis. This approach stresses argument and analysis as the base of the prophetic role that the church can play in addressing problems such as war, disarmament, economic exploitation, political oppression, and racism.

The second approach emphasizes the lived reality of Christian identity and experience. It attempts to describe the prophetic function of the church by beginning with the self-identity of the Christian community and the experience of Christians who are engaged in efforts to overcome injustice. The emphasis here is on the resources for public action that arise from the Christian's experience of life as shaped by the church as a community of belief in Jesus Christ. In recent Roman Catholic literature this second emphasis has been crystallized around the ancient theological motif of the church as the fundamental sacrament of Christ's active presence in the world. The living experience of Christian community is the fundamental sign of God's gracious intentions for the whole of humanity, not just for those who are formal members of the church.[5] This sacramental approach has parallels in modern Protestant theology. For example, Karl Barth has argued that the identity of the church as a community that exists to serve the kingdom of God is an identity that calls Christians "to regard the existence of the state as an allegory, as a correspondence and an analogue to the kingdom of God which the church preaches and believes in."[6] Both the recent Catholic sacramental approach and Barth's allegorical approach presuppose that the living experience of grace realized within the community of the church is in some way analogous to and correlated with the fundamental normative structure of social life.

These two theological approaches to the prophetic role of the church, that of principles and imperatives and that of identity and experience, are attempts to gain a perspective on the social roles of the Christian which avoid the twin pitfalls of privatism and individualism. They presume that either commonly shared ethical principles and generally plausible social analysis or common Christian identity and shared experience can counteract the cultural tendencies toward privatization and fragmentation. The disagreements in the recent theological literature reveal that both approaches contain serious difficulties.

Some Recent Approaches to the Prophetic Role of the Church

Recent discussions of the prophetic role of the church in society have been especially concerned with the common voice of the church as exercised through official statements and public moral teaching. In the Roman Catholic church, the questions of the teaching role of bishops, the pope, national and regional conferences, synods, and ecumenical councils have largely set the agenda for the discussion. This public teaching function has also received considerable attention from Protestant theologians, for what is at stake here is not simply the particular conception of moral and doctrinal authority found in recent Catholic tradition. More basically the question is that of the possibility of any Christian communion coming to that level of consensus on social and political problems that is necessary if prophetic statements are to be made in the name of the church as a whole. None of the participants in the discussions doubts that the church can and should speak to the moral values, attitudes, and general principles involved in public life. The disagreements concern the ability of the corporate voice of the church to propose concrete and particular actions as morally obligatory. There is also significant divergence of opinion on the way the church as a corporate body should come to conclusions about the demands of justice in society.

Paul Ramsey's writings, especially his polemical critique of the 1966 World Council of Churches' Conference on Church and Society,[7] present a vigorous argument against the drive toward detailed and particularized ethical prescriptions in public church statements. Ramsey regards the attempt of church bodies to prescribe concrete solutions in areas such as disarmament policy, nuclear strategy, and the Vietnam War as the result of a misinterpretation of the nature of political decision. It also stems from an overestimation of the practical wisdom of the church. The church does not have the political and technical competence to know either what is possible or what is best in such complex areas of international political life. Political decisions and policy-making are prudential decisions demanding knowledge of the real alternatives and the likely consequences of various courses of action. Though political decisions involve fundamental values and principles, in the end the formation of policy and the choice of concrete action are always the result of practical decision rather than of theoretical knowledge. Because of this prudential and contingent nature of political decisions, concrete directives for action cannot be unambiguously deduced from Christian faith. The possession of Christian faith does not give persons any special skills in international economics or diplomacy. In Ramsey's words: "Prudential political advice comes into the public forum with no special credentials because it issues from Christians or from Christian religious bodies."[8]

Thus the church's attempts to recommend policy and specific action are based on a confusion about the nature of both politics and the church. In Ramsey's view, the church's public function is the more limited but no less important task of providing perspectives on social and political issues that are rooted in and warranted by the Christian faith.[9] These perspectives, Ramsey is careful to note, must be more than pious generalities such as "feed the hungry" or "abolish war." They must be action-oriented and decision-oriented principles or directions (as opposed to specific directives) that positively illuminate the kinds of public decisions that in fact must be made. The public task before the church is the development of "decision-oriented or action-oriented (relevant) social and political analysis" that will serve to cultivate the political ethos of a nation and inform the consciences of its statesmen.[10] In Ramsey's view, therefore, it will only be on the rarest occasions that the church is in a position to advocate a specific and concrete form of social action as the only Christian alternative. The ordinary and more important function of its prophetic role in society is that of developing the principles and advocating the Christian perspectives that should shape the day-by-day decisions of citizens and public figures.

Ramsey believes that the move toward concrete and particularized statements in recent church documents has been the result of a rather superficial attempt to achieve ecumenical consensus on individual policy issues. This effort has distracted the churches from the more fundamental and important attempt to achieve consensus on basic ethical principles and action-oriented theological perspectives.[11] In Ramsey's view, the traditional Roman Catholic emphasis on general norms is more likely to produce genuine ecumenical consensus in the sphere of social justice. It is also more likely to have a lasting impact on perduring patterns of social relationship.

James M. Gustafson has written concerning the documents of the World Council of Churches in a similarly critical vein. Gustafson, with Ramsey, is dissatisfied with the lack of sufficient theological warrant for the particular moral judgments contained in these documents. The legitimacy of advocating any policy proposal or decision as Christian depends on showing how it fits into a moral vision of the world that is shaped by the central religious symbols and convictions that form the identity of the Christian community. As Gustafson put it, "If there is any common faith and loyalty in the Christian community, that faith and loyalty is the center from which moral outlooks and opinions ought to be formed."[12]

This stress on the theological center of Christian social opinions and strategy common to both Gustafson and Ramsey speaks not only to the Protestant churches but also to Roman Catholicism. In the modern Roman Catholic social tradition before the Second Vatican Council the chief warrants for specific ethical conclusions were drawn from a form of natural-law theory. This theory was used in a way that frequently reinforced traditional ethical conclusions. For example, the right to private property, the necessity of political inequality, the illegitimacy of contraception, and the subordination of woman to man in both family and society were all justified primarily by nontheological appeals to the law of nature. Theological and biblical appeals were then used to reinforce these nontheological arguments. It does not seem to be an accident that since Vatican II the more direct appeal to the central religious symbols of Christian faith has opened up Catholic social thought to a new period of creativity and moved many groups within the church toward a positive commitment to social change.[13] The use of biblical teachings concerning the love commandment, the actions and teachings of Jesus, the motifs of covenant and liberation, and the doctrine of Christian freedom have stimulated a new dynamism and critical spirit in Catholic social ethics.

The need for an explicitly Christian foundation for the church's public activity called for by Ramsey and Gustafson has been addressed in the writings of a group of European theologians, both Catholic and Protestant, who have come to be known as "political theologians." The three leading members of this group are Jürgen Moltmann, Wolfhart Pannenberg, and Johannes B. Metz. The eschatological promise of the final coming of the kingdom of God is the central theological motif that they use in interpreting the church-society relationship. Neither church nor society can be identified with the kingdom. Neither church nor society can be expected to be transformed into the kingdom on earth. The church, however, is the bearer of a vision of the ultimate and absolute future of all humanity—a vision of the kingdom of God which, "far from being a merely formalistic idea, is the utterly concrete reality of justice and love."[14] In the eschatological perspective of these writers this concrete justice and love has its reality as promise, a reality known through faith in the resurrection of Christ. Christian faith sees the world's ultimate meaning as based on the trustworthiness of this promise. The church's mission is that of pointing toward the kingdom which has not yet been fully achieved and offering humanity the hope that God will remain faithful to this promise of justice and love. The church's prophetic role, therefore, is to keep history open to the fulfillment of this promise. Its task is "to resist the institutional stabilizing of things, and by 'raising the question of meaning' to make things uncertain and keep them moving and elastic in the process of history."[15]

Consequently, Moltmann, Pannenberg, and Metz view the church's role as essentially that of offering a public critique of the institutions of society in the light of the kingdom. "The Church must always witness to the limitations of any given society. The very existence of the Church depends upon its playing this critical role. When this critical witness is abandoned, the Church becomes superfluous."[16] Prophecy, then, is the largely negative task of criticizing the ideological tendencies of all political and historical attempts to capture the transcendent meaning of justice and love within a political program or social system. The importance of this negative task, Metz maintains, should not be underestimated.

> There is to it an elementary positive power of mediation. Even if we cannot directly and immediately agree as to the positive content of freedom, peace, and justice, yet we have a long and common experience with their contraries, the lack of freedom, justice, and peace. This negative experience offers us a chance for consensus, less in regard to the positive aspect of the freedom and justice we are seeking, than in regard to our critical resistance against the dread and terror of no freedom and no justice. The solidarity which grows out of this experience offers the possibility of a common front of protest.[17]

Moltmann, Pannenberg, and Metz, therefore, have produced a strong theological argument for the engagement of the church in the struggle for the transformation of the structures of society. Because of the link they see between the kingdom of God and the future of all humanity, their theologies are strong arguments against the privatization of religion. It is not clear, however, that they provide a view of the church/society relationship that resists the pressure toward the fragmentation of Christian action that is exerted by modern institutional differentiation and specialization. This differentiation has revealed the relativity and partiality of all social roles, institutional structures, and specialized methods of social analysis. The recognition of this relativity is a prime source of the fear of ideology that runs through the new political theology, the fear of attaching even quasi-absolute significance to any concrete social institution. The stress on social critique as the primary public role of the church is a manifestation of this fear. Though the fear is legitimate, Metz's confidence that the corporate solidarity of Christian action in society can be built and sustained on this negative base seems unjustified. Corporate solidarity necessarily entails some positive intrahistorical loyalties. In other words, communal Christian action in society demands the presence of commitment to some norms for social life that concretize the Christian vision of social existence even though they do not provide a total description of the kingdom of God.

Both James Gustafson and Gustavo Gutierrez have voiced a somewhat similar criticism of Moltmann, Pannenberg, and Metz, though from two quite different perspectives. Gustafson believes that if the theological insights of this political theology are to have a genuine public relevance, its advocates must assume the intellectual responsibility for showing their positive social and political implications. The new political theology must be converted into a Christian social ethics. The critical approach is not enough, from either a pragmatic or theoretical point of view. Gustafson calls on the political theologians to recognize "the necessity of persuasive rational moral discourse which would convert what is said into terms and arguments that would be more effective in giving directions and control to various social policy proposals."[18] Gutierrez, from a different point of view, believes that this conversion of theological perspective into positive social commitment demands both experiential engagement in conflicts and struggles of society and a greater employment of the analyses of these conflicts provided by the social sciences.[19] Both Gustafson and Gutierrez argue that a theological perspective, though essential to the elaboration of the positive role of the church, must be correlated with philosophical and social-scientific reflection on the lived experiences of contemporary social struggles and problems.

Edward Schillebeeckx and Karl Rahner are in agreement with Gustafson and Gutierrez that human experience of the social struggle for justice must be correlated with philosophical and social-scientific reflection if the theological vision of Christianity is to have public influence.[20] They raise a number of questions, however, about the relation between the experiential and the theoretical components of this correlation. With Ramsey, neither Schillebeeckx nor Rahner conceives this correlation as a relation of logical entailment or rational deduction. One cannot produce a concrete and specific ethical conclusion about social policy by beginning with theological principles and then arguing syllogistically to an unavoidable decision for a specific action. The relation of theory and practice is not a relation between axioms or first principles and their necessary corollaries. Such a conception, Rahner states, is the foundation of a theological "integralism" or religious hegemony that is insufficiently aware of the freedom and creativity of all truly human action. In Rahner's words:

> Integralism in this sense implicitly presupposed that in his acts man simply puts his theory into practice, and that the world and its history, considered as the material field in which these acts of his are posited, is sufficiently predicable, malleable and submissive to his will, to make such a procedure possible. Integralism in this sense, therefore, entails a failure to recognize that the "practical intellect" has an element of the autonomous in it. Its act of apprehension can be achieved only within the context of the free decision as actually posited in hope.[21]

The acknowledgment of the presence of freedom within the practical intellect implies that the correlation of the theological, philosophical, and sociological theories with lived human experience is a synthetic art involving the creativity of human imagination. It is not an analytic act of dissection and deduction. The need for synthesis does not arise simply from the inadequacy of theological principles to produce specific determinations of concrete action. The same inadequacy is present in the principles of social theory and moral philosophy. In Schillebeeckx's view, theoretical formulations, whether theological, philosophical, or sociological, are always partial explications of the reality that is at stake in social interaction and the struggle for justice—the human person created and redeemed by God. It is precisely because the person has a worth and individual uniqueness that transcends the categories of theoretically elaborated principles that the decisions of practical reason are both necessary and possible. From this Schillebeeckx draws the following conclusion about the limited usefulness of general ethical principles in the public teaching of the church:

> Abstract pronouncements cannot seize hold of the reality simply *by themselves;* if they nevertheless possess a realistic value, this can only be derived from our total experience of reality. . . . Only and exclusively as intrinsically individualized is "being human" a reality and can it be the source of moral norms (which, in religious parlance, we can rightly describe as the will of God). Therefore, there is only one source of ethical norms, namely, the historical reality of the value of the inviolable human person with all its bodily and social implications. That is why we cannot attribute validity to abstract norms as such.[22]

Both Rahner and Schillebeeckx, therefore, affirm that the correlation of the theological, philosophical, and social-scientific insight must take place within the broader context of living experience of the social situation and of the dignity of the persons who live within this situation. For the church, moral principles retain an important role in shaping the decisions reached by practical reason, for they represent a theoretical crystallization of theological reflection on the past experience of the Christian community. In the present, however, the function of these principles is almost exclusively negative. They set limits for Christian action, but do not define a unique path of conduct for all Christians.[23] Moreover, many of the struggles of the human race that call out to the Christian conscience today are genuinely new. The need for common action in addressing problems such as world hunger, rapid population growth, nuclear warfare, and the changing roles of women in society will not be met by a simple reiteration of moral principles formulated in a world where such problems did not exist. Schillebeeckx has observed that these principles "are the tail end of a preceding history, while the future must be prepared by historical decisions and moral imperatives."[24]

Rahner and Schillebeeckx are concerned, then, with broadening the debate about the social role of the church beyond the theoretical domain where theological doctrines, philosophical analysis, and socioscientific theories can be interwoven without leading to a sense of direction for the church. Their concern is the same as Ramsey's, though they are much less confident than he that such a sense of direction can be discovered without some form of positive corporate commitment of the church to particular historical options. In Rahner's view, the development of any genuine ability to engage in common action depends not only on rational analysis but on "creative imagination" that engages freedom and affectivity.[25] It is through a kind of corporate creative imagination that the church is enabled to carry out its mission to the world.

Because of its creativity, imagination is a notoriously elusive notion. Its activity cannot be fully captured by theoretical reflection. Rahner sees the corporate creative imagination as the locus of the Holy Spirit's action within the church as it grapples with decisions about actions in society. It is the corporate counterpart to the charismatic "discernment of spirits" through which an individual person discovers his or her unique vocation and existential obligations.[26] Schillebeeckx stresses that this charismatic element in the Christian imagination is not an intervention of God that guides human action in a totally invisible or nonexperiential way. Rather, charismatic guidance and the creativity of the imagination emerge from the very heart of human experience. The charismatic insight arises from the simultaneous experience of the social situation and the call of the Christian faith. In situations where injustice is being done, this occurs in what Schillebeeckx calls a "contrast experience." The contrast is between the concrete reality of what is occurring and the concrete reality of one's experience of the Christian life. The creative insight comes in a concrete act of personal and affective synthesis, not simply on the rational level of principles and analysis. As Schillebeeckx describes the process, "the absence of 'what ought to be' is experienced initially, and this leads to a perhaps vague, yet real, perception of 'what should be done here and now.' "[27] The prophetic insight and voice of the church has its origin in the contrasts that exist within the living experience of those who are touched by actual injustice and who are struggling against it. Within the pretheoretical experience of those so engaged, concrete "moral pointers begin to stand out."[28] Prophetic insight, therefore, arises in the midst of practice. It is only after this experience has been weighed and tested that the theoretical reflection of theology, philosophy, and the social sciences can formulate the prophetic insight into ethical principles and coherent plans for social and political change.

These appeals to creative imagination, charismatic insight, and the lived experience of social struggle are all attempts by Rahner and Schillebeeckx to point the way toward a more positive and concrete approach to the church's prophetic role in society. Their arguments quite rightly emphasize that the prophetic function belongs not only to the individual Christian, but also to the church as a socially organized body. Within the institutional and corporate context, however, the appeal to imagination, charism, and experience must be given more clarity than either Rahner or Schillebeeckx has given it. In particular, the translation of their approaches from the individual to the corporate level depends on being able to identify some dimensions of the experience that are shared by all who are members of the community of belief. Without this identification of commonality, the appeal to experience and identity is a one-sided appeal to subjectivity. If a contrast experience of some persons is to be taken as the basis of an action proposal normative for all, then it must be shown that the proposal emerges from an identity that is normative for all. This clarification is essential if prophetic appeals are to have both communicative and persuasive power. Neither individual Christians, nor corporate bodies, nor official church leaders can expect their prophetic claims to be accepted as normative for other Christians unless they are prepared to advance reasons why they should be. On this point, Gustafson has remarked:

> It is, however, legitimate to engage prophets in nonprophetic discourse; some testing of their perceptions and of the theological convictions which both justify and empower their utterances is legitimate. Indeed, it is necessary if those who are not inclined to be moved by prophetic rhetoric are to be persuaded of its moral and theological validity. In a time of prophecy from the right and from the left it is even more important to engage in such discourse.[29]

From this review of some of the theological literature on the prophetic role of the Christian community several conclusions can be drawn. First, concrete proposals for social policy cannot be deduced from the general principles of Christian morality. These principles are useful for providing a direction for Christian action, but not for providing the specificity necessary if there is to be actual common action. Second, negative critique of society is an insufficient basis for the common engagement of the church in society. Third, some positive linkage between the fundamental structure of Christian identity and positive proposals for action must be shown if these proposals are urged as normative for the community as a whole. And, finally, this link between shared identity and shared action will be a link forged in a creative act of synthesis that occurs within the living experience of those who share a common Christian identity. The concluding section of this essay will argue that the sacramental life and the sacramental imagination that shape the living religious identity of Christians are a very important basis for such common prophetic action in society.

The Sacramental Church as a Source of Creative Imagination and Prophecy

If creative imagination, charism, and experience are the sources of both individual and corporate prophetic action for justice, then the public role of the church will be further clarified by reflection on the shape of the Christian imagination. The appeal to imagination and experience that has emerged in recent discussions of this question has a suggestion of irrationalism and subjectivism about it, especially to those who have been educated either in the Catholic tradition of neoscholasticism or in those forms of Protestant thought heavily influenced by the Enlightenment. This suspicion points out a genuine danger to which this kind of appeal could lead. But this fear would be justified only if imagination and experience are regarded as shapeless and uncontrollable. Such, however, is not the case. Neither the human mind nor the human heart is a *tabula rasa,* whimsically poised to move in any and every direction without preference. Human experience is shaped by the history of the person who experiences, and by the symbols or "root-metaphors" that provide identity and a means of communication within the community to which the person belongs.[30] The contrast between reason and experience is not a contrast of two contraries. The heart, too, has its reasons. As Iris Murdoch has stated: "A deeper realization of the role of symbols in morality need not involve (as certain critics seem to fear) any overthrow of reason. Reason must, however, especially in this region, appear in her other *persona* as imagination."[31] Imagination has a structure, a logic, or a kind of rationality that makes the claims of Rahner and Schillebeeckx far from antinomian irrationalism.

The moral imagination of Christians is shaped by all the fundamental symbols and doctrines of the Christian faith. The dimensions of this living imagination are most concretely shaped and revealed in those moments where the symbolic enactment of Christian belief is at its most intense—in the sacraments that are at the very heart of the church's life as a worshiping community. Sacraments are ritualized communal actions that not only express but also embody and realize religious meaning in the life of those who receptively and actively participate in them. Moreover, it is not simply "meaning," in the cognitive sense of this term, that is expressed and embodied in the sacramental event. It is the religious reality itself—God's saving grace and love—that enters into the life of the community of worshipers through a sacrament. Sacramental worship engages not only the mind but the heart. It touches the worshiper on the level of experience and concrete imagination. It is formed activity which, to borrow Bruno Bettelheim's phrase, creates and expresses an "informed heart." The initiation of a new member of the community at baptism and the celebration of the communion of faith at the Eucharist, for example, are not simply illustrations of doctrinal statements of the content of Christian belief. They are enactments of faith and experiential participation in faith. As David Power has put it:

> One can talk forever of the love of God in Jesus Christ but it takes a parable to make me ask whether this love is present in my daily actions and conduct. This is relevant to liturgy's claim to mediate reality. It claims not only to talk about it but to make it. It purports to allow the subject to express his relation to reality in a self-involving action. To be truly self-involving it must not only express the horizons of faith but must also involve the daily self in their pursuit.[32]

This simultaneous representation and realization of the all-pervasive reality of grace in the sacraments is expressed by Karl Rahner when he calls the sacraments "intrinsically real symbols."[33] It is also the meaning of the Council of Trent's statements that a sacrament is "the visible form of an invisible grace" and that sacraments contain the grace that they signify and signify the grace that they contain.[34] Sacraments, in other words, are an experienced synthesis of the ultimate reality in which Christians believe with the concrete life of a community. This synthesis occurs in the imaginative actions of baptism, the Eucharist, reconciliation, etc.

Thus the Roman Catholic sacramental principle suggests that the normative structure of Christian experience and Christian imagination is concretely expressed in symbolic actions of the church's sacramental life. I want to argue, therefore, that the structure of the church's sacramental life can serve as a touchstone for discerning the authenticity of prophetic statements that claim to be calls from God discovered by Christian imagination. More than this, both participation in and reflection on the structure of the sacramental life should be expected to stimulate such charismatic sensitivity. Such participation can orient the Christian community as a whole toward normative interpretations of the social process as, in Barth's terms, an allegory and analogue of the kingdom of God which is both anticipated and promised by God's already present grace.

This analogy between the internal life of the community, the structures of society, and the kingdom of God is not a relation that collapses into identity, as Barth forcefully argued. The Catholic sacramental principle does not imply that baptism and the Eucharist are realizations of the kingdom without eschatological remainder. The sacramental principle, however, serves as an important counterweight to the excessively futurist and critical approach of a purely eschatological theology or spirituality. The kingdom is already present, even though not fully so. The shape (though not necessarily the extent) of this presence is given its clearest expression in the sacramental life of the church.[35] Thus whenever the kingdom becomes visible it will have the shape outlined by this sacramental life. The claim that there is an analogy between the inner sacramental life of the church and the public life of society is not an argument for the reestablishment of Christendom. It is simply a claim that though neither church nor secular society is the kingdom, both can be *loci* in which the reality of the kingdom becomes visible and actual in human experience. It is to maintain that the church and secular society can both be partial realizations in history of the kingdom of God. Whether this realization occurs in the ecclesiastical or political spheres it will have the same imaginative contours. These contours are expressed in the sacramental symbols that give form to the church's life of worship.

Recent Catholic discussions of the sacramental dimensions of Christian life have stressed the fundamental unity of the sacramental principle rather than its differentiation into the seven sacraments enumerated by the Council of Trent. Contemporary discussions of the sacramental principle, in line with patristic thought, have highlighted the analogy that exists between the Father's love of humanity, the pattern of Jesus' life, death, and resurrection, the contours of the life of the church, and the shape of a humane and just society. Jesus Christ is the symbolic-real expression and embodiment of God's covenant of love with all of humanity. He is "the sacrament of the encounter with God."[36] The church, in turn, is the sacrament of Christ—the human community in which the saving grace of Christ is made visible and effective. Though the presence of grace is not restricted to those who are members of the church, this grace comes to its most explicit symbolic expression in the Christian community. God's covenant of love, moreover, extends to the whole of humanity. It is the most radical basis of the unity and solidarity of the human race. Therefore, as a community that both proclaims and attempts to live in this covenant, the church is, in the words of Vatican II, "the universal sacrament of salvation simultaneously manifesting and realizing the mystery of God's love for human beings," "a kind of sacrament or sign of intimate union with God, and of the unity of all humankind."[37] The sacramentalizing of divine presence and covenant, then, is not restricted to the traditional seven sacraments of the institutional church defined by Trent but occurs in the entire Christian life and the whole cosmos regarded as the symbolic manifestation of God's love. Louis Dupré has pointed out that this broader interpretation of sacramentality was common in the days before the polemics of the Reformation age caused its suppression:

> A clearer recognition of the intrinsic nature of religious symbolism could have constrained the bitter polemics among Christians over the number of sacraments. The positive, institutional element, peculiar to each faith, is undoubtedly more important than modernism and liberal Protestantism allowed, yet it should not eclipse the primary truth that sacramentality is a universal form of symbolism. It must not be restricted, then, to those particular forms of which we know the historical institution. Christian tradition itself professed the all-pervasive nature of sacramental symbolism in its respect for "sacramentals," now all but abolished by the institutional legalism of the last centuries. Another instance of sacramental symbolization is the veneration of images, so important in the cult of the Eastern Christian Churches. Far from being idolatrous, as some Byzantine emperors thought, the sacramental character of the Christian cosmos is directly implied in the incarnation. If God communicates himself in Christ, the image of God, then he also communicates himself in the images of that image.[38]

The range of the Christian sacramental imagination, then, is not restricted to the seven traditional sacraments. It is capable of seeing in the whole cosmos and in all human relationships a kind of symbolic realization of God's covenant with humanity. This, of course, does not imply that the entire cosmos and all human relationships are in fact realizations of the covenant love of the kingdom. To maintain this would be to maintain that the kingdom has already fully arrived. It is to maintain, however, that all of human existence is open to interpretation and action that rises not simply from the theoretical perspective of theology and the principles of social ethics but also from the Christian sacramental imagination.

Within this context the differentiation of the sacramental life of the Christian community into the traditional seven sacraments can be viewed in a way that gives it secondary but important relevance to the prophetic role of the church in society. Each of the seven sacraments places one of the key moments or events in human existence and the human life cycle within the symbolic-real world of Christian imagination. This is a world in which God's creating and redeeming covenant of love is seen as acting not only *on* human life but *within* it. The central events that provide the texture of human existence—birth, maturity, communion in a shared meal, marriage, vocation, forgiveness, and death—are all bearers of the grace of the new covenant. The seven sacraments are the concrete realization and enactment of the fundamental sacramental reality of the church in those events that give human life its shape. In Rahner's words, "A fundamental act of the church in an individual's regard, in situations that are decisive for him, an act which truly involves the nature of the church as the historical, eschatological presence of redemptive grace, is ipso facto a sacrament."[39] The sevenfold differentiation of the sacramentality of the church represents the historical differentiation of the church's awareness of key ways in which redemption is realized in human form. Though this differentiation is subordinate to the sacramentality of the entire fabric of human existence, it is a differentiation that provides a rough outline of the shape of the Christian imagination as it has evolved through history.

The relevance of this view of the sacraments to the public and prophetic role of the church is suggested by the fact that each of the sacraments is a specification of the fundamental sacramentality of the church that is called to be a sign of "the unity of all humanity."[40] The symbol of each sacrament points to the world beyond the sanctuary. Each of the seven sacraments has an intrinsic dynamism that carries the Christian imagination toward the perception of the grace of God's covenant love in social existence as well as in the interpersonal and private domains of human struggle and fulfillment. Each of the sacraments has a social relevance that arises from the universality of the grace it bears. The sacramentalizing of God's grace that occurs in the church is not solely for the benefit of the internal life of the Christian community but also for the whole world. Baptism expresses not only the call of a select few to the kingdom but the invitation that God's grace holds out to all persons. The Eucharist expresses not only the participation in the death and resurrection of Christ that is the source of Christian unity, but the radical source of the unity of the human race. Thus the Christian imagination whose contours are outlined by the sacramental system is an imagination that can shape existence and stimulate action in the whole of life, not just in the personal religious life of individual believers.

This social relevance of the sacraments has been largely absent from both sacramental theology and Christian ethics until very recently. A rediscovery of this relevance was begun in Henri de Lubac's great work, *Catholicism: A Study of Dogma in Relation to the Corporate Destiny of Mankind.* A contemporary American Protestant theologian, Langdon

Gilkey, has argued that the sacramental imagination of the Catholic tradition has the potential to make a major contribution to the struggle for justice and peace if it is allowed its full social range. In Gilkey's words:

> Strangely, in denying or abjuring—or being forced by the twentieth century to do so!—the great *temptations* of a sacramental form of religion to absolutize the relative and sanctify the ambiguous, Catholicism may discover the vast strength of a sacramental form of religion, namely, the divinely granted capacity to allow finite and relative instruments to be media of the divine and to endow all of secular and ordinary life with the possibility and the sanctity of divine creativity; and thus more than Protestantism, Catholicism may be able to bring Christianity alive and well through the turmoil of the modern world. However, if Catholicism or Protestantism is to achieve this task of mediating the divine grounding, judgment and possibility to our secular existence, it must widen the scope of both word and sacrament far beyond their present religious, ecclesiastical, dogmatic, and "merely redemptive" limits.[41]

This widening of scope for the sacramental imagination is called for by the pain and ambiguities of contemporary social life. It is more than a matter of attempting to insure the survival of Christianity in the future, however. This widening of scope for the sacramental imagination is called for by the nature of Christian faith itself.

The need for such a widening of the range of the sacramental imagination suggests that the influence of sacramental symbolism on secular life is not a one-way influence. The secular experience of Christians will influence their experience of worship and liturgical celebration. The way they understand and experience baptism, the Eucharist, marriage, ministry, forgiveness and death is not shaped solely by their experience within the worshiping community, but also by the contemporary social situation. Thus, once again, any effort logically to deduce a Christian approach to social and political action from the shape of the sacramental symbols is doomed to failure from the start. Worse than this, it would amount to an effort to impose a religious structure on secular life in an imperialistic and alienating way.

In arguing that the sacramental imagination is a central source of the church's prophetic action in society, I am not proposing that sacramental symbols drawn from the tradition be used as the first principles for a theory of the church's prophetic function in contemporary society. The imagination does not create by deduction. My suggestion is that the synthesis of the experience of the joys and struggles of life in all its dimensions with the experience of redemption and grace that occurs in communal sacramental worship is a synthesis that can and should provide insight into the concrete role that the church should play in society. There is a dialectical relation between the shape of the sacramental symbols of the worshiping community and the realities of the social community. This dialectic may be much more helpful for clarifying the relation between Christian faith and specific social options than are general moral principles. This is so because the dialectic between sacred and secular in the Christian imagination is *already* concrete. It does not have to *become* concrete by a process of deductive reasoning as is the case with general moral principles. It is a dialectic *within* concrete experience. To the extent that sacramental worship of the community is both true to itself and in touch with realities of contemporary society and culture it can lead to concrete communal action. On the basis of historical evidence Hans Bernhard Meyer has pointed out the kind of influence that sacramental liturgy can have in public life when it is thus related and open to secular experience:

> The more completely the expression of a culture is taken over for the liturgy, the more closely the language and symbols of the liturgy correspond with the social features of a period, the more likely it is that celebrations of the liturgy will have secondary effects which will be felt in the life of society outside worship. When this happens the liturgy can perform its function of providing meaning and motivation which will help to shape the lives, not only of individual believers, but also of the whole believing community, and go on to influence the wider society outside this.[42]

Though Meyer rightly calls this influence secondary, since sacramental worship is not social action, such an effect on society is an essential dimension of a form of faith that lives through sacraments.

The appeal to the sacramental imagination as a source of communal prophetic action in society was one of the central themes of the 41st International Eucharistic Congress whose theme was "The Eucharist and the Hungers of the Human Family." A main theme in the congress was the link between the symbolically shared meal of the Eucharist and the responsibility of the Christian community to take concrete action to alleviate world hunger. Some reflections on this theme will serve as an example of the function of the sacramental imagination envisioned in this essay.

The Eucharist is the representation and everlasting memorial of the new covenant God established with all of humanity through the death and resurrection of Jesus. This covenant is the source of Christian unity, and the Eucharist is the preeminent sacrament of unity. It both signifies and realizes the unity of the followers of Christ in a shared meal. In the concreteness and materiality of shared bread and wine the covenant between God and human beings becomes the covenant that forms the human community of the church.

The covenant sacramentalized in the Eucharist, however, is not an exclusive covenant with those who are members of the church. The new covenant is a universal covenant with all humanity. If the church is the "sacrament of the unity of humankind" and if the Eucharist is the primary enactment of the shape of that unity, then the shared meal is the preeminent symbol of God's will for the human race. Because of the presence of the universal grace of God's covenant in the sacramental sharing of food, the Christian imagination is drawn to both perceive and experience the relations between all persons as a covenant relationship, a relationship of partnership, communion, and solidarity only adequately expressed in the sharing of bread. This synthesis between the eucharistic faith and efforts to satisfy human hunger is essential if the symbolic reality of the Eucharist is to remain alive and authentic. Philip Rosato has made this point forcefully:

> The Eucharist would seem magical to many if it were understood as the only bright moment in an otherwise dark and godless world. . . . Christ's presence, then, in the hungry of the world (Mt. 25:35) and his presence in the Eucharist (I Cor. 12:23–26) must be seen as complementary. The Eucharist is not only the place where Christ encounters man, but it is the place where all of man's existential encounters with Christ—even in the suffering caused by human starvation—come together in one incandescent encounter with the crucified and glorified Lord.[43]

If an alienated and magical sacramentalism is to be avoided, the action of Christians in a hungry world must become eucharistic. And it will be eucharistic to the extent that it is action which brings food to the hungry.

This line of thinking does not exhaust the full significance of the Eucharist for the Christian imagination.[44] Nor does it spell out a policy for the solution of the tragic problem of world hunger. In the area of policy-making, however, this approach does provide the basis for corporate prophetic action by the church as a whole. In the Eucharist Christians are not presented with a moral ideal or general principle of human action. They are graced with a concrete manifestation of the shape of God's covenant with all humanity as a covenant that is *realized* in the sharing of food. This covenant, Christians believe, is a *fact,* not simply an ideal or a general norm. The covenant confronts Christians with a call or vocation, a call that has the weight of a moral imperative, but which also enters human experience as grace—as a gift that makes response to the imperative possible.

Consequently there is an intrinsic affinity between the Christian sacramental imagination and the assertion that all human persons have a "right to food." The affirmation of this right provides the intellectual foundation for quite specific policy proposals.

The existence of a "right to food" provides the basis for the proposals of the National Conference of Catholic Bishops' statement on "The World Food Crisis" and the "Statement of Policy" on the right to food issued by the ecumenical group Bread for the World.[45] These policy proposals include calls for specific action such as a national nutrition program in the United States, U.S. participation in a world food-reserve program, increase in U.S. food assistance, the separation of food policy from military policy, the lowering of trade barriers for imports from poor countries, and special preferences for their exports. These policy proposals are not deduced from the Eucharist. They do possess an imaginative affinity to the Eucharist, however. They "make sense" in a nonrationalistic way, in the context outlined here. Their very concreteness is one of the reasons why they make sense in this way, for the imagination is a concrete rather than abstractive faculty. The prophetic voice that the church addresses to the world food crisis thus has deep roots in the shared experience and identity of the Christian community. It can be defended as a normative expression of Christian faith.

The appeal to sacramental imagination does not absolve the church from the rigors of social, political, and theological analysis. All of these are essential if the imagination is to be informed by the realities of both the actual social world and of the Christian faith. There are times and situations, however, where the imagination can outrun this analysis and lead the church to corporate prophetic action that cannot strictly be "proven" to be the only Christian response. The sacramentalism of the Catholic tradition provides a framework within which it is possible to argue for the legitimacy of such prophecy in a way that will prevent the cultural tendencies toward the privatization and fragmentation of Christian faith from destroying the church's public influence. The link being drawn between the Eucharist and world hunger is just such a case. I believe that a similar impetus toward prophetic action can be discovered in the other sacraments. Examination of these other possible developments is not possible in an essay already too long. But further investigation and developments along these lines seem imperative if the church wants to act as a people and wants to do this in a public way. The pressures toward privatization and fragmentation of Christian behavior will continue to be present in our society. I have argued that the church possesses both the practical and theoretical resources that make common action for justice possible in spite of these pressures. These resources are in part to be found in the sacramental experience that has shaped the Roman Catholic identity. If Catholicism can tap the prophetic potential of its own identity, the entire ecumenical church stands to gain new insight and strength in its attempt to serve a struggling world.

Chapter 13

Preaching and Politics: The Problem of Consistency and Compromise

The relation between religion and politics has been front-page news in the United States throughout the 1980s. Hardly a day goes by without some highly visible report appearing in the media about the way churches and their ministers have become involved in public affairs. The previous chapters of this book have explored many of the theological and ethical developments since Vatican II that have stimulated such engagement by the Roman Catholic community. The U.S. Catholic bishops have become particularly vigorous participants in the debates over a host of public-policy questions. Other U.S. religious bodies are similarly engaged.

Many laypeople, however, remain uncertain how to respond to this activist engagement by religious leaders in the public sphere. In fact, most Americans are slightly schizophrenic about the relation between religion and politics. Americans are notably more religious than the citizens of any other advanced industrial society. Religion is pervasive in U.S. culture and constantly helps shape public affairs. Political leaders frequently seek to legitimize their stands by appealing to God for support. At the same time, Americans believe passionately in the separation of church from state and the right to religious freedom. Acceptance of the reality of pluralism is as much a part of the American character as is strong religious loyalty. Thus the relation between religion and politics will inevitably be a tense one in this country. The effort to relate religious vision to political life can produce unpredictable and potentially explosive results if it is not pursued with great care.

In recent years theologians, sociologists, and political scientists have been busily working to help clarify what such a careful approach to the public role of religion would look like. Very few of these authors, however, deal with the issues as they surface in the daily life of the parish. They rarely address the challenges that face pastors and preachers on the front lines of the church's ministry. This chapter will suggest three perspectives that may help already overburdened ministers think through the way their work in the parish relates to the political sphere, especially the particularly sensitive arena of electoral politics: 1. a *theological perspective* on the vocation of all Christians to relate their faith to their lives as citizens; 2. several practical suggestions about what this perspective implies for *preaching and other dimensions of parish ministry;* 3. some reflections on how much *consistency* the church can demand and how much *compromise* it can tolerate as its members participate in electoral politics.

A Theological Perspective: Christian Citizenship

Over the past quarter century—roughly since the pontificate of John XXIII and the Second Vatican Council—Catholic thought has been reexamining its understanding of the relationship between the domain of the spiritual and the religious to the order of the secular and the political. On the basis of a survey of the teachings of the magisterium during these years, Leslie Griffin has shown that there has been a subtle but important shift in the way this relationship is described in the official documents. She does not maintain that the shift has been from a stance that denies the importance of Christian engagement in the temporal and political spheres to one that affirms such engagement. Rather Griffin argues that the transition has been one in which "the spiritual and temporal aspects of human life have moved closer to each other, become more interrelated, more interdependent."[1] Without in any way identifying the sacred and the secular, the recent documents insist that there is an element of the sacred within the temporal and political domains.

Because the spheres of social and public life are not purely secular, the church's concern with the problems that arise within them is properly religious. Avery Dulles has succinctly summarized some of the key elements of the council's teaching on this intimate connection between religious faith and social responsibility:

> The church, rather than being a *societas perfecta* alongside the secular state, is seen as a pilgrim people, subject to the vicissitudes of history and sharing in the concerns and destiny of the whole human race (GS, 1). The church is linked to the world as the sacrament of universal unity (LG, 1), a sign and

> safeguard of the transcendence of the human person (GS, 76), a defender of authentic human rights (GS, 41). In a dynamically evolving world (GS, 4) social and political liberation pertains integrally to the process of redemption and hence is not foreign to the mission of the church. . . . The church's concern for human solidarity, peace, and justice, therefore, is not confined to the sphere of supernatural salvation in a life beyond.[2]

This vision has important consequences for the life of every Catholic and for the ordinary ministry of every parish that are only now becoming apparent over twenty years after the council. The social mission of the church is not simply a matter of bishops writing highly visible pastoral letters, testifying on legislation before Congress, or initiating social-advocacy projects on the diocesan level. These are important of course. But more important still is the need for laymen and women to recognize that living out their faith through engagement in the public affairs of community and nation is an integral part of their Christian vocations as well.

The council stressed that the Christian vocation to be a disciple of Christ is intimately linked with the active exercise of the rights and duties of citizenship. It called on all Christians "to appreciate their special and personal vocation in the political community. This vocation requires that they give conspicuous example of devotion to the sense of duty and of service to the advancement of the common good."[3]

Participation in public life and politics, when approached properly, are not activities in which individuals and groups simply pursue power and self-interest. Rather their objective is the enhancement of the quality of our life *together* in community. If we recognize the great dignity of public service and active citizenship, we will hold both our leaders and ourselves to a high standard of responsibility and integrity. Active citizenship, therefore, is part of the Christian vocation. It is integrally connected with the life of discipleship because it can be such an important way of serving one's neighbors.

This idea will seem odd or even unintelligible to many people in the United States today. For some, this is because they have not yet appropriated the renewed theological perspectives of the council. But there are also sociological sources of these difficulties as well. Citizenship has itself become a problematic concept in our time. The low percentage of Americans who exercise their right to vote is the most visible evidence for this. This is caused in part by a lack of confidence that individual people can have any meaningful influence in a political society as vast as ours. Many people, including many in the middle class, feel politically powerless.

Thus talk of a Christian vocation to active citizenship seems incongruous to them.

The U.S. bishops' pastoral letter on the economy also notes that there are deeper structural causes for this devaluation of citizenship. Modern societies are characterized by a division of labor into specialized jobs and professions. Our lives are further fragmented by the way family life, the work world, networks of friendship, and religious community are so often lived out in separate compartments. The bishops' letter observes that this makes it increasingly difficult to see how the kind of lives we lead can serve or impede the common good of the whole community. This in turn generates a heightened emphasis on personal concerns and private interests.[4] It also helps explain the growth of single-issue politics.

Thus the notion that active citizenship is part of the Christian vocation will go against the grain for many parishioners. This is not because they lack good will, but because the objective conditions of social life make it so difficult to sustain a vital sense of Christian citizenship. These difficulties are themselves theologically significant. The brokenness of our lives and our world is also part of the Christian interpretation of the human condition. "Getting it all together," both personally and socially, is not something Christians can expect to accomplish until God's reign is fully established. This somewhat sobering theological note should put us on guard against facile notions of developing a Christian politics that will lead to the establishment of a Christian republic.

Nevertheless, acknowledgment of the incomplete presence of the kingdom of God does not mean pessimistic resignation in the face of the difficulties of living out the vocation of Christian citizenship. Rather, it means that this vocation must be deeply rooted in faith, hope, and love: faith in the creator God who is the ultimate source of unity for our fragmented lives; hope that God's providence will guide our efforts despite limited knowledge and power; and love for our neighbors that seeks expression in public, political ways as well as in interpersonal relationships. In other words, living out the vocation of Christian citizenship is rooted first and foremost in truly hearing the Word of the gospel and allowing it continually to change our hearts. The power of the Word is the source of our empowerment to struggle with the difficult task of seeking the common good in the midst of all the complexities of our public world.

Thus parishes face the challenge of nurturing a broadened vision and deepened spirituality that will sustain active and critical participation in the political process. The economics pastoral letter states the need forcefully: "The virtues of citizenship are an expression of Christian love more crucial in today's interdependent world than ever before. These virtues grow out of a lively sense of one's dependence on the commonweal and obligations to it."[5] Despite the difficulty of developing such a vision and spirituality, it is an essential task for the church today. Laypeople will need all the help they can get from each other and from their pastors to respond to this challenge. Through mutual support in parish groups devoted to study, reflection, and active involvement in local and national affairs, the church can contribute to a revitalized sense of Christian citizenship. This is a task that must be taken up on all levels in the church, but the long-term impact of the council's vision will finally be determined by the way this vision becomes a living reality in parish communities.

The Tasks of Pastor and Preacher

How is this to be done concretely in the midst of the busy life of the parish? Vatican II provides the basic framework for addressing this practical pastoral question. I will add several more specific suggestions about the implications for preaching.

The council described the task of bishops and priests in the social sphere this way: They should "so preach the message of Christ that all the earthly activities of the faithful will be bathed in the light of the gospel."[6] This is a tall order. Clear thinking about its pastoral significance depends on noting the council's prime emphasis: *preach the message of Christ.* Whether in the pulpit, counseling, social-action activities, or educational programs, the minister's chief responsibility is to bear witness to the Good News in word, deed, tone, and style. Study and meditation on the scriptures and their social implications is at the heart of ministry in this as in all other areas.

Characteristically, however, the council goes on to stress that in order to preach and teach, pastors must also listen and learn. "By unremitting study they should fit themselves to do their part in establishing dialogue with the world and with people of all shades of opinion."[7] Again, this is a most demanding challenge. Fortunately this does not mean that every pastoral minister must be a full-time student of all the complex areas of social policy. The U.S. bishops' major pastoral letters and other policy statements are, however, based on such extensive study and dialogue. They provide some of the basic resources that ministers need to shed the light of the gospel on urgent and complex public matters. At the same time, the council also stressed that it is not the function of pastors to provide detailed, authoritative solutions for all the policy questions society must deal with in its public life. The task of the pastor and preacher, therefore, is the formation of conscience, not the prescription of political stances.

A difficult problem arises here. Often the most effective way of touching people's consciences is through very concrete discussion of social issues such as the increased number of children living in poverty, the human consequences of unemployment, the dangers of nuclear war, or the number of abortions performed since the 1973 Supreme Court decision. When faced with the struggle and anguish these problems involve, the instinct of both pastor and parishioner will be to ask what can be *done* about them. The council stated that "often enough the Christian view of things will itself suggest some specific solution in certain circumstances."[8] But it also noted that frequently no such specific solution flows from the gospel. How is the pastor or preacher to discern which is the case?

The matter is further complicated by the fact that the manner in which one preaches can *imply* that a specific solution is the Christian one even though this is not stated explicitly. This is especially true when the issue is a hot topic of public debate, in an electoral campaign for example. Therefore the pastor faces a dilemma when dealing with the actual moral choices that parishioners grapple with as citizens: how preach, teach, counsel, and organize parish programs in ways that forcefully address urgent issues without turning the pulpit into a political stump or the church basement into a caucus room?

One way around this dilemma is for pastors to confine themselves to the statement of general moral and religious principles, leaving their concrete application to lay Christian citizens. This may be the best solution in some circumstances. But it is not the path that the U.S. bishops have chosen to follow on questions such as nuclear strategy, economic justice, abortion, and human rights.

Archbishop Rembert Weakland has provided a helpful discussion of why the statement of general moral principles is not always adequate pastorally.[9] First, a clean break between moral principles and concrete applications doesn't do justice to the way we actually reason and act in the moral sphere. Moral decisions are not reached simply by first learning theoretical principles and then applying them deductively. The meaning of a principle can remain vague until at least some of its concrete implications are spelled out, and many moral principles are inductively arrived at by reflection on concrete moral choices. Theory and practice cannot be completely separated from each other. Second, the church is not divided into a lay branch for concrete questions and a clergy branch for theoretical principles. Though this may appear to have the advantage of keeping pastors insulated from many controversies, it can bring what Karl Rahner called a "terrifying sterility"[10] to pastoral activity. It can remove the pastor from genuine engagement in the struggles the laity must face. And though the function of the pastor is to help parishioners form their consciences and not to dictate political options, does it make pastoral sense implicitly to tell the laity that their pastors can be of no help when it comes to concrete choices? This is certainly not the way we proceed in areas such as marriage preparation or the ministry of health care. Why should it be so in questions involving the exercise of Christian citizenship?

An alternative approach is suggested by the way the U.S. bishops have gone about drafting their recent pastoral letters. These letters present the biblical perspectives and ethical principles that should shape policy choices on war and economics. These perspectives and principles provide a distinctive angle of vision on the complex issues the pastoral letters address. They make the bishops particularly sensitive to the human dimensions of these problems that narrower perspectives might ignore or overlook. On the basis of careful study of the facts, combined with theological and ethical reflection shaped by the church's long tradition, the bishops then propose several specific steps they believe will promote peace and human dignity, such as a nuclear test-ban treaty and a series of initiatives to create jobs. These concrete proposals make their letters existentially challenging. They show that the message of the gospel can speak vividly to our lives as citizens when we take up its challenge faithfully and intelligently. But the proposals are set forward in a way that acknowledges that they do not have the status of dogmas and that Christians of good will can legitimately disagree with them. However, the bishops also ask those who disagree to come forward with alternative proposals for how to reduce the risk of nuclear war and bring down unemployment. The bishops' pastoral strategy is to stimulate dialogue on the implications of Christian faith for policy in these areas.

This model of pastoral leadership can shed light on many of the aspects of parish ministry. In particular it suggests a fruitful way of dealing with the religious and moral dimensions of political questions from the pulpit. Let me suggest several guidelines.

1. In preaching, the Good News is the center of everything that is said. If the word about to be spoken from the pulpit cannot be regarded as Good News, don't say it. This does *not* mean speaking only "smooth words." The gospel is a challenge to conversion, sometimes even a word of judgment. However, it is the vision of a loving God, who loves justice, that should be at the heart of every homily. It is this love that calls, challenges, and invites whatever social response should be forthcoming. Avoid guilt trips.

2. Social issues are best addressed in the context of a regular pattern of preaching that frequently adverts to the public implications of the gospel.

"Social-justice homilies" should not stick out in a pattern of preaching as something unrelated to the parish's regular liturgical rhythm.

3. It goes without saying that "proof-texting" is to be avoided. Thus "You cannot serve God and money" should not be used to condemn financial success or capitalism as such. A text like this must be seen in the context of biblical teaching on the goodness of creation, the charge to till the earth, the need to care responsibly for one's family, etc. It is a warning of the dangers of wealth, not a condemnation of the wealthy. Similarly "the poor you will always have with you" is not a justification for accepting current levels of poverty. In context it is a call to assist the poor who *are* with us. Thus the preacher must know the real meaning of the text being preached and have interiorized an integral theology and spirituality of the whole of the gospel message, including its social implications.

4. Have deep respect for the experience, competence, and struggles of one's congregation. People in the congregation already know a lot about the struggles of social life. Very frequently they have a lot more expertise than the preacher in business, politics, family life, etc. What is frequently most needed is encouragement, vision, and support.

5. Provide examples of possible ways to grapple with and act upon the question considered in the homily. Do not leave people with the sense that there is something having to do with salvation at stake, but with no sense of what to do about it. But carefully distinguish the word of the gospel and the teaching of the church about fundamental moral principles from prudential judgments about what these imply for concrete policies or actions. This applies whether these judgments are those of the hierarchy or the preacher's own. When it comes to the concrete, the congregation should be able to recognize that the preacher is a fellow Christian pursuing the right course of action in light of the gospel. Pastorally, sounding like a pundit is the kiss of death.

6. See preaching about social justice as an integral part of the whole social mission of the parish, to be accompanied by all the other parts. If a congregation does not yet have a lively social-action ministry it will be that much harder to preach about social questions. This is a chicken-and-egg problem. Pastoral discernment and living experience of the fabric of a parish's life is the touchstone for deciding on how much to say about a controversial issue, and when to say it. This means that visiting preachers should be especially prudent about starting fights they don't have to finish.

7. Preachers should recognize that they are human—earthen vessels—and not be afraid to make mistakes. If God is leading the church and its ministers to tackle this new and very challenging form of proclaiming the

Word, then God is surely ready to deal with the fact that we are only beginning to learn how to do it.

Consistency and Compromise

The pluralism of religious and moral convictions held by the citizens of the United States poses an additional challenge in the effort to realize the council's vision of the church in the world. As has already been noted, the council stated that the vocation of all Christians in the political order is "service to the advancement of the common good." This immediately confronts us with the problem that there is no agreement in our society about precisely what the common good is. How, then, are Christian citizens to advance the common good without running roughshod over the convictions of their fellow citizens? In particular, how are they to do this when they participate in electoral politics as voters, candidates, or officeholders?

The council, of course, unambiguously affirmed that religious freedom is a human and civil right of all persons. It clearly stated that the content of this right is an immunity from coercion in matters religious. All politics, particularly the use of the vote and the passage of legislation, involves the use of power that is at least potentially coercive. When electoral or legislative politics touch issues on which there is basic religious and moral disagreement the question of religious freedom is necessarily engaged.

The council, however, also taught that the right to religious freedom has a positive content: "It comes within the meaning of religious freedom that religious bodies should not be prohibited from freely undertaking to show the special value of their doctrine in what concerns the organization of society and the inspiration of the whole of human activity."[11] Religious freedom cannot be invoked to exclude the churches or Christian citizens from efforts to shape public policies in accord with their values. How to do this while respecting the rights of those whose convictions are different is proving to be one of the most difficult pastoral problems faced by the church as it addresses the religious and moral dimensions of American public life.

Pastorally, the issue is twofold. First, how does the pastor assist people to express their faith and moral convictions in a consistent way as they live their lives as citizens? Second, how help members of the parish discern when they may come to legitimate political compromise on candidates, issues, or legislation out of respect for the freedom of their fellow citizens or in the interest of political effectiveness? Several distinctions can help address this thorny set of questions.

First, the Catholic theological understanding of the relation between the kingdom of God and our present life in society sheds some light on the problem. The full Christian vision of the common good of society is shaped by the promise of the coming of the kingdom of God, where all things will be made new and every tear washed away. The good society is a community of persons with one another and with God, characterized by the fullness of love, justice, and peace. This reign has already been initiated among us, but it is not yet complete. Thus, in the words of the pastoral letter on the economy, Christians should "embody in their lives the values of the new creation while they labor under the old."[12] There is to be no passive acceptance of the injustice and sinfulness of our world, but active and hopeful efforts to transform it. This is an ethic that calls Christians to accept responsibility for the complexities inevitably involved in such efforts at transformation. It resists the notion that fidelity to the gospel can be achieved only in a community of the perfect, in a kind of sect or ghetto untouched by the conflicts and tradeoffs that are so much part of the political world. Consistency, therefore, means exercising such responsibility with rational coherence and personal integrity. It does not mean creating a world apart where hard choices do not exist.

Second, Catholic moral theology, going back to Augustine and Thomas Aquinas, distinguishes the roles of civil law and morality in the quest for the common good. Civil law must reflect and embody morality. A law that does positive injustice or compels citizens to engage in immoral action violates this essential link between the legal and the moral. Thus St. Thomas declared that such a law is not law at all "but rather a kind of violence."[13] In this sense the slogan "you can't legislate morality" is false. Nevertheless Augustine and Aquinas also insisted that it is not the task of civil law to enforce *all* of morality, but only that part of it necessary for the maintenance of a just and well-ordered society. Law and government are to secure fundamental human rights and the minimal demands of justice for all members of the commonwealth. Working for this objective is the moral responsibility of all public officials. And as the economics pastoral letter states, "this obligation also falls on individual citizens as they choose their representatives and participate in shaping public opinion."[14]

Over the past several years, Cardinal Joseph Bernardin has delivered a number of important speeches developing a moral perspective on the interconnection between these fundamental human rights and basic demands of justice. He has called this perspective "a consistent ethic of life."[15] Its purpose is to show that the bishops' efforts to influence public policy are guided by a single moral vision and supported by coherent moral argument. Their approach to topics such as abortion, nuclear-weapons policy, capital punishment, meeting the basic needs of the poor, and care for the terminally ill are not ad hoc and disconnected. Though there are important differences among all these issues, they all concern the fundamental requirements of human dignity. They are all in that domain of morality that is properly the concern of citizens, legislators, and the law. The bishops are seeking to show how they are linked on the moral level, and are urging that this linkage be translated into a consistent set of public policies.

Here the pastoral task of assisting Christian citizens to discern how best to pursue these basic moral objectives becomes acute. It is clear that Christians have a duty to work for the elimination of the vast number of abortions that occur in our country, for the reduction of the risks of nuclear war, for the elimination of poverty and hunger, and for the other moral purposes set forward in the consistent ethic of life. It is not always clear how to do this in the midst of a pluralistic society where disagreement exists both on these moral objectives and on the best means to attain them. The bishops have explicitly acknowledged that faithful Christians may legitimately disagree with some of the specific policy recommendations they have made in their pastoral letters on nuclear strategy and economics. The bishops conference has itself varied in its recommendations on policy regarding abortion, at one time calling for an amendment to the U.S. Constitution banning all abortions, at another time recommending that the setting of legal norms for abortion be returned to the jurisdiction of the several states. This recognition of legitimate pluralism on how to translate moral commitment to human dignity and rights into law and public policy is not a form of moral capitulation. It is based on a clear-eyed recognition that it is not possible to deduce wise policy directly from moral principle. Wise policy depends on political wisdom as well as moral uprightness. It may in some circumstances call for compromise and a willingness to make political choices among competing goods. It may sometimes mean choosing the lesser of two evils.

For example, how are voters to deal with an election in which all of the candidates depart from one or more of the bishops' prudential judgments about the policy implications of the consistent ethic? Such situations have already arisen in a number of campaigns and, to put it mildly, have generated considerable controversy and confusion. One candidate may be in strong agreement with the bishops' policy recommendations on nuclear strategy, capital punishment, and aid for the poor, while dissenting from their conclusions about what is legislatively achievable and responsibly enforceable on abortion. Another candidate for the same office may stand with the bishops on abortion but oppose them on capital punishment, the role of government in generating jobs, or the appropriate stance on arms control. What does consistency mean for the voter in such an election?

Traditional Catholic moral theology provides several helpful guidelines for such choices. Many of the theologians in the manualist tradition of pre-Vatican II moral theology discussed the question of whether a Christian could ever vote for an "unworthy" candidate for office. By unworthy candidate they did not mean someone whose personal character was corrupt or dubious. Rather they were dealing with the question of the morality of voting for candidates whose political positions were at least in part opposed to the church's teaching. The manualists argued that there would be a presumption against voting for such a candidate. But there could be exceptions. Over fifty years ago, Dominic Prümmer summarized the consensus among these theologians in language that is rather quaint but nonetheless very much to the point: "Nearly all modern theologians concede that the election of an unworthy representative is not something intrinsically evil, and furthermore is sometimes *per accidens* licit to avoid a greater evil."[16] If one were to substitute the phrase "representative who departs from one or more of the bishops' set of prudential judgments" for "unworthy representative," the implications are evident.

For example, this principle would be of help in an election where one candidate is in favor of federal aid to private schools but opposed to serious arms-control measures, while the other candidate holds opposite positions on both of these issues. The Christian citizen must weigh the importance of these two issues in deciding how to vote. This choice, I submit, is a relatively simple one from the viewpoint of the consistent ethic because of the extreme importance of the nuclear question. Also, only government is in a position to deal with nuclear strategy, while private education can be supported without government assistance, even though with difficulty. If the abortion question is introduced into this hypothetical example, it becomes less hypothetical and more difficult. Nonetheless the same sort of weighing of relative goods and relative evils is called for. The only alternative is not to vote at all. And this, I believe, would generally be contrary to the Catholic theological commitment to seek to transform society and not to withdraw from it.

Another example, this one from a 1921 pastoral letter by the archbishop of Paris, shows that we are not the first people to struggle with the question of consistency and compromise in relating Christian morality to electoral politics. Cardinal Léon Adolphe Amette, in a difficult period of church-state relations in France, called Parisian Catholics to recognize their duty to vote, to vote honestly, and to vote wisely. By wisely he meant "in such a way as not to waste your votes." The cardinal went on to say that this might mean voting for candidates whose views left something to be desired from the church's point of view. Such a path would be justified even if there were other candidates running for office whose "program would indeed be more perfect" but "whose almost certain defeat might open the door to the enemies of religion and the social order."[17] In other words, political judgment about the effectiveness of the possible uses of one's vote in securing religious and ethical values is part of responsible Christian citizenship.

These judgments of political prudence must be made by all in the church—bishops, priests, and laity alike. As I have argued above, they are not simply a problem for laypersons. The issue of prudential judgment arises not only within a single area of public policy, such as the complex questions of nuclear strategy. It also arises as one tries to apply a consistent concern for human life, dignity, and rights across a spectrum of issues. This needs to be acknowledged in all the pastoral activities of the parish as well—in preaching, in education, and in organized social action. It would be a serious pastoral mistake for preachers or pastors to communicate directly or indirectly that there is one and only one acceptable way for Christians to deal with these complex questions in the political forum, especially the forum of electoral politics. The pastor can suggest options and invite serious moral reflection on these questions of consistency and compromise. This is perhaps often best done in forums such as adult education or parish reflection and study groups rather than in the pulpit. The aim should be to stimulate serious engagement with questions that are of high importance but that often do not have a single right answer.

By way of summary, the pastoral challenge facing Catholic pastors and parishes as they seek to live out the council's vision of the place of the church in the modern world is a great one. The challenge is equally great for laymen and women in their lives as citizens. With mutual support, intelligent leadership, and the guidance of the Spirit we can find the way to respond. And in the process, we can be hopeful that the church will come more fully alive to the reality of God and God's world.

Chapter 14

Courage and Patience: Education for Staying Power in the Pursuit of Justice

The previous essays in this book make it clear that the church is in the midst of a major renewal of its mission to promote the cause of justice. The importance of Christian commitment to the pursuit of justice is evident on many fronts. It has been strongly emphasized in official church teachings. It is the central theme of liberation theology, one of the most creative developments in Christian thought to occur in our century. The meaning of justice in the North American context has been probed by social scientists, philosophers, and theologians in the context both of interdisciplinary dialogue and that of their Christian faith. These new intellectual developments are most encouraging and need to be carried forward vigorously. They deserve the serious attention of all religious educators as new patterns of education for justice are explored. Despite their importance, however, another aspect of the task of education for justice will be the central focus of this essay. We might call it the education of the heart, that part of the person where "the joys and the hopes, the griefs and the anxieties"[1] of the people of our day are experienced and felt by those actively struggling for justice.

Though the idea of justice and the meaning of justice in our society are crucial foci for the educational task, they are not its sole concern. This is so because justice is not merely an idea. It is an action, a matter of practice, a structured reality that must be created by human freedom and choice. Lack of knowledge of the meaning of justice and of the demands of justice in the concrete situation will surely prevent the Christian community from contributing to the creation of a just society. But though the possession of such knowledge is a necessary condition for effective advocacy of the cause of a more human world, it is not a sufficient condition for such effectiveness. For example, Lawrence Kohlberg has built his model of moral education on the centrality of the norm of justice. Christian religious educators can and should be in full agreement with this emphasis. However, when Kohlberg goes on to affirm that "he (she) who knows the good chooses the good,"[2] both theological and educational questions must be raised.

Much of Christian social thought, particularly in its Roman Catholic form, rests on strongly intellectualist presuppositions which emphasize that *knowledge* of the good is central to the moral life. Thus there is considerable room for agreement between Christian approaches to education for justice and Kohlberg's cognitive approach to moral development. Nevertheless, even in moral theologies that strongly stress the importance of knowing what is just, such as those of Thomas Aquinas and his contemporary disciples, cognition alone cannot guarantee that justice will be done. States of the heart such as fear, desire, anxiety, boredom, resentment, anger, sadness, or exhaustion can lead men and women to fail to do what they know will contribute to greater justice. Such states of feeling can even lead them to do what they know to be unjust. By the same token, doing what is known to be just can be greatly facilitated by the presence of confidence, hope, energy, and magnanimity. Knowledge of the good is not in itself sufficient to produce these states of the heart. This is so because human beings are not pure mind. Also, there is a rift or conflict in the center of the human person that Christian theology calls original sin.[3] This conflict is not only within the interior heart of the person but also between the desires of the heart and the good of justice that the mind perceives. This rift is less fundamental than the unity and goodness of the human person as the image of God. It must, however, be taken into account by religious educators, theologians, and indeed all Christians as they rethink their roles and responsibilities in the Christian mission for social change.

In what follows a few modest suggestions about the education of the heart for the pursuit of justice will be outlined. First, a major problem that threatens to undermine much of the personal and corporate progress that has been made in the Christian community's quest for justice will be briefly described. This is the experience of powerlessness or loss of hope and energy among social-justice advocates. Second, we will look briefly at a resource in the Christian tradition that can increase our understanding of ways to improve staying power and combat the feeling of powerlessness. This resource is the traditional analysis of the virtues of courage and patience found in Catholic moral theology. Third, several suggestions will be made about how courage and patience can be fostered and deepened among contemporary Christians. And finally a few words will be said about the deeper religious and theological significance of courage and patience in the quest for justice.

The Experience of Powerlessness

The problem of staying power in the commitment to justice has emerged as an important question for the Christian community because of the experience of the lack of such power in recent years. Despite the signs of real progress in the church's social ministry during the last decade, there have also been signs that this work is more arduous and costly than it might have seemed in the early days of renewal. The cost is most tragically visible in the harassment, imprisonment, and even the torture and execution of Christians in a number of countries where the church is in conflict with economic elites or political ruling groups.[4] In many of these situations injustice is evident and tangible and the needed direction of change is palpable. The struggle Christians face as they prepare to act is an inner struggle between fear and daring, between hope and despair, rather than a struggle to know what justice demands. It is as much an affair of the heart as it is of the mind.

In the North American context the difficulties faced by agents of change are less dramatic, but nonetheless very real. Among the hazards that sometimes accompany sustained work for justice are not physical violence or imprisonment, but emotional and psychological exhaustion. Frustration levels among those pursuing the work of justice in North American society seem almost always to be quite high. This is not simply a result of psychological problems of social-justice advocates. It is related to the kind of society they work in. The United States is a highly differentiated, pluralist society in which the causes of injustice are neither single nor simple. The patterns of cause and effect in the dynamics of social change are governed by multiple variables. As a result, moral choice is rarely rooted in a simple confrontation between good and evil or between oppressors and oppressed. The complexity of the mechanisms of change make moral choice less a clear-cut decision between justice and injustice than is sometimes the case in less complex societies.

The social system that exists in the United States has a distinctive impact on the emotional and affective dimensions of moral choice. Where choices to be made in the pursuit of justice are relatively simple and clear, one can put one's whole heart into one's action without having to exert large amounts of psychological energy to do so. When the choices are less clear or when every choice demands that many factors be held together in balanced tension, we tend to hedge our affective bets a bit. The structures of a complex pluralistic society lead to a certain emotional distancing of social agents from their actions in society. Sociologists call the extreme form of this distancing anomie, a situation in which action loses all normative and affective significance. When such significance is undermined, so is the likelihood of commitment and choice.

This social context exacts a high cost from men and women who pursue the cause of justice over a sustained period of time. All members of advanced industrial societies have problems finding unified meaning and emotional integrity in the chopped-up world they live in.[5] Those who set out to address the problems of injustice inherent in these societies must carry additional burdens. First, they must deal either directly in experience or indirectly in reflection with the pain and suffering of the victims of injustice. The experience of these negative aspects of social reality make it that much more difficult to maintain an integrated world of meaning and the wholeness of heart that is rooted in such meaning. In addition the social-justice advocate must also regularly deal with the conflicts and contradictions within the social system itself. These conflicts become part of experience and take up residence within the mind and heart. Finally, deepening awareness of the scope of injustice can combine with frustration over the slow pace of change to produce a smouldering anger. This anger may be the only emotionally effective way that the activist can avoid surrendering to the anomie or loss of affective significance with which modern society threatens everyone.

In short, because the social-justice advocate is consciously dealing with the negativities of contemporary social reality, he or she is particularly vulnerable to some of these negativities. If they get the upper hand within the heart of a person dedicated to the quest for justice, the final outcome can be a state of emotional burnout that renders further action impossible. Alfred Kammer has described this state as "a physical, emotional, psychological phenomenon—an experience of personal fatigue, alienation, failure."[6] It seems to be a threat not only to Christian social activists but also to persons of various beliefs and competencies who are professionally engaged in helping the victims in our complex industrial society.[7] These different emotional dangers are as much a threat to the quest for justice in North America as are the physical threats and dangers of violence in other parts of the world. As psychologist James Gill has pointed out, there is deep irony in the fact that persons who have the highest level of commitment to helping others in our society are the very persons most in danger of disillusionment and burnout. In Gill's words, "Those who altruistically enter the helping professions and devote themselves unstintingly and enthusiastically to meeting the needs of others are the ones likely to experience frustration and disillusionment, find their energy exhausted, distance themselves from people (even friends), regard their efforts as failure, and, in some cases, even abandon their work."[8] This irony is the result of the emotional price that modern industrial society exacts from those who seek to change it. Both the full-time specialist in work for social justice and American Christians in general are in need of help if they are to avoid burnout and develop staying power in their commitment and action. Since the threat is a matter of the heart rather than the head, the defense must address the heart as well.

The Virtues of Courage and Patience

In the tradition of Christian moral thought the quality of heart that enables persons to do what is just in the face of difficulty or adversity is called the virtue of courage. In the writings of Thomas Aquinas, for example, courage is not simply a discrete virtue that a person could develop independent of concern for the doing of justice. Courage is not simply strength of will, fearlessness, or the ability to endure in the face of hardship. It is strength of will *in the pursuit of justice*. It is the ability to undertake daring action for justice in spite of the presence of well-founded fear. It is patient endurance of either pain or tedium in the pursuit of justice. In St. Thomas's words, "Now courage in civil affairs establishes a man's spirit in human justice, to preserve which he endures mortal danger; and in the same way the courage which is a gift of grace strengthens the human mind in the good of God's justice, which is won through faith in Jesus Christ."[9] In the Thomistic account of the moral life, then, courage is founded on knowledge of what is just. But it goes beyond knowledge by disposing the spirit to act for justice in the face of opposition.

Courage has two principle forms: daring and endurance. Thomas argues that endurance in the face of adversity is the highest form of courage. Endurance in the cause, even to the point of laying down one's life, is the noblest example of courageous action. Thomas cites the scriptures to support this contention: "Blessed are they who suffer persecution for justice sake, for theirs is the kingdom of heaven" (Matt 5:10). This courage of endurance to the point of martyrdom is both the great challenge and the great gift of Christians who are faced with violent opposition in their pursuit of justice.

But St. Thomas is quite clear that the patient endurance of evil is not the whole of courage. It is also vigorously active. As he puts it, "Courage ought not merely to endure unflinchingly the pressure of difficult situations by restraining fear, it ought also to make a calculated attack, when it is necessary to eliminate difficulties in order to win safety for the future. Such action appears to belong to daring. Therefore courage is concerned with fears and acts of daring, restraining the first and measuring the second."[10] Courageous action is daring directed by the norm or measure of justice. It involves passion and even anger. Following Aristotle, Thomas argues that the most natural form of courageous action is an attack against evil provoked by anger. Such rightly directed anger, he says, "is true courage."[11] Thus, in Thomistic thought, assertiveness in the cause of justice is part of the virtuous life of the Christian.

Educating the Heart

Both the active courage of assertiveness and the patient courage of endurance are needed if Christians are to develop the staying power needed in the quest for justice today. There is no simple psychological or educational recipe for producing such virtues in others or even in oneself. Just as knowledge of justice does not produce justice of itself, so knowledge of the importance of courage does not produce courageous action. Nevertheless some suggestions can be made about resources that make courageous staying power more likely in the pursuit of justice.

First, some immediate experience of the suffering of the victims of injustice is important if one's heart is to remain sensitive to the continuing need for action. The effective agent of social justice needs to feel and taste the reality of injustice. This experience is the foundation of the rightly directed anger that St. Thomas sees as the "most natural" source of courageous action. In American society some continuing exposure to these harsh realities will serve as an antidote to the experience of social complexity that tends to paralyze the will. Persons entering into the task of seeking justice need such experience if their hearts as well as their minds are to be attuned to the evil they seek to combat. Those who have been working at the task for a long time, especially if they are in administrative positions in social agencies or teaching positions in academia or the church, also need some continuing firsthand experience of the struggles of the victims of our society. Such experience can help sustain the affective significance of their work. This suggests that both students and teachers in programs of education for justice need to spend at least a part of their time in personal contact with the poor and other marginalized persons in our society. This will help develop courage and staying power.

Second, courage depends on what might be called knowledgeability or practical wisdom. This is the quality of mind that has traditionally been called prudence by moral theologians and philosophers. It is the ability to discern the possibilities for greater justice as they exist in the concrete situation. It is therefore more than an understanding of the general principles of social ethics. It depends on an understanding of the conflict and change at work in the area one seeks to address. Since these dynamics are almost inevitably complex and multileveled in our society, prudence includes the ability to live with such complexity. So it is in fact a quality of heart as well as of mind. Having practical wisdom means that one is able to sustain protracted analysis of complex issues without leaping to a premature division of the world into groups of villains and groups of victims. It also calls for a theological awareness that in human history the wheat and the tares are growing together and that the task of separating them completely should be left to God on the day of judgment. When humans attempt to do so, they misunderstand the nature of their own abilities and usually fail to promote that form of justice that is within their power to effect. Thus discerning prudence has the humility, patience, and wisdom to seize the opportunities for justice as they are offered rather than insisting that these opportunities should appear in simpler form. Complexity is a characteristic of the struggle for justice both in social fact and in the proper theological interpretation of this social reality. Recognition of the reality and inevitability of this complexity is a condition for sustained and courageous action.

Religious education for justice should thus resist the frequently strong impulse to reduce this complexity to simple, clear-cut interpretations of injustice. Whether in outlining the politics of an issue or in sketching its theological significance, the fullest possible understanding is necessary if the appropriate action is to be taken. Education for justice thus needs to encourage participants to develop this discerning practical wisdom that rests on an ability to see the world as it is.

A third means that can assist in the development of courage and staying power in the quest for justice is involvement in a supportive community of peers and co-workers. Experience of injustice and a willingness to live with complexity are necessary qualities of the person who is committed to the long-term task of seeking justice in society. But these indispensable qualities can exact a heavy emotional and psychological price. Close friends and trusted colleagues in the work for justice can assist one another to bear these burdens. They can also provide encouragement and a sense of hope to one another. Their mutual support can stimulate both the daring and the patience that the work demands. Advocates of justice are much more likely to sustain the struggle over the long haul if they help one another do so. The solitary warrior for the cause of right may be a romantic image for some who are dedicated to the tasks of social ministry.

Those who try to live according to this image, however, are prime candidates for disillusionment and burnout. Indeed, part of courage is the admission that one cannot really even begin this kind of work without a lot of help and guidance from others. Even though every community is touched by the reality of sin and is therefore to some extent in itself unjust, persons cannot become effective agents of change without truly communal support. As David Baily Harned has remarked, "Courage is courageous enough to ask for assistance from the same communities and powers that threaten the self with captivity, and it is courageous enough not to desert its responsibilities there."[12]

Courage and staying power depend on the presence of hope. Communal support is itself a powerful source of hope in human life. To the extent that such support is present, even the triumph of great injustice in a particular situation is not the final verdict on the case. Education for justice thus should be education for collaboration, cooperation, and community. It should include collaboration and cooperation between the students themselves in their activities and assignments. Collaboration between students and those outside the classroom who are involved in similar concerns may also be a useful way to foster this goal. And a cooperative relationship between teacher and student will be of great educational benefit as well.

A fourth factor in the development of courage and staying power is the experience that some success in the struggle for justice has been and remains possible. Though the final victory of justice is an eschatological hope, perseverance in such hope depends on seeing signs of its presence already in history. And indeed there *are* victories of justice over injustice in our world. Seeing these victories, hearing the stories of how they came to pass, getting to know the people who made them possible, and helping to bring them about are all sources of the courage and patience that is so important in the quest for justice. Developing such courage depends in part, therefore, on undertaking tasks where there is at least some hope of success. Estimation of the chance of success is, of course, related to how large one's vision and confidence already are. A magnanimous person will dare much greater efforts than will a pusillanimous one. Those who already have some taste of confidence are thus enabled to risk more and achieve more. From an educational point of view, this suggests that attention to achievements in the history of the struggle for justice is as important as focusing on the most oppressive and violent injustices in the world today. The theological principle that we can only experience conversion because of the presence of grace makes good educational sense as well. We can develop the courage to dare great things only by experiencing the possibility of achievement in our lives and the lives of others.

A fifth quality of the courageous and patient advocate of justice is a confident and serene acknowledgment of the limits of one's capabilities, energy, time, and wisdom. Magnanimity is not the same as the effort to ape God by becoming responsible for everything that happens on the face of the earth. Because we human beings are finite and limited creatures, human courage includes the ability to accept our honest limits. Daring and endurance will acquire true focus to the extent that these limits are accepted. Such acceptance is the beginning of the courage truly to be oneself and truly to give oneself to the struggle for justice. Educationally this implies that religious education for justice needs to be education in self-knowledge as well.

Courage and Faith

All five of these suggestions for ways of fostering courage are a reminder of the fact that the final victory of justice is not fully within our power to achieve. There is a gap between every human effort and the final achievement of true justice. It is precisely because there is such a gap that courage remains a constant necessity. The final source of courage, therefore, is not a trust that one's energy, or anger, or one's successes and the support one receives from co-workers will finally usher in the kingdom of justice and peace. Confidence in these powers alone is not courage but foolhardy illusion. If courage is truly to be courage at all, it must rest on a movement beyond ourselves, in which we entrust ourselves to God and regain from God the courage to act with steadfastness. As theologians such as Karl Rahner, Paul Tillich, and Leo O'Donovan have pointed out, true courage is ultimately not only rooted in faith but even identical with faith.[13]

Courage is a trust that in the act of self-surrender that all work for justice demands we will not finally be destroyed. Rather we will be saved, along with those whose burdens we seek to alleviate. As Leo O'Donovan has put it, "Our courage, accordingly, is meant to have the same course as the courage of Christ: for the sake of life into the danger of death and then, through a power which belongs to God alone, through death to eternal life. The price we are willing to pay for our greatest hopes about life can be nothing less than life itself; the love we learn for our fellow human beings and for our world can only be fulfilled if it is put to the test of what seems to be the end of love."[14] Courage is thus not simply a moral virtue to be cultivated by techniques of self-improvement. These techniques, including the five just suggested in this essay, are important parts of every Christian life. But if courage is to have a really trustworthy foundation, it must be founded ultimately on faith in God and love for God as revealed in Jesus Christ. Just as contemporary theologians can identify true courage with true faith, so Augustine saw courage as one aspect of our love of God and neighbor. And the traditions of Christian spirituality, drawing on scriptural sources, have long known that courage is one of the gifts of the Holy Spirit, poured into our hearts by the grace of Christ. Similarly, the enduring courage we call patience is one of the fruits of the presence of the Spirit in our hearts.

From a theological point of view, therefore, we can see that the development of courage in the quest for justice is a religious and spiritual task as much as it is a moral one. This is not to say that religious faith is somehow a substitute for the arduous task of developing the capacity to act in the face of frustration or to endure in the face of setbacks in the quest for justice. Rather, it is simply to point out that education for justice can help foster genuine courage to the extent that it is genuinely Christian education. Its final goal is not to indoctrinate students with the appropriate ideology or to form in them the appropriate instincts. Its ultimate goal is to introduce them to the reality of the God who is revealed in Jesus Christ and whose Spirit is present working for justice in the world today. To the extent that religious education forgets this primary purpose, it seems likely to fail to lead students both to justice and to courage. To the extent that it faithfully pursues this primary goal, it will be led to undertake all its other tasks in the service of justice as well.

Notes

Frequently Cited Church Documents

Church documents that are cited repeatedly in these notes are taken from the following sources. In some cases the translations have been revised, using language that is inclusive of both genders.

Ad gentes. Vatican Council II, "Decree on the Church's Missionary Activity." In Walter M. Abbott and Joseph Gallagher, eds., *The Documents of Vatican II*. New York: Guild Press/America Press/Association Press, 1966.

The Challenge of Peace: God's Promise and Our Response. National Conference of Catholic Bishops, 1983 pastoral letter on the nuclear issue. Washington, DC: United States Catholic Conference, 1983.

Dignitatis humanae. Vatican Council II, "Declaration on Religious Freedom." In Abbott and Gallagher, eds., *The Documents of Vatican II*.

Divini redemptoris. Pope Pius XI, encyclical letter on "Atheistic Communism." In Claudia Carlin, ed., *The Papal Encyclicals*, 5 vols. (Wilmington, NC: McGrath Publishing Company, 1981), vol. 2.

Economic Justice for All: Pastoral Letter on Catholic Social Teaching and the U.S. Economy. National Conference of Catholic Bishops. Washington, DC: United States Catholic Conference, 1986.

Gaudium et spes. Vatican Council II, "Pastoral Constitution on the Church in the Modern World." In Abbott and Gallagher, eds., *The Documents of Vatican II*.

Justitia in mundo. Synod of Bishops, Second General Assembly, 1971. In Gremillion, ed., *The Gospel of Peace and Justice: Catholic Social Teaching since Pope John*. Maryknoll, NY: Orbis Books, 1976.

Laborem exercens. Pope John Paul II, 1981 encyclical letter "On Human Work." Washington, DC: United States Catholic Conference, 1981.

Lumen gentium. Vatican Council II, "Dogmatic Constitution on the Church." In Abbott and Gallagher, eds., *The Documents of Vatican II*.

Mater et magistra. Pope John XXIII, 1961 encyclical letter, "Christianity and Social Progress." In Gremillion, ed., *The Gospel of Peace and Justice*.

Octogesima adveniens. Pope Paul VI, 1971 apostolic letter on "The Eightieth Anniversary of 'Rerum Novarum'." In Gremillion, ed., *The Gospel of Peace and Justice*.

Pacem in terris. Pope John XXIII, 1963 encyclical letter "Peace on Earth." In Gremillion, ed., *The Gospel of Peace and Justice.*

Populorum progressio. Pope Paul VI, 1967 encyclical letter "On the Development of Peoples." In Gremillion, ed., *The Gospel of Peace and Justice.*

Quadragesimo anno. Pope Pius XI, 1931 encyclical letter, "On Reconstruction of the Social Order." In Carlen, ed., *The Papal Encyclicals,* vol. 2.

Quod apostolici muneris. Pope Leo XIII, 1878 encyclical letter "On socialism." In Carlen, ed., *The Papal Encyclicals,* vol. 1.

Redemptor hominis. Pope John Paul II, 1979 encyclical letter, "Redeemer of Man." Washington, DC: United States Catholic Conference, 1979.

Rerum novarum. Pope Leo XIII, 1891 encyclical letter "On the Condition of Workers." In Carlen, ed., *The Papal Encyclicals,* vol 1.

Sacrosanctum concilium. Vatican Council II, "Constitution on the Sacred Liturgy." In Abbott and Gallagher, eds., *The Documents of Vatican II.*

1. The Church's Social Mission in a Pluralistic Society

Reprinted by permission of the publisher from *Vatican II: The Unfinished Agenda,* ed. Lucien Richard with Daniel J. Harrington and John W. O'Malley (New York: Paulist Press, 1987). © by Lucien Richard

1. J. Bryan Hehir, "Church-State and Church-World: The Ecclesiological Implications," *Proceedings of the Catholic Theological Society of America* 41 (1986), p. 56.

2. *Aeterni patris,* no. 9, in *The Church Speaks to the Modern World: The Social Teachings of Leo XIII,* ed. Etienne Gilson (Garden City, NY: Doubleday Image Books, 1954), p. 38.

3. Johann Baptist Metz, *Faith in History and Society,* trans. David Smith (New York: Seabury, 1980), pp. 18–19.

4. *Gaudium et spes,* no. 4.

5. See David Hollenbach, *Claims in Conflict: Retrieving and Renewing the Catholic Human Rights Tradition* (New York: Paulist, 1979), p. 122. For parallel, though in some ways quite different, views, see also Alasdair MacIntyre, *After Virtue: A Study in Moral Theory* (Notre Dame, IN: University of Notre Dame Press, 1981), and Roberto Mangabeira Unger, *Knowledge and Politics* (New York: Free Press, 1975).

6. *Gaudium et spes,* nos. 10 and 11.

7. For an overview of many of these theological developments, see Mark Schoof, *A Survey of Catholic Theology, 1800–1970* (Glen Rock, NJ: Paulist Newman Press, 1970).

8. Metz, *Faith in History and Society,* p. 19.

9. For discussion of recent debates about the proper way to express the unbreakable link between social mission and the church's core identity, see Charles M. Murphy, "Action for Justice as Constitutive of the Preaching of the Gospel: What Did the 1971 Synod Mean?" *Theological Studies* 44 (1983), pp. 298–

311, and Francis Schüssler Fiorenza, *Foundational Theology: Jesus and the Church* (New York: Crossroad, 1985), part III.

10. *Gaudium et spes*, no. 42.

11. Ibid., no. 40.

12. Ibid., no. 22. See John Paul II, *Redemptor hominis*, nos. 8, 13, and 14, and passim. Referring to the passage from *Gaudium et spes* cited here, Josef (now Cardinal) Ratzinger has written: "We are probably justified in saying that here for the first time in an official document of the magisterium a new type of completely Christocentric theology appears. On the basis of Christ this dares to present theology as anthropology and only becomes radically theological by including man in discourse about God by way of Christ, thus manifesting the deepest unity of theology" ("The Dignity of the Human Person," in *Commentary on the Documents of Vatican II*, ed. H. Vorgrimler, vol. 5 [New York: Herder and Herder, 1969], p. 159). This implies, I take it, that any suggestion that the church's mission to defend the dignity of the human person is not essential to the preaching of the gospel of Christ would be a threat to this unity of theology.

13. *Gaudium et spes*, no. 32.

14. Ibid., no. 42.

15. Ibid., no. 34.

16. Ibid., no. 39.

17. Ibid., no. 38.

18. See, for example, John A. Coleman, "The Situation for Modern Faith," *Theological Studies* 39 (1978), pp. 601–32.

19. *Gaudium et spes*, no. 43.

20. See note 9 above.

21. Karl Rahner, "Theological Reflections on the Problem of Secularization," *Theological Investigations*, vol. 10 (New York: Herder and Herder, 1973), p. 322.

22. *Dignitatis humanae*, no. 2.

23. Ibid., no. 4.

24. John Courtney Murray, *The Problem of Religious Freedom*, Woodstock Papers, No. 7 (Westminster, MD: Newman Press, 1965), pp. 20–22.

25. *Gaudium et spes*, no. 44.

26. Ibid., no. 43.

27. Karl Rahner, *The Shape of the Church to Come*, trans. Edward Quinn (New York: Seabury, 1974), p. 76.

2. Modern Catholic Teachings Concerning Justice

Reprinted by permission of the publisher from *The Faith That Does Justice*, ed. John Haughey (New York: Paulist Press, 1977). © by The Missionary Society of St. Paul the Apostle in the State of New York.

1. Synod of Bishops, *Justitia in mundo*, no. 6.

2. For an illuminating discussion of alternative definitions of justice, see Chaim Perelman, *The Idea of Justice and the Problem of Argument*, trans. John

Petrie (London: Routledge and Kegan Paul, 1963). For an overview of diverse philosophical theories, confer John Arthur and William H. Shaw, eds., *Justice and Economic Distribution* (Englewood Cliffs, NJ: Prentice-Hall, 1978). See also Gene Outka, *Agape: An Ethical Analysis* (New Haven: Yale University Press, 1972), pp. 88–92, and Karen Lebacqz, *Six Theories of Justice* (Minneapolis: Augsburg, 1986) for more theological analyses. The analysis here, though different from Outka's in important ways, is heavily indebted to him. Chapter 5 below considers the Catholic ethical approach to justice in relation to recent discussions in American moral and political philosophy.

3. *The Republic of Plato*, trans. Francis MacDonald Cornford (New York: Oxford University Press, 1945), no. 432.

4. *Nicomachean Ethics*, trans. Martin Ostwald (Indianapolis: Bobbs-Merrill, 1962), no. 1131a.

5. *Second Treatise on Civil Government*, in *Social Contract: Essays by Locke, Hume, and Rousseau*, ed. Sir Ernest Barker (New York: Oxford University Press, 1962), no. 124.

6. "Critique of the Gotha Program," in *Basic Writings on Politics and Philosophy: Karl Marx and Friedrich Engels*, ed. Lewis S. Feuer (Garden City, NY: Doubleday Anchor, 1949), p. 119.

7. *A Theory of Justice* (Cambridge, MA: The Belknap Press of Harvard University Press, 1971), pp. 60–61.

8. Some of these concerns are treated in Peter L. Berger and Richard John Neuhaus, eds., *Against the World for the World: The Hartford Appeal and the Future of American Religion* (New York: Seabury, 1976).

9. *Rerum novarum*, nos. 1–3.

10. *Mater et magistra*, no. 219.

11. William A. Luijpen, *Phenomenology of Natural Law* (Pittsburgh: Duquesne University Press, 1967), p. 180.

12. See, for example, William Frankena, *Ethics*, 2nd ed. (Englewood Cliffs, NJ: Prentice-Hall, 1973), pp. 56–59; Joel Feinberg, *Social Philosophy* (Englewood Cliffs, NJ: Prentice-Hall, 1973), p. 89; Gene Outka, *Agape*, chap. 3.

13. *On the Morals of the Catholic Church*, chap. 15, in *Basic Writings of St. Augustine*, vol. I, ed. Whitney Oates (New York: Random House, 1948).

14. *Divini redemptoris*, no. 49.

15. *Quadragesimo anno*, no. 88.

16. Ibid., no. 137.

17. *Rerum novarum*, no. 3.

18. *Justitia in mundo*, nos. 3 and 10.

19. See Ramsey's discussion of in-principled love in *War and the Christian Conscience* (Durham, NC: Duke University Press, 1961). The same need for moving to a more concrete level of normative discourse is made in James Gustafson, *Can Ethics Be Christian?* (Chicago: University of Chicago Press, 1975), pp. 148–64. My reading of the Catholic documents has been influenced in important ways by both Ramsey and Gustafson.

20. There are parallels to this type of quest for specificity in modern Protestant

theology. The orders of creation, the ordinances of the Creator, and the mandates of God in the world are counterparts to the notion of natural law to be found in the writings of Brunner, Barth, and Bonhoeffer. Catholicism, however, has exhibited a much greater confidence in its ability to identify these specific moral demands in detail.

21. *Gaudium et spes*, no. 29; *Quod apostolici muneris*, no. 5.

22. *The Nature and Destiny of Man* (New York: Scribner's, 1943), vol. 2, p. 253. Charles Curran makes the same point from within the Catholic tradition: "There was always the danger of identifying a particular order or structure as the immutable order of God when in reality it was only an historically and culturally conditioned attempt to respond as well as possible to the needs of a particular period and very often manifested the desires of the dominant power group in the society rather than the eternal order of God" (*Catholic Moral Theology in Dialogue* [Notre Dame, IN: Fides, 1972, p. 121]).

23. *Octogesima adveniens*, no. 40.

24. *Gaudium et spes*, no. 53.

25. On this point the recent developments of the Catholic tradition again seem to have come fairly close to accepting one of Reinhold Niebuhr's most basic points. *Gaudium et spes* views human beings as both boundless and at the same time radically limited. The tension between these two aspects of humanity is seen as one that leads to sin and injustice (nos. 10 and 13). This anthropology could fittingly be expressed by a well-known passage from Niebuhr: "Man is tempted by the situation in which he stands. He stands at the juncture of nature and spirit. The freedom of his spirit causes him to break the harmonies of nature and the pride of his spirit prevents him from establishing a new harmony. . . . The Christian view of human nature is involved in the paradox of claiming a higher stature for man and of taking a more serious view of his evil than other anthropology" (*The Nature and Destiny of Man*, vol. 1, pp. 17–18).

26. *Gaudium et spes*, no. 53.

27. Paul VI puts the matter this way: "These sciences are a condition at once indispensable and inadequate for a better discovery of what is human. They are a language which becomes more and more complex, yet one that deepens rather than solves the mystery of the heart of the human person, nor does it provide the complete and definitive answer to the desire which springs from his innermost being" (*Octogesima adveniens*, no. 40).

28. Ibid., nos. 36ff.

29. *Gaudium et spes*, no. 4. See *Mater et magistra*, no. 206.

30. "The Relevance of Historical Understanding," in *Toward a Discipline of Social Ethics*, ed. Paul Deats, Jr. (Boston: Boston University Press, 1972), p. 67.

31. For discussions of these three types of justice see the following examples of the extensive literature on Catholic social thought: Charles Antoine, *Cours d'économie sociale*, 4th ed. (Paris: Felix Alcan, 1908), chap. 5, "Justice et Charité"; Johannes Messner, *Social Ethics*, rev. ed., trans. J. J. Doherty (St. Louis: B. Herder, 1965), pp. 314–24; Thomas Gilby, *Between Community and Society* (London: Longmans, Green, 1953), chap. 8; John A Ryan, *Distributive Justice*

(New York: Macmillan, 1927), chap. 16; Oswald von-Nell Breuning, *Reorganization of Social Economy,* trans. Bernard W. Dempsey (New York: Bruce, 1939), pp. 170–91; Thomas E. Henneberry, "On Definitions of Social Justice," S.T.D. dissertation, Woodstock College, 1941.

32. See *Rerum novarum,* nos. 43–45; John Paul II, *Laborem exercens,* no. 19.

33. In the words of Leo XIII: "As regards the state, the interests of all, whether high or low, are equal. The members of the working class are citizens by nature and by the same right as the rich; they are real parts living the life which makes up, through the family, the body of the commonwealth. . . . Among the many and grave duties of rulers who would do their best for the people, the first and chief is to act with strict justice—with that justice which is called distributive—toward each and every class alike" (*Rerum novarum,* no. 33).

34. For discussion of the tension between the hierarchical and egalitarian aspects of Leo XIII's thought, see John Courtney Murray, "Leo XIII: Two Concepts of Government," *Theological Studies* 14 (1953), pp. 551–67; Murray, "Leo XIII: Two Concepts of Government. II. Government and the Order of Culture," *Theological Studies* 15 (1954), pp. 1–33; Arturo Gaete, "Socialism and Communism: History of a Problem-Ridden Condemnation," *LADOC* 4, no. 1 (September 1973), pp. 1–16.

35. *Rerum novarum,* no. 22.

36. A major exception to this statement is the tradition's continued adherence to a hierarchical conception of the relations and roles of men and women. For an excellent treatment of this question, see Margaret A. Farley, "New Patterns of Relationship: The Beginnings of a Moral Revolution," *Theological Studies* 36 (December 1975), pp. 627–46. Farley's general approach to the definition of justice, as expressed in this article and elsewhere, has been influential in shaping the analysis presented here.

37. Quoted in *Gaudium et spes,* no. 69, note 233, in the Abbott-Gallagher edition of *The Documents of Vatican II.*

38. *Justitia in mundo,* no. 18.

39. Mt. 25:40.

40. The quotations are from *Justitia in mundo,* nos. 30–35.

41. *Justitia in mundo,* no. 6.

42. This way of stating the distinctiveness of a Christian ethic is parallel to that argued for by James Gustafson's *Can Ethics Be Christian?*

43. Paul VI acknowledges the utopian dimensions of a Christian vision of justice and notes that such dimensions are especially important in a world starved for the imagination necessary "both to perceive in the present the disregarded possibility hidden within it and to direct itself toward a fresh future" (*Octogesima adveniens,* no. 32).

44. See *Populorum progressio,* no. 79.

3. Human Work and the Story of Creation

Reprinted from *Co-Creation and Capitalism: John Paul II's Laborem Exercens,* ed. John W. Houck and Oliver F. Williams (Washington, DC: University Press of America, 1983).

1. Hannah Arendt, *The Human Condition* (Garden City, NY: Doubleday Anchor Books, 1959), p. 49.

2. *Laborem exercens,* no. 25.

3. Ibid.

4. Karl Barth, *Church Dogmatics* III/4, trans. A. T. MacKay et al. (Edinburgh: T. and T. Clarke, 1961), p. 482.

5. *Laborem exercens,* no. 25.

6. Ibid., no. 1.

7. Ibid., no. 6.

8. Ibid., no. 12.

9. Ibid., no. 14.

10. Ibid., no. 18.

11. Ibid., no. 1. For an analysis of the claim to unbroken continuity in the modern Catholic social tradition, see Richard McCormick, "Notes on Moral Theology 1981," *Theological Studies* 43 (1982), pp. 97–102, and John Coleman "Development of Church Social Teaching," *Origins* 11 (1981), pp. 33–41.

12. *Laborem exercens,* no. 4.

13. René Coste, "Le travail et l'homme. L'encyclique 'Laborem exercens,'" *Esprit et vie,* January 21, 1982, p. 37.

14. *Laborem exercens,* no. 4.

15. Ibid., no. 4.

16. See Harold L. Creager, "The Divine Image," in *A Light unto My Path: Old Testament Studies in Honor of Jacob M. Myers,* ed. Howard N. Bream et al., Gettysburg Theological Studies IV (Philadelphia: Temple University Press, 1974), pp. 103–18.

17. See *Gaudium et spes* no. 17.

18. The prime modern representative of this interpretation is Karl Barth. See *Church Dogmatics* III/1, pp. 193 ff. and III/2, p. 324. This notion is also found in the teaching of the Second Vatican Council. See *Gaudium et spes,* no. 12. A forceful argument that Barth has misread Genesis in developing this interpretation has been developed by Phylis Bird in "'Male and Female He Created Them': Gen 1:27b in the Context of the Priestly Account of Creation," *Harvard Theological Review* 74 (1981), pp. 129–59.

19. *Laborem exercens,* no. 4.

20. See, for example, Lynn White Jr., "The Historical Roots of Our Ecologic Crisis," *Science* 155 (1967), pp. 1203–7.

21. See James Barr, "Man and Nature: The Ecological Controversy and the Old Testament," *Bulletin of the John Rylands Library* 55 (1972–73), pp. 9–32; and Bernhard W. Anderson, "Human Dominion over Nature," in *Biblical Studies in Contemporary Thought,* ed. Miriam Ward (Somerville, MA: Greeno, Hadden, 1975), pp. 27–45.

22. *Redemptor hominis,* no. 15.

23. *Laborem exercens,* no. 6.

24. Ibid., no. 7.

25. Paul Ricoeur, *The Symbolism of Evil*, trans. Emerson Buchanan (Boston: Beacon Press, 1967), p. 232.

26. Ibid., p. 233.

27. Claus Westermann, *Creation*, trans. John J. Scullion (Philadelphia: Fortress Press, 1974), pp. 12–13.

28. Ibid., p. 11.

29. See *Laborem exercens*, no. 9.

30. The most evident instance of the limits of *Laborem exercens*' use of Genesis occurs in its single reference to the Tower of Babel story. In a list of various professions which are referred to in the Old Testament, *Laborem exercens* includes the work of "the builder" (no. 26). The footnote cites Gen 11:3, a text which describes the preparations for the construction of the tower: "And they said to one another 'Come, let us make bricks, and burn them thoroughly.' And they had brick for stone and bitumen for mortar." One could not easily find a less appropriate text to support the encyclical's basic perspective, for the Genesis myth attributes all the conflicts of world history to this construction project.

31. See Phyllis Trible, *God and the Rhetoric of Sexuality* (Philadelphia: Fortress Press, 1978), pp. 126–28.

32. Westermann, *Creation*, p. 19.

33. For a thorough and perceptive reflection on this problem, see David H. Kelsey, *The Uses of Scripture in Recent Theology* (Philadelphia: Fortress Press, 1975).

34. Gerhard von Rad, *Genesis: A Commentary*, rev. ed., trans. John H. Marks (Philadelphia: Westminster, 1972), p. 25.

35. Bernard W. Anderson, *Understanding the Old Testament*, 3rd ed. (Englewood Cliffs, NJ: Prentice-Hall, 1975), p. 434.

36. See Westermann, *Creation*, p. 51.

37. John Paul II, "Address to UNESCO," June 2, 1980, in *The Person, the Nation and the State: Texts of John Paul II (October 1978–January 1980)*, ed. William Murphy (Vatican City: Pontifical Commission Justitia et Pax, 1980), p. 48.

38. Von Rad, *Genesis*, p. 152.

39. Jean-Jacques Rousseau, *The Social Contract*, in *Social Contract: Essays by Locke, Hume, and Rousseau*, ed. Sir Ernest Barker (New York: Oxford University Press, 1967), p. 167.

40. Ricoeur, *The Symbolism of Evil*, p. 251.

41. Ibid.

42. *Laborem exercens*, no. 8.

43. *Laborem exercens*, nos. 17 and 18.

44. Pope John Paul II, *Original Unity of Man and Woman: Catechesis on the Book of Genesis* (Boston: St. Paul Editions, 1981), p. 24.

45. For an analysis of the limits of ontological thinking as a vehicle for the expression of Christian faith, see Johann Baptist Metz, *Faith in History and Society: Toward a Practical Fundamental Theology*, trans. David Smith (New York: Seabury, 1980).

46. See Paul Ricoeur, *Fallible Man: Philosophy of the Will,* trans. Charles Kelbley (Chicago: Henry Regnery, 1967), p. 217.

4. Unemployment and Jobs: A Social, Theological, and Ethical Analysis

Reprinted from *Catholic Social Teaching and the U.S. Economy: Working Papers for a Bishops' Pastoral Letter,* ed. John W. Houck and Oliver F. Williams (Washington, DC: University Press of America, 1984).

1. National Conference of Catholic Bishops, *Economic Justice for All: Pastoral Letter on Catholic Social Teaching and the U.S. Economy* (Washington DC: U.S. Catholic Conference, 1986).
2. Paul A. Samuelson, *Economics: An Introductory Analysis,* 6th ed. (New York: McGraw-Hill, 1964), p. 572.
3. See Paul Bullock, *CETA at the Crossroads: Employment Policy and Politics* (Los Angeles: Institute of Industrial Relations, University of California at Los Angeles, 1981).
4. See Barry Bluestone and Bennett Harrison, *The Deindustrialization of America: Plant Closings, Community Abandonment and the Dismantling of Basic Industry* (New York: Basic Books, 1982), pp. 233–40 and passim.
5. Lester C. Thurow, *The Zero-Sum Society: Distribution and the Possibilities for Economic Change* (New York: Penguin Books, 1981), pp. 77–82.
6. See the very interesting debate on this issue between Thurow, Bluestone, and Harley Shaiken, "Reindustrialization and Jobs," *Working Papers* 7 (November/December, 1980), pp. 47–59.
7. The *Business Week* Team (Seymour Zucker et al.), *The Reindustrialization of America* (New York: McGraw Hill, 1982).
8. "Blueprint for a Working America," *Solidarity,* May 16–31, 1983.
9. *The Reindustrialization of America,* p. 185.
10. "Blueprint," p. 11.
11. *The Reindustrialization of America,* p. 77.
12. Robert B. Reich, "The Next American Frontier," *Atlantıc Monthly,* March 1983, p. 46.
13. *The Reindustrialization of America,* p. 160.
14. Barry Bluestone and Bennett Harrison, "Economic Development, the Public Sector, and Full Employment: An Outline for a Plan," in *The Federal Budget and Social Reconstruction: The People and the State,* ed. Marcus Raskin (Washington, DC: Institute for Policy Studies, 1978), pp. 416ff.
15. See George Gilder, "A Supply-Side Economics of the Left," and Amitai Etzioni, "The MITIzation of America?" *The Public Interest* 72 (1983), pp. 29–43 and 44–51.
16. Gregory Baum, ed., *Work and Religion* (New York: Seabury, 1980), pp. vii-viii.
17. Herbert Marcuse, *Eros and Civilization: A Philsophical Inquiry into Freud* (New York: Vintage, 1961). The internal quotation is from C.B. Chisholm, "The

Psychiatry of Enduring Peace and Social Progress," *Psychiatry* 9, no. 1 (1946), p. 31.

18. Francis Schüssler Fiorenza, "Religious Beliefs and Praxis: Reflections on Catholic Theological Views of Work," in Baum, ed., *Work and Religion,* p. 98. For a fuller discussion of recent analyses and interpretations of the contemporary Western experience of work, see Marie Jahoda, *Employment and Unemployment: A Social-Psychological Analysis* (Cambridge: Cambridge University Press, 1982).

19. See *Laborem exercens,* no. 1.

20. Contra Marcuse, *Eros and Civilization,* chap. 11.

21. See Jahoda, *Employment and Unemployment,* pp. 58–61.

22. See Claus Westermann, "Work, Civilization and Culture in the Bible," in Baum, ed., *Religion and Work,* pp. 81–91.

23. *Pacem in terris,* no. 18.

24. *Gaudium et spes,* no. 67.

25. U.S. Catholic Conference, "The Economy: Human Dimensions," statement of November 20, 1975, in *Quest for Justice: A Compendium of Statements of the United States Catholic Bishops on the Political and Social Order 1966–1980,* ed. J. Brian Benestad and Francis J. Butler (Washington, DC: United States Catholic Conference, 1981), pp. 264–65.

26. Three examples of this testimony are the interventions of Bishop James S. Rausch, Bishop Eugene A. Marino, and Archbishop Thomas A. Donnellan, published in *Full Employment and Economic Justice: Resources for Education and Action,* ed. John Carr (Washington, DC: U.S. Catholic Conference, 1977), pp. 19–38. See the commentary on these church initiatives by Ronald Krietemeyer, "The Genesis and Development of the Right to Work," in *Unemployment and the Right to Work,* ed Jacques Pohier and Dietmar Mieth (New York: Seabury, 1982), pp. 27–33. A detailed discussion of the evolution of the Humphrey-Hawkins bill can be found in Helen Ginsburg, *Full Employment and Public Policy: The United States and Sweden* (Toronto: D. C. Heath, 1983), chap. 3.

27. *Gaudium et spes,* no. 60.

28. *Laborem exercens,* no. 18.

29. Dietrich Bonhoeffer, *Ethics,* ed. Eberhard Bethge, trans. N. H. Smith (New York: Macmillan Paperback Edition, 1965), p. 269.

30. Henry Shue has argued cogently that the distinction between the two types of rights should not be interpreted as an opposition. I fully agree. But the distinction does have its usefulness. See Henry Shue, *Basic Rights: Subsistence, Affluence and U.S. Foreign Policy* (Princeton: Princeton University Press, 1980), esp. pp. 35–40. A helpful discussion of the evolution of the understanding of the right to work as a social right within Catholic social thought can be found in Friedhelm Hengsbach, "The Church and the Right to Work," in Pohier and Mieth, eds. *Unemployment and the Right to Work,* pp. 40–49.

31. Reinhold Niebuhr, *The Nature and Destiny of Man,* vol. 2 (New York: Scribner's, 1964), p. 72.

32. Leo XIII, *Rerum novarum,* no. 2.

33. *Justitia in mundo,* no. 18.

34. Pius XI, *Divini redemptoris,* no. 51. The Carlen edition through a typographical error, replaces "from" with "for" in this quotation. The error produces a significantly different meaning.

35. See Nicholas Rescher, *Distributive Justice* (Indianapolis, IN: Bobbs-Merrill, 1966), pp. 12–18.

36. *Octogesima adveniens,* no. 24. See also *Gaudium et spes,* no. 74.

37. *Quadragesimo anno,* no. 79.

38. See the proposals from the UAW and from the *Business Week* team referred to in notes 7 and 8 above. See also Felix Rohatyn, "Time for a Change," *New York Review of Books* 30, no. 13 (August 18, 1983), pp. 46–49.

5. Justice as Participation: Public Moral Discourse and the U.S. Economy

Reprinted from *Community in America: The Challenge of Habits of the Heart,* ed. Charles H. Reynolds and Ralph V. Norman (Berkeley, CA: University of California Press, 1988).

1. James M. Gustafson, "The Church as a Community of Moral Discourse," in *The Church as Moral Decision-maker* (Philadelphia: Pilgrim, 1970), pp. 83–95.

2. Robert N. Bellah, Richard Madsen, William M. Sullivan, Ann Swidler, and Stephen M. Tipton, *Habits of the Heart: Individualism and Commitment in American Life* (Berkeley, CA: University of California Press, 1985).

3. John Courtney Murray, *We Hold These Truths: Catholic Reflections on the American Proposition* (New York: Sheed and Ward, 1960), pp. 15–16.

4. Michael Novak, "McGovernism among the Bishops," *Washington Times,* October 25, 1985.

5. Murray, *We Hold These Truths,* p.12.

6. Alasdair MacIntyre, *After Virtue: A Study in Moral Theory* (Notre Dame, IN: University of Notre Dame Press, 1981), p. 6.

7. Ibid., pp. 104–5.

8. Ibid., p. 245.

9. National Conference of Catholic Bishops, *Economic Justice for All: Catholic Social Teaching and the U.S. Economy,* no. 27.

10. Stanley Hauerwas, *The Peaceable Kingdom: A Primer in Christian Ethics* (Notre Dame, IN: University of Notre Dame Press, 1983), pp. 112–13.

11. Ibid., pp. 99–102.

12. *Economic Justice for All,* no. 61.

13. George Lindbeck, "The Sectarian Future of the Church," in *The God Experience: Essays in Hope,* ed. Joseph P. Whalen (Westminster, MD: Newman, 1971), pp. 226–43.

14. Murray, *We Hold These Truths,* p. 10, emphasis added.

15. Walter Lippmann, *The Public Philosophy* (Boston: Little, Brown, 1955).

16. William M. Sullivan, *Reconstructing Public Philosophy* (Berkeley, CA: University of California Press, 1982), p. 9. See Bellah et al., *Habits of the Heart,* Appendix, "Social Science as Public Philosophy," pp. 297–307.

17. Murray, *We Hold These Truths,* p. 8.
18. Ibid., p. 87.
19. John Rawls, *A Theory of Justice* (Cambridge, MA: Harvard University Press, 1971); Robert Nozick, *Anarchy, State, and Utopia* (New York: Basic Books, 1974); Michael J. Sandel, *Liberalism and the Limits of Justice* (New York: Cambridge University Press, 1982); Michael Walzer, *Spheres of Justice: A Defense of Pluralism and Equality* (New York: Basic Books, 1983). See also Bruce Ackerman, *Social Justice in the Liberal State* (New Haven: Yale University Press, 1980); William A. Galston, *Justice and the Human Good* (Chicago: University of Chicago Press, 1980); Amy Gutmann, *Liberal Equality* (New York: Cambridge University Press, 1980).
20. Rawls, "Justice as Fairness: Political not Metaphysical," *Philosophy and Public Affairs* 14 (1985), p. 231.
21. Ibid., pp. 246–47.
22. Walzer, *Spheres of Justice,* p. 31.
23. Rawls, "Justice as Fairness: Political not Metaphysical," p. 233.
24. *Economic Justice for All,* no. 77.
25. Ibid., no. 141.
26. Walzer, *Spheres of Justice,* pp. 76, 79.
27. *Economic Justice for All,* no. 27.

6. Global Human Rights: An Interpretation of the Contemporary Catholic Understanding

Reprinted from *Human Rights in the Americas: The Struggle for Consensus,* ed. Alfred T. Hennelly and John Langan (Washington, DC: Georgetown University Press, 1982)

1. See Bernard Plongeron, "Anathema or Dialogue? Christian Reactions to Declarations of the Rights of Man in the United States and Europe in the Eighteenth Century," in *The Church and the Rights of Man, Concilium,* no. 124, ed. Alois Müller and Norbert Greinacher (New York: Seabury, 1979), pp. 39–47; and Arturo Gaete, "Socialism and Communism: History of a Problem-Ridden Condemnation," *LADOC* 4, no. 1 (September 1973), pp. 1–16.
2. See Müller and Greinacher, eds., *The Church and the Rights of Man,* pp. 77–121; Alfred Hennelly and John Langan, eds., *Human Rights in the Americas: The Struggle for Consensus* (Washington, DC: Georgetown University Press, 1982).
3. *Dignitatis humanae,* no. 1.
4. John Courtney Murray, "Commentary and Notes on the Declaration on Religious Liberty," in Abbot and Gallagher, *The Documents of Vatican II,* p. 677, n. 4. See also Murray, "Vers une intelligence du dévelopment de la doctrine de l'Église sur la liberté religieuse," in *Vatican II: La Liberté Religieuse* (Paris: Cerf, 1967), pp. 111–47.
5. *Pacem in terris,* no. 9.

6. Karl Rahner, "Towards a Fundamental Interpretation of Vatican II," *Theological Studies* 40 (1979), p. 717.

7. For a fuller discussion of this shift and its implications for the structure, function, and self-understanding of the Catholic Church, see Joseph Gremillion, *The Gospel of Peace and Justice* (Maryknoll, NY: Orbis, 1976), pp. 57–68; idem, *Harvard Seminar on Muslim, Jewish, Christian Faith Communities as Transnational Actors for Peace and Justice: Report and Interpretation* (Washington, DC: Interreligious Peace Colloquium, 1979, privately circulated), pp. 20–29 and passim; J. Bryan Hehir, "The Roman Catholic Church as Transnational Actor: Amending Vallier," Unpublished paper, International Studies Association, Washington, DC, October 1979.

8. John Langan, "Defining Human Rights: A Revision of the Liberal Tradition," in Hennelly and Langan, eds. *Human Rights in the Americas,* p. 70.

9. Ibid., p. 72.

10. See Gremillion, *The Gospel of Peace and Justice,* section 2, "The Church as a Social Actor," pp. 125–32.

11. See John Haughey, "Individualism and Rights in Karl Marx," in Hennelly and Langan, eds., *Human Rights in the Americas,* pp. 102–41.

12. See Drew Christiansen, "Basic Needs: Criterion for the Legitimacy of Development," in Hennelly and Langan, pp. 245–88; and John Weeks and Elizabeth Dore, "Basic Needs: Journey of a Concept," in *Human Rights and Basic Needs in the Americas,* ed. Margaret E. Crahan (Washington, DC: Georgetown University Press, 1982), pp. 131–49.

13. *Pacem in terris,* nos. 9–27. See also Pontifical Commission Justice and Peace, *The Church and Human Rights* (Vatican City: Vatican Polyglot Press, 1975); David Hollenbach, *Claims in Conflict: Retrieving and Renewing the Catholic Human Rights Tradition* (New York: Paulist, 1979), pp. 62–69, 89–100.

14. Pope Paul VI, *Octogesima adveniens,* nos. 27, 36.

15. For an analysis of this ambivalence, see Gregory Baum, "The Meaning of Ideology," in *Proceedings of the Catholic Theological Society of America* 34 (1979), pp. 174–75.

16. *Mater et magistra,* no. 219.

17. For a more detailed discussion of these warrants, see Hollenbach, *Claims in Conflict,* pp. 107–37.

18. For a somewhat similar though not identical argument, see Bruno Schüller, "Die Personwürde des Menschen als Beweisgrund in der normativen Ethik," *Theologie und Glaube* 53 (1978), pp. 538–55.

19. See John Courtney Murray, "The Problem of State Religion," *Theological Studies* 12 (1951), p. 170.

20. For an account of this history of modern Catholic reflections on the specific rights essential to the protection of human dignity, see Hollenbach, *Claims in Conflict,* chap. 2, pp. 41–106.

21. *Justitia in mundo,* no. 15.

22. Ibid., no. 18.

23. What is said here is argued in somewhat greater detail in Hollenbach, *Claims in Conflict*, pp. 187–207.

24. J.P. Pronk, "Human Rights and Development Aid," *International Commission of Jurists Review* 18 (June 1977), pp. 35–36. See also Patricia Weiss Fagan, "The Links Between Human Rights and Basic Needs," *Background* (Center for International Policy) Spring 1978.

7. Religious Freedom and Economic Rights: A Note on an Unfinished Argument

Reprinted from *America* 153 (November 30, 1985).

1. *Dignitatis humanae*, no. 1.
2. Gregory XVI, *Mirari vos arbitramur*, in H. Denzinger and A. Schönmetzer, *Enchiridion symbolorum*, 32nd ed., no. 2730; *Dignitatis humanae*, no. 2.
3. See John Courtney Murray, *The Problem of Religious Freedom* (Westminster, MD: Newman Press, 1965), pp. 28–30.
4. John Courtney Murray, "The Declaration on Religious Freedom": A Moment in Its Legislative History," in Murray, ed., *Religious Liberty: An End and a Beginning* (New York: Macmillan, 1966), p.35.
5. Murray, *The Problem of Religious Freedom*, p. 30.
6. *Dignitatis humanae*, no. 7.
7. Ibid., no. 4.
8. Michael Novak, "Economic Rights: The Servile State," *Catholicism and Crisis* 3, no. 10 (October 1985), p. 10.
9. Murray, "Leo XIII: Two Concepts of Government," *Theological Studies* 14 (1953), p. 559.

8. Human Rights in the Middle East: The Impact of Religious Diversity

Reprinted from *The Human Rights Quarterly* 4 (1982), by permission of Johns Hopkins University Press.

1. See Joel Feinberg, *Social Philosophy* (Englewood Cliffs, NJ: Prentice-Hall, 1973), p. 85.
2. Jürgen Moltmann, "A Christian Declaration on Human Rights," in *A Christian Declaration on Human Rights*, ed. Allen O. Miller (Grand Rapids, MI: Eerdmans, 1977), p. 135.
3. See Alan S. Rosenbaum, ed., *The Philosophy of Human Rights: International Perspectives* (Westport, CT: Greenwood Press, 1980).
4. See Adamantia Pollis and Peter Schwab, eds., *Human Rights: Cultural and Ideological Perspectives* (New York: Praeger, 1979), and Jorge I. Dominguez, Nigel Rodley, Bryce Wood, and Richard Falk, *Enhancing Global Human Rights* (New York: McGraw-Hill, 1979).

5. Jeane Kirkpatrick, "US Security and Latin America," *Commentary* 71 (January 1981), p. 40.

6. Wilfred Cantwell Smith, "Divisiveness and Unity," in *Food/Energy and the Major Faiths,* ed. Joseph Gremillion (Maryknoll, NY: Orbis Books, 1978), p. 73.

7. Smith, "Divisiveness and Unity," p. 74.

8. Jacques Maritain, "Introduction," *Human Rights: Comments and Interpretations,* ed. UNESCO (New York: Columbia University Press, 1949), pp. 15–16. See Maritain, *Man and the State,* 1949 Charles R. Walgreen Foundation Lectures (Chicago: University of Chicago Press, 1971), p. 106.

9. Richard McKeon, "The Philosophic Bases and Material Circumstances of the Rights of Man," in UNESCO, ed., *Human Rights,* p. 35.

10. For a discussion of this development see Jacob Katz, *Exclusiveness and Tolerance: Jewish-Gentile Relations in Medieval and Modern Times* (New York: Schocken, 1962).

11. Christopher Dawson, "The Origins of European Disunity," *Dublin Review* 207 (1940), p. 144.

12. See John Courtney Murray, "The Problem of State Religion," *Theological Studies* 12 (1951), p. 170.

13. Krister Stendahl, "Towards World Community," in *Jewish-Christian Dialogue,* published by the International Jewish Committee on Interreligious Dialogue and the World Council of Churches' Subunit on Dialogue with the People of Living Faiths and Ideologies (Geneva: 1975), p. 60.

14. For a succinct and lucid analysis of this interaction, see Shlomo Avineri, "Zionism as a National Liberation Movement," *Jerusalem Quarterly* 10 (1979), pp. 133–44.

15. See Ben Halpern, "Jewish Nationalism: Self-Determination as a Human Right," in *Essays on Human Rights: Contemporary Issues and Jewish Perspectives,* ed. David Sidorsky (Philadelphia: Jewish Publication Society of America, 1979), pp. 309–35.

16. Uriel Tal, "Structures of Fellowship and Community in Judaism," in *Jewish Christian Dialogue,* pp. 32, 35.

17. Ahmad Zaki Yamani, *Islamic Law and Contemporary Issues* (Jidda: Saudi Publishing House, 1388 A.H.), p. 16.

18. Seyyed Hossein Nasr, *Ideals and Realities of Islam* (London: George Allen and Unwin, 1966), pp. 29–30.

19. Syed Abul 'Ala Maudoodi, *Islamic Law and Constitution,* ed. Kurshid Ahmad (Karachi: Jamaat-e-Islami Publications, 1955), p. 193.

9. Nuclear Weapons and Nuclear War: The Shape of the Catholic Debate

Reprinted with deletions from *Theological Studies* 43 (1982), by permission of the editor.

1. Two helpful summaries of the evolution of the nuclear debate in the West

are Michael Mandelbaum, *The Nuclear Question: The United States and Nuclear Weapons, 1946–1976* (Cambridge: Cambridge University Press, 1979), and Lawrence Freedman, *The Evolution of Nuclear Strategy* (New York: St. Martin's, 1983).

2. This seems clear before the year 170. Toward the end of the second century and well into the third, E. A. Ryan concludes, "Christian conscripts and even volunteers were . . . joining up in appreciable numbers" ("The Rejection of Military Service by the Early Christians," *Theological Studies* 13 [1952], p.30).

3. Roland H. Bainton, *Christian Attitudes toward War and Peace: A Historical Survey and Critical Re-evaluation* (New York: Abingdon Press, 1960), pp. 63 and 89.

4. For a classic analysis of this cause of the widespread growth of monasticism, see Ernst Troeltsch, *The Social Teaching of the Christian Churches,* vol. 1, trans. Olive Wyon (New York: Harper Torchbooks, 1960), esp. pp. 161–64.

5. Bainton, *Christian Attitudes,* p. 89.

6. James W. Douglass, *The Non-violent Cross: A Theology of Revolution and Peace* (New York: Macmillan, 1968) pp. 177–78.

7. Thomas Aquinas, *Summa Theologiae,* IIa–IIae, q. 40, art. 2. (The translation is that of the Fathers of the English Dominican Province.)

8. See Vatican Council II, *Lumen gentium* (Dogmatic Constitution on the Church), chap. 5, "The Call of the Whole Church to Holiness."

9. For an important analysis of the relevant passages on love of enemy, see Luise Schottroff, "Non-Violence and the Love of One's Enemies," in Schottroff et al., *Essays on the Love Commandment,* trans. Reginald H. and Ilse Fuller (Philadelphia: Fortress Press, 1978), pp. 7–39.

10. See Oscar Cullmann, *Jesus and the Revolutionaries* (New York: Harper, 1970); and Hans Küng, *On Being a Christian,* trans. Edward Quinn (Garden City, NY: Doubleday, 1976) pp. 177–213.

11. Stanley Hauerwas, "Work as Co-Creation," in *Co-Creation and Capitalism,* ed. John W. Houck and Oliver F. Williams (Washington, DC: University Press of America, 1983), p. 50. See also John Howard Yoder, *The Politics of Jesus* (Grand Rapids, MI: Eerdmans, 1972). James Douglass has also written eloquently on the relation between the death of Christ and an ethic of nonviolence: "The logic of non-violence is the logic of crucifixion and leads the man of non-violence into the heart of the suffering Christ" (Douglass, *The Non-Violent Cross,* p. 71).

12. James T. Johnson, "On Keeping Faith: The Use of History for Religious Ethics," *Journal of Religious Ethics* 7 (1979), p. 112. See Johnson's excellent book-length works on the subject: *Ideology, Reason and the Limitation of War* (Princeton: Princeton University Press, 1975) and *Just War Tradition and the Limitation of War* (Princeton: Princeton University Press, 1981).

13. *Summa Theologiae,* IIa–IIae, q. 40, art. 1.

14. Johnson, "On Keeping Faith," p. 113.

15. James Childress, "Just-War Criteria," in *War or Peace? The Search for New Answers,* ed. Thomas A. Shannon (Maryknoll, NY: Orbis Books, 1980), pp. 40–58.

16. Pope John Paul II, "1982 World Day of Peace Message," nos. 9 and 12, *Origins* 11 (1982), pp. 476, 478.

17. See "Peace in the OT" and "Peace in the NT," *Interpreter's Dictionary of the Bible*, vol. 3, pp. 704–6.

18. I have not been able to locate the source of this statement, which has become something close to the motto of recent American pacifist groups. It is cited without reference in John Howard Yoder, *Nevertheless: A Meditation on the Varieties and Shortcomings of Religious Pacifism* (Scottdale, PA: Herald Press, 1971), p. 68.

19. Edward Schillebeeckx, *Christ: The Experience of Jesus as Lord*, trans. John Bowden (New York: Crossroad, 1980) pp. 695–96.

20. Yoder, *The Politics of Jesus*, p. 240.

21. Gordon Zahn, "Afterword," in Shannon, ed., *War or Peace?*, p. 241.

22. Childress, "Just-War Criteria," p. 40.

23. For some further very useful reflections on the pluralism about this question in the church today and the implications of this pluralism for policy debate, see J. Bryan Hehir, "The Just-War Ethic and Catholic Theology: Dynamics of Change and Continuity," in Shannon, ed., *War or Peace?*, pp. 15–39.

24. John XXIII, *Pacem in terris*, no. 127.

25. *Gaudium et spes*, no. 80.

26. Ibid.

27. Pope John Paul II, Homily at Coventry Cathedral, May 30, 1982, no. 2, *Origins* 12 (1982), p. 55.

28. Hehir, "The Just-War Ethic and Catholic Theology," pp. 19–22. Paul Ramsey has pointed out that the diversity of interpretations is in part the result of an erroneous translation of *Pacem in terris*, no. 127. See Paul Ramsey, *The Just War: Force and Political Responsibility* (New York: Scribner's, 1968) pp. 192–98.

29. Douglass, *The Non-Violent Cross*, p. 176.

30. See ibid., chaps. 4, 5, and 6.

31. *Gaudium et spes*, no. 79; John Paul II, "1982 World Day of Peace Message," no. 12. See Hehir, "The Just-War Ethic and Catholic Theology," pp. 22–23.

32. For a careful elaboration of the meaning and function of these criteria, see Childress, "Just-War Criteria," pp. 45–50 and passim.

33. See James T. Johnson, "Weapons Limits and the Restraint of War: A Just War Critique," *The Society of Christian Ethics 1980 Selected Papers* (Waterloo, Ontario: Council on the Study of Religion, 1980), p. 89.

34. *Gaudium et spes*, no. 80.

35. See Colin S. Gray and Keith Payne, "Victory Is Possible," *Foreign Policy* 39 (Summer 1980), pp. 14–27.

36. Spurgeon M. Keeny, Jr., and Wolfgang Panofsky, "MAD versus NUTS: Can Doctrine or Weaponry Remedy the Mutual Hostage Relationship of the Superpowers?" *Foreign Affairs* 60, no. 2 (Winter 1981–82), p. 294.

37. See U.S. Department of Defense, *Annual Report, Fiscal Year 1981* (Washington, DC: U.S. Government Printing Office, 1980), esp. pp. 65–67.

38. A helpful collection of these statements from U.S. bishops and a variety of other church sources, both Catholic and Protestant, is in *Nuclear Disarmament: Key Statements of Popes, Bishops, Councils and Churches*, ed. Robert Heyer (New York: Paulist Press, 1982).

39. McGeorge Bundy, George F. Kennan, Robert S. McNamara, and Gerard Smith, "Nuclear Weapons and the Atlantic Alliance," *Foreign Affairs* 60, no. 4 (Spring 1982), p. 756.

40. Ibid., p. 757.

41. See Karl Kaiser, Georg Leber, Alois Mertes, and Franz-Josef Schultze, "Nuclear Weapons and the Preservation of Peace: A Response to an American Proposal for Renouncing the First Use of Nuclear Weapons," *Foreign Affairs* 60, no. 5 (Summer 1982), pp. 1157–70; "Debate over No First Use," *Foreign Affairs* 60, no. 5 (Summer 1982), pp. 1171–80.

42. Bundy et al., "The Authors Reply," *Foreign Affairs* 60, no. 5 (Summer 1982), p. 1180.

43. See, for example, Richard McCormick and Paul Ramsey, eds., *Doing Evil to Achieve Good: Moral Choice in Conflict Situations* (Chicago: Loyola University Press, 1978), and John R. Connery, "Catholic Ethics: Has the Norm for Rule-Making Changed?" *Theological Studies* 42 (1981) 232–50.

44. For an interesting parallel argument, see Johnson, *Just War Tradition and the Limitation of War,* pp. 219–24.

45. See, for example, Edward N. Luttwak, "How to Think about Nuclear War," *Commentary* 74, no. 2 (August 1982), pp. 21–28.

46. The view of Colin Gray and Keith Payne is representative of this approach: "An adequate US deterrent posture is one that denies the Soviet Union any plausible hope of success at any level of strategic conflict; offers a likely prospect of Soviet defeat; and offers a rasonable chance of limiting damage to the United States. . . . As long as the United States relies on nuclear threats to deter an increasingly powerful Soviet Union, it is inconceivable that the US defense community can continue to divorce its thinking on deterrence from its planning for the efficient conduct of war and defense of the country. Prudence in the latter should enhance the former" ("Victory Is Possible," pp. 26–27). See also U.S. Department of Defense, *Annual Report, Fiscal Year 1981*, pp. 65–67.

47. *Gaudium et spes*, no. 81.

48. See Joseph Fahey, "Pax Christi," in Shannon, ed., *War or Peace?*, p. 63: "Pax Christi USA seeks to foster both nuclear and general disarmament. It believes that the construction and possession of nuclear weapons represents a profound immorality in the contemporary world." See also Joan Chittister's response to the first draft of the pastoral letter on war and peace of the National Conference of Catholic Bishops: "My hope is that in the final draft of this much needed pastoral, the bishops will complete the prophetic work they have begun. Let them say a clear no to nuclear war and the possession and manufacture of nuclear weapons as well" ("Stepping Tentatively between Prophetism and Nationalism," *Commonweal* 109 [1982], p. 429).

49. National Conference of Catholic Bishops, *To Live in Christ Jesus: A*

Pastoral Reflection on the Moral Life (Washington, DC: U.S. Catholic Conference, 1976), p. 34. See the analysis of the ambiguities present in this statement in Hehir, "The Just-War Ethic and Catholic Theology," pp. 28–29.

50. John Cardinal Krol, "Testimony before the Senate Foreign Relations Committee, September 6, 1979," *Origins* 9 (1979), pp. 195–99.

51. For examples of these two responses, see Joan Chittister, "Stepping Tentatively," p. 429, and Robert L. Spaeth, "Disarmament and the Catholic Bishops," *This World* 2 (Summer 1982), pp. 5–17.

52. John Cardinal Krol, "Testimony before the Senate Foreign Relations Committee," section 1.

53. Ibid.

54. There is an illuminating parallel between the way the concept of toleration has been used in the Krol testimony and the way it was used by preconciliar theologians opposed to the church's acceptance of the right of religious freedom. The chief problem with both of these uses of the notion of toleration is their separation of moral and historical judgment. What I am proposing here regarding deterrence policy is analogous to the revision that John Courtney Murray made in the religious-freedom argument: the recognition that moral judgments cannot be made in an unhistorical way.

10. *The Challenge of Peace* in the Context of Recent Church Teachings

Reprinted from *Catholics and Nuclear War: A Commentary on The Challenge of Peace, the U.S. Catholic Bishops' Pastoral Letter on War and Peace,* ed. Philip J. Murnion (New York: Crossroad, 1983).

1. National Conference of Catholic Bishops, *The Challenge of Peace: God's Promise and Our Response,* no. 64.
2. Ibid.
3. *The Challenge of Peace,* Third Draft, *Origins* 12 (1983), p. 704, col. 3.
4. Pius XII, Christmas Message 1948, cited in *The Challenge of Peace,* no. 76.
5. Pius XII, Christmas Message 1956, in *The Major Addresses of Pope Pius XII,* vol. 2, ed. Vincent A. Yzermans (St. Paul: North Central Publishing Co., 1961), p. 225. For an analysis of this papal message, see John Courtney Murray, *Morality and Modern War* (New York: Council on Religion and International Affairs, 1959).
6. *The Challenge of Peace,* no.118.
7. See ibid., no. 75.
8. Ibid., no. 74.
9. Ibid., no. 14.
10. Ibid., nos. 124–25.
11. Ibid., no. 122.
12. Ibid.
13. Ibid., nos. 120–21.
14. Ibid., no. 60.

15. Ibid., no. 80.

16. Pius XII, Address to the International Office of Documentation for Military Medicine, October 19, 1953, in *Peace and Disarmament: Documents of the World Council of Churches and the Roman Catholic Church* (Vatican City: Tipographica Poliglotta Vaticana, 1982), p. 128.

17. Ibid.

18. Pius XII, Address to the Eighth Congress of the World Medical Association, September 30, 1954, in *Peace and Disarmament*, p. 131. This passage is cited in *The Challenge of Peace*, no. 147.

19. John XXIII, *Pacem in terris*, no. 127.

20. *Gaudium et spes*, no. 80.

21. *The Challenge of Peace*, no. 148.

22. John Paul II, Homily at Coventry Cathedral, May 30, 1982, no. 2, in *Origins* 12 (1982), p. 55.

23. *The Challenge of Peace*, no. 152.

24. Ibid., no. 159.

25. Ibid., no. 161.

26. *Gaudium et spes*, no. 81.

27. John Paul II, "Message to the Second Special Session of the United Nations General Assembly Devoted to Disarmament," (June 1982), 8. Cited in *The Challenge of Peace*, no. 173.

28. *The Challenge of Peace*, no. 195.

29. Ibid., no. 190.

30. Ibid., no. 122.

11. Ethics in Distress: Can There Be Just Wars in the Nuclear Age?

Reprinted by permission of the publisher from *The Nuclear Dilemma and the Just War Tradition*, ed. William V. O'Brien and John Langan (Lexington MA: Lexington Books, D. C. Heath, 1986).

1. "The French Bishops' Statement: Winning Peace," *Origins* 13, no. 26 (1983), p. 442, col. 3.

2. Ibid., p. 443, col. 2.

3. Ibid.

4. Ibid.

5. Ibid., note 20.

6. Joint Pastoral Letter of the German Bishops, *Out of Justice, Peace* (Dublin: Irish Messenger Publications, 1983), p. 61.

7. Ibid., p. 39.

8. Ibid., p. 61.

9. Ibid.

10. Ibid., pp. 61–62.

11. Thomas Aquinas, *Summa Theologiae*, Ia–IIae, q. 91, art. 2.

12. Michael Walzer, *Just and Unjust Wars* (New York: Basic Books, 1977), p. 129.

13. Ibid., p. 153.

14. Ibid., p. 133.

15. Ibid., p. 252.

16. Ibid., p. 260.

17. Ibid., p. 323.

18. Ibid., p. 324.

19. See, for example, the recent study by Stephen E. Lammers, "Area Bombing in World War II: The Argument of Michael Walzer," *Journal of Religious Ethics* 111 (1983), pp. 96–113.

20. John C. Ford, "The Morality of Obliteration Bombing," *Theological Studies* 5 (1944), p. 268.

21. Lawrence Freedman, *The Evolution of Nuclear Strategy* (New York: St. Martins Press, 1981), pp. 3–21.

22. For a helpful discussion of some of the dimensions of this qualitative transition, see Michael Howard, "Bombing and the Bomb," in his *Studies in War and Peace* (New York: Viking Press, 1971), pp. 141–53.

23. Lammers, "Area Bombing," p. 104.

24. Walzer, *Just and Unjust Wars,* p. 272.

25. Ibid., p. 274.

26. Ibid., p. 282.

27. Alasdair MacIntyre, *After Virtue: A Study in Moral Theory* (Notre Dame, IN: University of Notre Dame Press, 1981), p. 6.

28. Ibid., pp. 104–5.

29. Ibid., pp. 244–45.

30. See Stanley Hauerwas, "On Surviving Justly: An Ethical Analysis of Nuclear Disarmament," in *Religious Conscience and Nuclear Warfare,* the 1982 Paine Lectures in Religion, ed. Jill Raitt, privately printed by the University of Missouri-Columbia, p. 19.

31. For a helpful discussion of this, see Ronald Green, *Religious Reason: The Rational and Moral Basis of Religious Belief* (New York: Oxford University Press, 1978), chap. 3.

32. See Stanley Hauerwas, *A Community of Character* (Notre Dame, IN: University of Notre Dame Press, 1981), p. 101.

33. Ibid., p. 106.

34. See Paul Ramsey, *War and the Christian Conscience: How Shall Modern War Be Conducted Justly?* (Durham, NC: Duke University Press, 1961), chaps. 2 and 3.

35. Walzer, *Just and Unjust Wars,* p. 278.

36. Lawrence Freedman, *The Evolution of Nuclear Strategy,* p. 400.

37. Stanley Hoffmann, "Le cri d'alarme de l'église americaine," *Le Monde,* November 19, 1983, p. 1.

38. See, most recently, Wohlstetter's reply to his critics in "Morality and Deterrence: Wohlstetter and Critics," *Commentary,* December 1983, pp. 13–22.

39. See Colin Gray and Keith Payne, "Victory Is Possible," *Foreign Policy* 39 (Summer 1980), pp. 14–27.

40. William V. O'Brien, *The Conduct of Just and Limited War* (New York: Praeger, 1981), p. 135.

41. Albert Wohlstetter, "Optimal Ways to Confuse Ourselves," *Foreign Policy* 20 (Autumn 1975), p. 198.

42. For several views of it, see Philip J. Murnion, ed., *Catholics and Nuclear War: A Commentary on The Challenge of Peace, The U.S. Catholic Bishops' Pastoral Letter on War and Peace* (New York: Crossroad, 1983); Michael Novak, *Moral Clarity in the Nuclear Age* (Nashville: Thomas Nelson, 1983).

43. National Conference of Catholic Bishops, *The Challenge of Peace: God's Promise and Our Response,* no. 178.

44. Ibid., no. 185.

45. Ibid., nos. 188–190.

46. Ibid., no. 191.

12. A Prophetic Church and the Sacramental Imagination

Reprinted by permission of the publisher from *The Faith That Does Justice,* ed. John Haughey (New York: Paulist Press, 1977). © by The Missionary Society of St. Paul the Apostle in the State of New York.

1. *Lumen gentium,* no. 9.

2. Max Weber "Science as a Vocation," in *From Max Weber,* ed. H. H. Gerth and C. Wright Mills (New York: Oxford University Press, 1967), p. 155.

3. Karl Rahner, "Theological Reflections on the Problem of Secularization," in *Theological Investigations,* vol. 10, trans. David Bourke (New York: Herder and Herder, 1973), p. 318.

4. For a parallel discussion of the two approaches, see James M. Gustafson, "Two Approaches to Theological Ethics," in his *Christian Ethics and the Community* (Philadelphia: Pilgrim Press, 1971), pp. 127–38.

5. For a synthetic discussion of the recent literature on the church as sacrament, see Avery Dulles, *Models of the Church* (Garden City, NY: Doubleday, 1974), chap. 4.

6. Karl Barth, *Community, State and Church* (Garden City, NY: Doubleday Anchor, 1960), p. 169.

7. Paul Ramsey, *Who Speaks for the Church? A Critique of the 1966 Geneva Conference on Church and Society* (Nashville: Abingdon, 1967).

8. Ibid., p. 34.

9. Ibid., pp. 17 and 152.

10. Ibid., pp. 16 and 149.

11. Ibid., p. 169, no. 4.

12. James M. Gustafson, "Moral Authority of the Church," *The Chicago Theological Seminary Register* 61, no. 4, (1971), p. 6.

13. For a general account of these recent developments and the official docu-

ments that reflect them, see *The Gospel of Peace and Justice: Catholic Social Teaching Since Pope John,* presented by Joseph Gremillion (Maryknoll, NY: Orbis Books, 1976), esp. pp. 7–10 and 531–67.

14. Wolfhart Pannenberg, *Theology and the Kingdom of God,* ed. Richard John Neuhaus (Philadelphia: Westminster Press, 1969), p. 79.

15. Jürgen Moltmann, *Theology of Hope: On the Ground and Implications of a Christian Eschatology,* trans. James W. Leitch (London: SCM Press, 1967), p. 324.

16. Pannenberg, *Theology and the Kingdom,* p. 83.

17. Johannes B. Metz, *Theology of the World,* trans. William Glen-Doepel (New York: Herder and Herder, 1969), pp. 123–24.

18. Gustafson, "Moral Authority," p. 11.

19. Gustavo Gutierrez, *A Theology of Liberation: History, Politics and Salvation,* trans. Sister Caridad Inda and John Eagleson (Maryknoll, NY: Orbis Books, 1973), pp. 224–25.

20. See Rahner, "On the Theological Problems Entailed in a 'Pastoral Constitution,'" in *Theological Investigations,* vol. 10, pp. 293–317, and Edward Schillebeeckx, "Church, Magisterium and Politics," in *God the Future of Man,* trans. N. D. Smith (New York: Sheed and Ward, 1968), pp. 141–66.

21. Rahner, "Theological Reflections on the Problem of Secularization," p. 322. See also Rahner, "On the Theological Problems Entailed in a Pastoral Constitution," p. 303.

22. Schillebeeckx, "Church, Magisterium and Politics," p. 151.

23. See ibid., p. 152, and Rahner, "Theological Reflections on the Problem of Secularization," p. 330.

24. Schillebeeckx, "Church, Magisterium and Politics," p. 156.

25. Rahner, "Theological Reflections on the Problems of Secularization," p. 331.

26. Rahner, "On the Theological Problems Entailed in a Pastoral Constitution," pp. 304–6.

27. Schillebeeckx, "Church, Magisterium and Politics," p. 154.

28. Ibid., p. 159.

29. Gustafson, "Moral Authority," pp. 9–19.

30. The place of symbol and root-metaphor in Christian theology and ethics has been analyzed in a seminal way by H. Richard Niebuhr, *The Responsible Self: An Essay in Christian Moral Philosophy* (New York: Harper and Row, 1963), Appendix A, "Metaphors and Morals."

31. Iris Murdoch, "Vision and Choice in Morality," in *Christian Ethics and Contemporary Philosophy,* ed. Ian T. Ramsey (London, SCM Press, 1966), p. 212, n. 37.

32. David Power, "The Song of the Lord in an Alien Land," in *Concilium,* n. s., vol. 2, no. 2 (February 1974), "Politics and Liturgy," p. 92.

33. Karl Rahner, "The Church and the Sacraments," in *Inquiries* (New York: Herder and Herder, 1964), p. 219.

34. H. Denzinger and A. Schönmetzer, eds., *Enchiridion symbolorum,* 35th ed., nos. 1639 and 1606.

35. Joseph Gelineau has pointed out the complex relation of simultaneous continuity and discontinuity between the sacramental and eschatological realization of the kingdom in a way that is relevant here: "There is a dialectic of continuity-rupture-communion at the basis of liturgical dynamics. But the liturgy is practice rather than theory. It does not stop at the level of -ologies (anthropology, theo-logy); it is concerned with the order of -urgies (liturgy). It is symbolic action and an inductive force; it institutes a new existence. That is the way to look for its political power and liberating power" (Joseph Gelineau, "Celebrating the Paschal Liberation," *Concilium,* n.s., vol. 2, no. 2, p. 112).

36. The phrase is taken from the title of Schillebeeckx's important and influential study, *Christ the Sacrament of the Encounter with God* (New York: Sheed and Ward, 1963).

37. *Gaudium et spes,* no. 45; *Lumen gentium,* no. 1. See also *Gaudium et spes,* no. 42: *Lumen gentium,* nos. 9 and 48, *Sacrosanctum concilium,* no. 26, *Ad gentes,* no. 5. For recent discussion of these texts, see Dulles, *Models of the Church,* chap. 4; Juan Luis Segundo, *The Community Called Church,* trans. John Drury (Maryknoll, NY: Orbis Books, 1973), chap. 4; Edward Schillebeeckx, *God the Future of Man,* chap. 4; idem, *The Mission of the Church,* trans. N. D. Smith (New York: Seabury, 1973), chap. 3; Richard P. McBrien, *Church: The Continuing Quest* (New York: Newman Press, 1970): Louis Dupré, *The Other Dimension: A Search for the Meaning of Religious Attitudes* (Garden City, NY: Doubleday, 1972), chap. 4.

38. Dupré, *The Other Dimension,* p. 185.

39. Rahner, "The Church and the Sacraments," p. 223.

40. *Lumen gentium,* no. 1.

41. Langdon Gilkey, *Catholicism Confronts Modernity: A Protestant View* (New York: Seabury, 1975), pp. 196–97.

42. Hans Bernhard Meyer, "The Social Significance of Liturgy," *Concilium,* n.s., vol. 2, no. 10, p. 37.

43. Philip J. Rosato, "World Hunger and Eucharistic Theology," *America* 135 (August 7, 1976), p. 48.

44. For a reflection on the relation between this emphasis and the more familiar Catholic stress on the themes of presence and sacrifice in the context of shifting social and cultural structures, see William J. Byron, "Eucharist and Society," *America* 135 (August 7, 1976), pp. 43–46.

45. National Conference of Catholic Bishops, "The World Food Crisis—a Pastoral Plan of Action," November 21, 1974; and "The Right to Food," in Arthur Simon, *Bread for the World* (New York/Grand Rapids: Paulist/Eerdmans, 1975), pp. 165–72. For an analysis of these documents from a perspective similar to that adopted here, see Drew Christiansen, "Society and Ethics: The Church and World Hunger," The Catholic Theological Society of America, *Proceedings of the Thirtieth Annual Convention* (1975), pp. 129–39.

13. Preaching and Politics: The Problem of Consistency and Compromise

Reprinted with changes from *Church* 3 (1987). © National Pastoral Life Center.

1. Leslie Griffin, "The Integration of Spiritual and Temporal: Contemporary Roman Catholic Church-State Theory," *Theological Studies* 48 (1987), p. 249.
2. Avery Dulles, "The Gospel, The Church, and Politics," *Origins* 16 (1987), pp. 637–46, at p. 641.
3. *Gaudium et spes,* no. 75.
4. *Economic Justice for All,* no. 22.
5. Ibid., no. 66.
6. *Gaudium et spes,* no. 43.
7. Ibid.
8. Ibid.
9. Rembert G. Weakland, "The Church in Worldly Affairs: Tensions between Clergy and Laity," *America,* October 18, 1986, pp. 201–16.
10. Karl Rahner, *The Shape of the Church to Come* (New York: Seabury, 1974), chap. 7, "A Church of Concrete Directives," pp. 76–81.
11. *Dignitatis humanae,* no. 4.
12. *Economic Justice for All,* no. 55.
13. Thomas Aquinas, *Summa theologiae,* Ia–IIae, q. 93, art. 3.
14. *Economic Justice for All,* no. 122.
15. See Cardinal Joseph Bernardin, "The Consistent Ethic: What Sort of Framework?" *Origins* 16 (1986), pp. 345–50. The side-bar on p. 347 of this issue of *Origins* contains the references to other speeches on this topic by Cardinal Bernardin.
16. Dominicus Prümmer, O.P., *Manuale theologiae moralis,* 3 vols., 7th. ed. (Friburg, 1928–1933), vol. 2, p. 604.
17. Quoted in John A. Ryan and Francis J. Boland, C.S.C., *Catholic Principles of Politics* (New York: Macmillan, 1950), pp. 207–8.

14. Courage and Patience: Education for Staying Power in the Pursuit of Justice

Reprinted from *Education for Peace and Justice,* ed. Padraic O'Hare (San Francisco: Harper and Row, 1983).

1. *Gaudium et spes,* no. 1.
2. Lawrence Kohlberg, "Education for Justice: A Modern Statement of the Platonic View," in James Gustafson et al., *Moral Education: Five Lectures* (Cambridge, MA: Harvard University Press, 1970), p. 58. This essay has been reprinted under the revised title, "Education for Justice: A Modern Statement of the Socratic View," in Kohlberg, *The Philosophy of Moral Development: Essays in Moral Development,* vol. 1 (New York: Harper and Row, 1981).
3. For a very helpful analysis of the theological discussion of original sin, see

Brian O. McDermott, "The Theology of Original Sin: Recent Developments," *Theological Studies* 38 (1977) pp. 478–512. Reinhold Niebuhr's critique of John Dewey's philosophy rests on Niebuhr's reappropriation of the doctrine of original sin. See Padraic O'Hare, "Religious Education for Social Justice," *Religious Education* 75 (January/February, 1980), pp. 76–89. Contemporary justice-oriented education could well benefit from a similar reappropriation, though that is a task that goes beyond the scope of this essay.

4. For moving narratives of the lives of five Christians who gave their lives in response to the Christian vocation to promote justice, see William O'Malley, *The Voice of Blood: Five Christian Martyrs of Our Time* (Maryknoll, NY: Orbis Books, 1980).

5. See Peter Berger, Brigitte Berger, and Hansfried Kellner, *The Homeless Mind: Modernization and Consciousness* (New York: Vintage Books, 1973), especially chap. 3.

6. Alfred C. Kammer, "'Burn-out'—A Contemporary Dilemma for the Jesuit Social Activist," *Studies in the Spirituality of Jesuits* 10, no. 1 (January 1978), p. 1.

7. See Jerry Edelwich and Archie Brodsky, *Burnout: Stages of Disillusionment in the Helping Professions* (New York: Human Sciences Press, 1980).

8. James J. Gill, "Burnout: A Growing Threat in Ministry," *Human Development* 1, no. 2 (Summer 1980), p. 22.

9. St. Thomas Aquinas, *Summa Theologiae,* IIa–IIae, q. 124, art. 32 ad 1. The translation is that of the Blackfriar's edition, vol. 42 (New York: McGraw-Hill, 1966).

10. Ibid., q. 123, art. 3.

11. Ibid., art. 11, ad 3.

12. David Baily Harned, *Faith and Virtue* (Philadelphia: Pilgrim Press, 1973), p. 143.

13. See Karl Rahner, "Faith as Courage," in *Meditations on Freedom and the Spirit,* trans. Rosaleen Ockenden (New York: Seabury, 1978), pp. 5–29; Paul Tillich, *The Courage to Be* (New Haven: Yale University Press, 1952); Leo J. O'Donovan, "The Courage of Faith: An Essay in Honor of William F. Lynch's Seventieth Birthday," *Thought* 53 (1978), pp. 369–83.

14. O'Donovan, "The Courage of Faith," p. 382.

Index